THE HISTORY OF FREEMASONRY

ITS LEGENDS AND TRADITIONS

ITS CHRONOLOGICAL HISTORY

BY ALBERT GALLATIN MACKEY, M.D., 33°

VOLUME SIX

CHAPTER LV

HISTORY OF THE INTRODUCTION OF FREEMASONRY INTO EACH STATE AND TERRITORY OF THE UNITED STATES

The First Lodges and the Grand Lodges

Ohio.

THE introduction of Masonry into Ohio is due to the fact that soon after the close of the War of the Revolution, the Master, Jonathan Heart, and some of the members of American Union Lodge settled near Marietta.

The Charter of that lodge, which had been granted by the St. John's Grand Lodge of Massachusetts, February 15, 1776, by John Rowe, Grand Master (in the Connecticut Line of the Army),[1] was held by the Master, and he claimed that it was a lodge at large and not under the jurisdiction of any Grand Lodge, and in fact "it was invested with every power necessary to constitute, rule, and govern" Masonry in the Territories.

It had been recognized "by the Grand Lodge of Massachusetts, Pennsylvania, and New York, as a constituent of the Grand Lodge of Massachusetts." This lodge worked for several years until its Charter was burned; a revival of it was asked for from the Grand Lodge of Pennsylvania, which was declined, "except as one of its constituent" Application to the Grand Lodge of Massachusetts was made, which authorized the lodge to resume work under a copy of the original

---

[1] Shortly after, the lodge having removed to New York, asked for a Confirmation of their Charter, from the D.G.M., Dr. Middleton; but a new Warrant was granted under the name of Military Union, No. 1. - Gould's "History," vol. vi., P. 415.

Charter, "with the express provision that the charter should be of force only until a Grand Lodge should be formed in the territory in which it was located."

The Grand Lodge of Ohio was organized January 7, 1808.

The lodges represented were American Union, No. 1, at Marietta; Cincinnati, No. 13, warranted by the Grand Lodge of New Jersey as Nova Cesaraea, No. 10, now known as N.C. Harmony, No. 21; Sciota, No. 2, and Chillicothe, warranted by the Grand Lodge of Massachusetts in 1805, now known as No. 6; Erie, No. 47, at Warren, warranted by the Grand Lodge of Connecticut, March 16, 1804, now known as Old Erie, No. 3; and Amity, No. 105, at Zanesville, warranted by the Grand Lodge of Pennsylvania in 1804, now No. 5. January 4, 1808, a preliminary convention of the delegates from all the lodges then in Ohio - six in number - was held in Chillicothe to deliberate upon the propriety of forming a Grand Lodge, and to inaugurate measures for the organization of such a body.

The convention continued its deliberations four consecutive days, which resulted in the unanimous adoption of a resolution proposed by Brother Lewis Cass, viz.: "that it is expedient to form a Grand Lodge of the State of Ohio."[2]

A few rules, couched as resolutions, were adopted for the formation of a Grand Lodge, and appointed the first Monday in January, 1809, as the time, and Chillicothe as the place for holding the first Grand Communication of said Grand Lodge.

The Grand Lodge met at Chillicothe, January 2, 1809, and duly organized with representatives from four lodges.

In consequence of the absence of the representatives of American Union Lodge, No. 1, there being but four lodges represented, it was thought that a Grand Lodge could not be legally organized.

The Grand Lodge adjourned from day to day, and, finally, on January 5th, it adopted pro tempore the Constitution of the Grand Lodge of Kentucky, having decided that under their peculiar circumstances it would be right and proper to organize a Grand Lodge with only four lodges represented.

Brother Rufus Putnam, who had been chosen Grand Master at the convention held in 1808, wrote a letter to the Grand Lodge declining the office, on account of his great age, which was accepted, and Bro. Samuel Huntington was duly elected Grand Master.

---

[2] Proceedings of the Grand Lodge of Ohio.

Previous to the reception of this letter all the other Grard Officers elected the last year had been installed, and upon the election of the Grand Master he also was immediately installed, and all the other Grand Officers who had just been elected at the same time with the Grand Master.

The Grand Lodge closed its sessions on January 7, 1709, having completed all things necessary to its proper work in Masonry.

Louisiana.

The introduction of Freemasonry in the Territory of Louisiana is principally due to the political condition of that Territory and the circumstances connected with the affairs in San Domingo, both counties at that period being somewhat, if not exclusively, settled by the Latin race and their negro slaves.

Masonry had been introduced upon the Island of San Domingo from the Grand Orient of France, also by charters from the Grand Lodge of Pennsylvania.

When the insurrection occurred in San Domingo, in 1791, the white refugees spread themselves in many of the cities in the United States; a very large number settled in New Orleans, and among them were many Masons, and in 1793 several of these residing in New Orleans organized into a lodge and received a Charter from the Grand Lodge of South Carolina by the name of "Parfaite Union, No. 29," the officers being installed in the York Rite on March 30, 1794. In the same year several Brethren of the French, or Modern Rite, formed themselves into a lodge called "Etoile Polaire" (Polar Star), and applied for a Charter from the Grand Orient of France.

The Grand Orient having suspended its labors, in consequence of the political condition of France, could not issue a Charter.

The Brethren, however, obtained a provisional Charter or dispensation from the Provincial Lodge La Parfaite Sincerile at Marseilles in 1796, and intrusted the same to Dominique Mayronne, with authority to constitute the new lodge and install the officers, which was done under the French Rite, December 27, 1798.

When the Grand Orient resumed labor in 1803, a Charter was issued to Polar Star Lodge, No. 4263, in 1804, and Ch. Tessier was deputed to deliver the Charter and heal their work, which was done, and officers were installed, November 11, 1804, by A. Pinard and A.Marmillion.

The early records of "Perfect Union" and "Polar Star" can not be found, but the above information has been obtained by Brother James

H. Scot, the historian of the Grand Lodge of Louisiana, from the "Manuel Maconnique," a very rare work, published in New Orleans in 1828.

It is very probable that these lodges were formed about the same time, "but in the absence of the original records it is impossible to decide the question."[3]

It is thought that the Brethren who formed these two lodges were from the Island of Guadaloupe, which was involved in the horrors of the negro insurrection of 1791.

In consequence of political differences among the French inhabitants in Louisiana, growing out of the French Revolution, difficulties arose which resulted in the refusal of the members of these two lodges to hold any Masonic intercourse with each other.

Some of the former members of "Candor Lodge, No. 12," in Charleston, S.C., which was extinct, having settled in New Orleans, applied to the Grand Lodge of Pennsylvania and obtained a Charter, dated May 18, 1801, as Candor Lodge, No. 90.

It is possible that this lodge did not survive very long, if it ever was duly constituted, as on March 1, 1802, the Grand Lodge of Pennsylvania granted a Charter to Charity Lodge, No. 93, having the name of N. Definieto, W. M., who was the W.M. of Candor, No. 90.

This Charter was not received until 1804, and on May 13th of that year the lodge was duly constituted and the officers were installed in the York Rite.

On October 1, 1800, by treaty, Spain retroceded the whole of the territory of Louisiana to France, which held an actual possession of only twenty days, as on December 20, 1803, the United States flag was raised in New Orleans, France having sold the whole territory to the United States.

This change in the political condition made equally a change in Masonic affairs, and from that date on, viz., 1804, Masonry assumed quite a different attitude in Louisiana.

A change also in the Island of San Domingo caused a very large number of the refugees of 1791 to return to their old homes, and the French contingent among the Masons in New Orleans was greatly reduced.

The American element, which had in Masonic matters been much in the minority, began to increase and soon prevailed.

---

[3] James H. Scot, "History of Masonry in Louisiana."
archives, etc., had been destroyed.

A duplicate Charter from the Grand Orient of France was received, July 20, 1807, bearing date of February 17, 1806, by the Lodge "La Union Desiree," No. 3013, which had been under the auspices of the Grand Orient of France, at Port au Prince, April 16, 1783. During the revolution Of 1791 the Charter, the members who had fled to New Orleans in 1791, and had returned to San Domingo in 1802, had been again compelled to flee to New Orleans the second time.

In 1806 Masons from the Northern part of the United States applied for and obtained a Charter from the Grand Lodge of New York, on September 2, 1807, now Louisiana Lodge, No. 2. In the "Manuel Maconnique" it is No. 101, which is an error of the author.

This was the first lodge in New Orleans that worked in the English language, and its first W. M. was the celebrated jurist Edward Livingstone.

Polar Star Lodge, No. 4263, applied to the Grand Orient of France and obtained a Charter to hold a Chapter of Rose Croix, which was constituted and officers installed, May 24, 1807, as " La Vertu Recompensee, No. 5001."

On September 15, 1808, a York Rite Charter was issued to some of the members of Lodge La Reunion Desiree, No. 3829, by the same name but numbered 112, by the Grand Lodge of Pennsylvania.

This lodge dissolved March 23, 1812.

This much of the early history in Louisiana must suffice, as to continue a specific notice of all the lodges chartered and the various contests which grew out of the various rites in use, and the "Cumulation" thereof, would utilize our entire remaining pages of this chapter, hence must proceed to the organization of the Grand Lodge.

It appears from the records that twelve lodges had received charters in New Orleans prior to the organization of a Grand Lodge, as will appear in the following:[4]

---

[4] Of these lodges, Candor, No. 90, York Rite, was perhaps never organized; Reunion Desiree, No. 3829, French Rite, ceased to work, November 27, 1808; Polar Star, No. 4293, French Rite, adjourned sine die, October 13, 1811; Reunion Desiree, No. 112, York Rite, dissolved, March 23, 1812; and Bienfaisance, No. 1, Scottish Rite, affiliated with Concord, No. 117, May 27, 1812, leaving seven lodges in full activity and all working the York Rite, viz.: Numbers 1, 4, 6, 8, 9, 10, 11, and 12, in the above table.

Name of Lodge	No.	By Whom Chartered	Date of Charter
Perfect Union	29	Grand Lodge of South Carolina	March 30, 1794
Polar Star	4263	Pro. Lodge Sincerite, Marseilles Reconstructed by Grand Oriental of France	December 27, 1798 November 11, 1804
Candor	90	Grand Lodge of Pennsylvania	May 18, 1801
Charity	93	Grand Lodge of Pennsylvania	March 1, 1802
Reunion Desiree	3829	Grand Orient of France	February 17, 1807
Louisiana	1	Grand Lodge of New York	September 2, 1807
Reunion Desiree	112	Grand Lodge of Pennsylvania	September 15, 1808
Concord	117	Grand Lodge of Pennsylvania	October 7, 1810
Perseverance	118	Grand Lodge of Pennsylvania	October 7, 1810
Harmony	122	Grand Lodge of Pennsylvania	November 19, 1810
Polar Star	129	Grand Lodge of Pennsylvania	June 3, 1811
Bienfaisance	1	Grand Consistory of Jamaica	June 22, 1811

Louisiana was admitted as a State by Act of Congress, April 8, 1812, to take effect after April 30th.

This change politically had a corresponding result masonically.

Perfect Union Lodge, No. 29, had the honor of taking initiatory steps toward the organization of a Grand Lodge, which resulted in a meeting, April 18, 1812, of the delegates of Perfect Union Lodge, No. 29; Charity Lodge, No. 93; Louisiana Lodge, No. 1; Concord

Lodge, No. 117; Perseverance Lodge, No. 118; Harmony Lodge, No. 122; and Polar Star Lodge, No. 129.

These delegates organized themselves into a "General Committee of the State of Louisiana to provide for the establishment of a Grand Lodge in the City of New Orleans." P. F. Dubourg was the first President.

On May 16th following a second meeting was held, Charity Lodge, No. 93, not being represented; and a communication was received from Louisiana Lodge, No. 1, saying that in their opinion "it would be inexpedient at present" to join in the proposed formation of a Grand Lodge; whereupon a resolution was passed requesting the W. Master of the Senior of the regular lodges in the State, Perfect Union, No. 29, to issue his summons[5] to the Masters, Past Masters, and Officers of the several Ancient and regularly constituted lodges in the State to meet in convention to take into consideration the interests of the true Craft, and to deliberate on the necessity of establishing a Grand Lodge in the State, which was accordingly done, and the convention met June 13, 1812, and the following representatives were present, viz.: Perfect Union, No. 29; Charity, No. 93; Concord, No. 117; Perseverance, No. 118; Polar Star, No. 129.

As soon as the convention was organized the President, Brother Dubourg, stated that he had received a communication from Harmony Lodge, No. 122, which had withdrawn from the convention.

The convention adjourned to meet June 20th next.

June 20, 1812, the Grand Convention then met and elected the Grand Officers; P.F. Dubourg being elected Grand Master, who was duly installed after the election of the Grand Officers, and by a resolution adopted, the Grand Master installed all the other Grand Officers on July 11th following.

At a communication held August 15, 1812, the committee appointed for that purpose reported a draft of a Constitution which was adopted.

At a quarterly communication held March 27, 1813, the Grand Master announced that a Grand Royal Arch Chapter had been organized and attached to the Grand Lodge of Louisiana.

The Grand Chapter had been organized, March 8, 1813, by Concord and Perseverance R.'. A.'. Chapter, working under charters from the Grand Chapter of Pennsylvania and attached to the lodges of the same name.

---

[5] Ancient term for Notification.

On March 13th the Grand Officers were elected and installed.

To follow the history of the Grand Lodge of Louisiana would require more space than can be permitted; here we must close with the date of March, 1813.

Tennessee.

Warrants to organize lodges had been issued from the Grand Lodge of North Carolina as early as 1796 and one from Kentucky.

These lodges held a convention at Knoxville in December, 1811, and adopted the following:

"Resolved, That in the opinion of this Convention the number of Ancient York Masons in this State as well as the state of society, require the formation of a Grand Lodge within the same for the better regulation and extension of the Craft.

"Resolved, That a Committee be appointed for the purpose of drawing up an address to the Grand Lodge of North Carolina, soliciting their assent to the establishment of a Grand Lodge in the State of Tennessee."

The Grand Lodge of North Carolina granted this request; and the convention again met October 14, 1813, and the Grand Lodge was constitutionally established and the Grand Officers were elected and installed.

Mississippi.

The first lodge in Mississippi which received a Warrant from the Grand Lodge of Kentucky was Harmony, No. 33; originally No. 7, by a Charter October 16, 1801.

Two other lodges, viz.: Andrew Jackson, No. 15, and Washington, No. 17, received their warrants from the Grand Lodge of Tennessee July 27, 1818.

A convention was held in the city of Natchez, when it was resolved that it was necessary and expedient to form a Grand Lodge for the State of Mississippi.

On August 25th following, the convention again met, and the Grand Lodge was regularly constituted.

Henry Toohey was elected Grand Master.

Illinois.

The Grand Master of Pennsylvania, Israel Israel, issued a dispensation for six months to Western Star Lodge, No. 107, to be located at Kaskaskia, situated near the mouth of the Okaw (now

Kaskaskia) River, where it empties into the Mississippi River, September 24, 1805.

At that period Illinois was in the Indian Territory.

This lodge received its Charter, which was granted June 2, 1806, and on September 13th following, the lodge was regularly constituted.

This lodge was doubtless the first one established in that Territory - now comprising the States of Wisconsin and Illinois and a part of Minnesota.

The Grand Lodge of Kentucky issued a Charter, August 28, 1815, to Lawrence Lodge, to be located at Shawneetown; the Grand Lodge of Tennessee issued a Charter, October 6, 1819, to Libanus Lodge, at Edwardsville; June 20, 1820, the Grand Master of Tennessee issued a dispensation to Temple Lodge, at Belleville, St. Clair County, which was surrendered in 1821.

From the Grand Lodge of Missouri at various dates in 1822 the following warrants were granted: October 3, 1822, Olive Branch, No. 5, at Alton, Ill. ; October 8, 1822, Vandalia, No. 8, at Vandalia; October 9, 1822, Sangamon, No. 9, at Springfield; October 24, 1822, Union, No. 10, at Jonesborough; October 8, 1822, Eden, No. 11, at Covington.

The Grand Master of Indiana issued a dispensation, March 12, 1822, to Albion Lodge, at Albion.

All the above lodges except Sangamon sent delegates to a convention at Vandalia which met December 9, 1822.

They adopted a constitution, which was sent to the lodges for their consideration.

Eight of these lodges were represented at a convention held December 1 1823, and a Grand Lodge was duly organized.

The Grand Master was installed by Dr. Hardage Lane, of St. Louis, Mo., the Deputy Grand Master of the Grand Lodge of Missouri.

In 1827 the Grand Lodge of Illinois went out of existence, and after June 24, 1827, "every Lodge in the State was so effectually blotted out that no trace of any of them has been found."

It is supposed that as the anti-Masonic excitement had, about that time, begun to work its way to the West, the Masons were more or less lukewarm in the cause, and politics being somewhat mixed up in the affair, the Brethren let the matter drop for a while.

The Grand Lodge of Kentucky issued a dispensation to Bodley Lodge, No. 97, at Quincy, Ill., there being at that time no working lodge in the State. That lodge was warranted August 30, 1838.

That Grand Lodge likewise warranted Equality Lodge, No. 102, at Equality, in Gallatin County, August 29, 1837; and Ottawa, No. 114, at Ottawa County, of Lasalle, September 1, 1740.

The Grand Master of Kentucky issued a dispensation to Friendship Lodge at Dixon in 1840.

The Grand Lodge of Missouri warranted:

Franklin Lodge, at Alton, in 1827 Harmony Lodge, at Jacksonville, in 1838 Springfield Lodge, at Springfild, in 1839 Temperance Lodge, at Vandalia, in 1839 Far West Lodge, at Galena, in 1839 Mount Moriah Lodge, at Hillsboro, in 1840 Clinton Lodge, at Carlisle, in 1840 a dispensation to Columbus Lodge, No. 20, at Columbus, in 1839.

Delegates from several of the subordinate lodges on January 30, 1840, held a convention in Jacksonville, when it was resolved to form a Grand Lodge.

A committee was appointed to correspond with the lodges in the State and ask their assistance, and to send delegates to a convention to be held at Jacksonville, April 6, 1840, which convention was held on that date and six of the eight chartered lodges and one under dispensation were represented, and the Grand Lodge was then organized.

At the meeting held April 28th, the Grand Master, Abraham Jonas, was installed by proxy.[6] Warrants were issued to the lodges represented and numbered according to their dates of constitution - some of them, however, did not get their new warrants until sometime in 1844.

In consequence of the business relations existing between many of the towns in Illinois and the city of St. Louis in Missouri, some of the lodges in those towns much preferred to hold their warrants from Missouri Grand Lodge, as the representatives could attend the Grand Lodge of Missouri in St. Louis, and at the same time transact their commercial business in that city.

---

[6] The "Reprint of the Proceedings for 1840 to 1860," published 1874, shows: April 6, 1840, at Jacksonville, "M.W. Abraham Jonas was elected G.M." April 28th, "called from refreshment to labor." The name of Abraham Jonas does not appear as being present.
James Adams, D.G.M., presided.
The minutes say: "On motion all but Past Masters having retired a convocation of Past Masters was declared open, and the M.W. Grand Master was installed by proxy, and the grand honors paid him agreeable to ancient form and usage."

The writer was an officer of the Grand Lodge of Missouri in 1841-42-43 and well remembers that those Brethren from Illinois were urged to withdraw from our Grand Lodge and unite with the Grand Lodge in their own State.

They, however, declined for the reason above stated.

We can bear witness to this as a justification of the conduct of the Grand Lodge of Missouri, for they could not drive away their Brethren of Illinois.

Finally, however, those lodges did withdraw and unite with the Grand Lodge of Illinois, as also did several of the lodges in Iowa, about that time, which had been chartered by the Grand Lodge of Missouri, and they formed the Grand Lodge of Iowa.

On February 10 1850, a fire occurred in Peoria by which was destroyed, in the office of the Grand Secretary, all the books, papers, and records of the Grand Lodge of Illinois.

To remedy the loss as far as possible, the Grand Lodge was convened in Springfield, April 8, 1850.

Of the lodges aiding in the organization of the second Grand Lodge, four are now alive, viz: Bodley, No. 1; Equality, No. 2; Harmony, No. 3; and Springfield, No. 4.

In 1889, October 1st and 2d, the fiftieth anniversary was celebrated.

The Grand Lodge of Illinois, in her growth since its organization in 1839, has kept even pace with the increase of population, and now stands in membership among the first in the United States, in 1897 the membership number being 53,452, number of lodges, 722. In her influence for good and the reputation of her personnel she is primus inter pares (first among her equals).

Missouri.

The first settlers of Upper Louisiana, as the now State of Missouri was originally called, were French, who came by the way of Canada, and were companions of Cartier, La Salle, and Father Hennepin, who traversed the vast wilderness that extended between the boundaries of Canada and the settlements of the French on the Lower Mississippi.

In November, 1763, Pierre Liguiste Laclede arrived at St. Genevieve, and finding no place suitable for the storage of his good, he proceeded up the Mississippi River; and on February 15, 1764, he and his party landed where the city of St. Louis now stands, which he named in honor of Louis XV. of France.

In that early day the merchants who were in St. Louis and St. Genevieve procured their goods in Philadelphia, where they went once every year.

Many of these merchants became Masons and were made in the French Lodge, No. 73, in Philadelphia.

As the Masons in the Territory increased in numbers, they resolved to organize a lodge, and in 1807-8 having applied for, they received a Warrant of Constitution from the Grand Lodge of Pennsylvania for a lodge in the town of St. Genevieve, as Louisiana Lodge, No. 109. Otho Strader was the first Master.

Among its members were many of those who afterward became prominent merchants of St. Louis, as Pierre Chouteau and Bartholomew Berthold, who became the founders of the great Fur Company.[7]

This was the first lodge established in Missouri.

In 1811-12 Gen. H. Dodge presided over this lodge as W. Master, but owing to the unsettled condition of the Territory in consequence of the late war with Great Britain, the lodge ceased to work about 1825.

In 1809-10 the Grand Lodge of Pennsylvania granted a Warrant to a lodge in St. Louis as No. 111. There is no record whatever of this lodge remaining.

A dispensation was issued by the Grand Lodge of Indiana in 1820 for a lodge in Jackson, now in Cape Gerardeau County.

This lodge was subsequently chartered by the Grand Lodge of Missouri.

October 18, 1816 the Grand Lodge of Tennessee granted a Charter to a lodge in St. Louis as Missouri Lodge, No. 12, which is still in existence as No. 1.

That Grand Lodge also granted charters to the following lodges, viz.: October 6, 1819, to Joachim Lodge, No. 25, at Herculaneum, and on same date to St. Charles Lodge, No. 28, at St. Charles on the Missouri River.

February 23, 1821, by an invitation sent by Missouri Lodge, No. 12, to the several lodges in the State, the following lodges, by their representatives, met in St. Louis, and a committee having been appointed to draft a constitution and code of bylaws they adjourned until April 23d following, to meet at the same place to organize a Grand Lodge.

---

[7] Geo. F. Gouley, "History of Grand Lodge of Missouri."

Prior to this date (April 23, 1821), a convention of Masons met, pursuant to previous notice given by the convention of delegates, at the lodge-room of Missouri Lodge, No. 12, April 23d, Anno Lucis, Year of Light, 5821, for the purpose of organizing the Grand Lodge of the State of Missouri.

Opened in the third degree in due form, with Wor. Edward Bates,[8] Master, and others.

After reading the proceedings of the convention held February 22d last, adjourned until 24th inst. April 24, A.L. 5821. Present as before.

An election for the officers for the ensuing year was held and resulted as follows

Brother Thos. F. Riddick, M.W.G.M.
Brother James Kennerly, S.G.W.
Brother William Bates, J.G.W.
Brother Archibald Gamble, G. Treasurer.
Brother William Renshaw, G. Secretary.
Adjourned to May 4th next.

May 4th A.L. 5821, Semi-Annual Convocation was held, a procession was formed and proceeded to the Baptist Church, where the solemn ceremony of consecration and installation was performed, in conformity with the ancient landmarks and customs of the Fraternity.

The Grand Lodge then returned to the lodge-room and adjourned until next day.[9]

The first annual communication was held October 1, 1821.

At this communication Brother Frederick Bates was elected Grand Master, who, not being present, was notified by a committee, but declined accepting the office.

Grand Lodge adjourned until October 10, 1821, at which time the Grand Lodge resumed labor and elected Brother N.B. Tucker M.W. Grand Master, and Edward Bates G.S.W.

The Grand Lodge then adjourned until 7 P.M., when at the request of Bro. Thos. F. Riddick, Brother Douglass took the Chair and installed Brother Nathaniel B. Tucker Most Worshipful Grand Master of the Grand Lodge of Missouri in ample form, and the Past Master's Lodge was closed, and the other Grand Officers were duly installed into their respective offices.

---

[8] Hon. Edward Bates was Attorney-General in Mr. Lincoln's Cabinet, 1861-64. Nearly every member of this Grand Lodge was personally known to the present writer in 1837.

[9] Geo. F. Gouley, "History of Grand Lodge of Missouri."

Thus the Grand Lodge of Missouri was constituted and has continued to the present day, and the writer, who the commencement of his own Masonic career, January 18, 1840, could personally testify to the character and standing, in the community of the State of Missouri, to nearly every member of that distinguished body of men and Masons, upon whose shoulders the interests of our noble institution, at that time, were placed by the Grand Lodge.

In the year 1841 the writer was appointed the Senior Grand Deacon of the Grand Lodge by Hon. Priestly H. McBride, Grand Master, and was reappointed in 1842 and 1843.

A very large proportion of those who organized the first Grand Lodge continued as members and officers of the Grand Lodge up to the year 1844, when by accessions of lodges which had been chartered from 1821 to 1840, the number had increased from four to twenty-five, which was Naphtali, and in which we received the three degrees.

In 1841-42 several lodges had been chartered in Iowa, and among them was Iowa Lodge, No. 42, of which our very distinguished Brother Theodore S. Parvin was Wor. Master, and we mention this circumstance to state that he and the writer are the only surviving members of that Grand Lodge of 1841 to 1844.

Indiana.

As early as 1795 members of the Fraternity who had been connected with lodges in the army on the northwest frontier, introduced Free Masonry into the Territory.

The first lodge, however, was organized by a dispensation from the Grand Lodge of Kentucky, August 31, 1808, at Vincennes, by the name of Vincennes Lodge, No. 15.

The following lodges were also granted warrants by the Grand Lodge of Kentucky: At Madison, Union Lodge, No. 29, August 31, 1815; at Charlestown, Blazing Star, No. 36, August 25, 1816; at Salem, Melchizedeck, No. 43; Lawrenceburg, Lawrenceburg, No. 44; and at Corydon, Pisgah, No. 45, all August 25, 1817.

The Grand Master of Kentucky, after the annual meeting of the Grand Lodge, issued a dispensation for the Lodge at Switzerland, and one for Rising Sun Lodge, at Rising Sun.

A dispensation for lodge Brookville Harmony, No. 41, at Brookville, was issued by the Grand Master of Ohio in 1816 or 1817.

A general convention of the representatives of the following lodges of Ancient York Masons of the State of Indiana was held at Corydon on December 3, 1817, viz.:

Name of Lodge.	No.	Location.	Representative.
Vincennes	5	Vincennes	G.W. Johnston.
Lawrenceburg	44	Lawrenceburg	James Dill
Switzerland	U.D. of Ky	Vevay	Hezekiah B. Hull.
Rising Sun	U.D. of Ky	Rising Sun	A.C. Pepper.
Madison Union	29	Madison	H.P. Thornton.
Blazing Star	36	Charlestown	Jos. Bartholomew. John Miller.
Brookville Harmony.	41	U.D.Ohio. Brookville	Stephen C. Stevens.
Salem	43	Salem	Christ Harrison.
Pisgah	45	Corydon	Davis Floyd.

Brother Alexander Buckner was unanimously chosen President, and Davis Floyd unanimously elected Secretary.

The convention then adopted the following:

"Resolved, That it is expected and advisable that a Grand Lodge should be at this time formed in the State of Indiana."

All the above representatives voted in the affirmative except those of Harmony and Pisgah.

The convention then adopted the following:

"Resolved, That a committee of four members be appointed to inform the M.W. Grand Masters of Kentucky and Ohio that a constitutional number of chartered lodges have determined in general convention to form a Grand Lodge in this State, and consequently will secede from their Mother Lodge so soon as a Grand Lodge is organized."

The convention also

"Resolved, That the several subordinate lodges here represented do appoint one or more delegates to meet at Madison on the second Monday in January next, for the purpose of opening a Grand Lodge for the State of Indiana; and that a Communication be forwarded to the rest of the lodges in this State unrepresented in this convention, of the above determination."

This resolution was adopted:

Harmony, No. 41; Lawrenceburg, No. 44; Switzerland, U.D.; Rising Sun, U.D.; and Madison, No. 29, voted in the affirmative, five.

Vincennes No. 15; Salem, No. 43; Pisgah, No. 45; and Blazing Star, No. 36, voted in the negative, four.

A Grand Communication of the subordinate lodges of the State of Indiana was held Monday, January 12, A.L. 5818.

Representatives of the following lodges were present: Rising Sun, U.D.; Union, No. 29; Switzerland, U.D.; Blazing Star, No. 36.

Delegates were reported by the Committee on Credentials, and admitted as being duly appointed by their respective lodges, viz.: Harmony Lodge, Brookville, U.D., from Grand Lodge of Ohio; Lawrenceburg, No. 44; Vincennes, No. 15; Melchizedeck, No. 43; Pisgah, No. 45.

The following resolution was adopted: "Resolved, That the chartered lodges here represented do now separate for a time from the lodges under dispensation, and proceed immediately to organize a Grand Lodge for the State of Indiana."

Brother Alexander A. Meek, being the oldest Past Master present, was called to the Chair.

Melchizedeck Lodge surrendered her Charter but declined having a new one.

January 13th the Grand Officers were duly elected, M.W. Alexander Buckner, Grand Master.

The representatives from lodges Nos. 15, 29, 36, 43, 44, 45, holding charters from the Grand Lodge of Kentucky, surrendered the same, and asked to have charters granted to their respective lodges by the Grand Lodge of Indiana, which was accordingly done on the 14th, viz.:

Vincennes Lodge, No. 1, Vincennes; Union Lodge, No. 2, Madison; Blazing Star Lodge, No. 3, Charlestown; Lawrenceburg Lodge, No. 4, Lawrenceburg; Melchizedeck Lodge, No. 5; Pisgah Lodge, No. 6, Corydon; which lodges received their charters at this communication.

The Grand Constitution was adopted January 15th.

The illustrations of Masonry of Thomas Smith Webb were adopted for the government of the Grand Lodge, and were recommended to be adopted by all the subordinate lodges of the State for the government of the same.

Charlestown was selected as the site for the meeting of the Grand Lodge for the present.

The Junior Grand Warden being a member of Melchizedeck Lodge, which declined a Charter, the office became vacant and an election was held to fill the same, and Brother Benjamin V. Becks was duly elected.

The Grand Lodge met in various towns and cities until 1828, when it removed to Indianapolis, and has continued to do so ever since.

Alabama.

The first lodge in Alabama was Madison, No. 21, at Huntsville, which was chartered by the Grand Lodge of Kentucky, August 28, 1812. The Grand Lodge of Tennessee granted a Charter to Alabama Lodge, No. 21, at Huntsville, October 6, 1818.

The Grand Lodge of South Carolina granted a Charter to Alabama Lodge, No. 51, at Clairborne, in 1819; the Grand Lodge of Tennessee granted a Warrant to Rising Virtue Lodge, No. , at Tuskaloosa, October 5, 1818; and the Grand Master of Tennessee issued a dispensation to Halo Lodge, at Cahawba, April 4, 1820, and which continued until October, 1821; but the Grand Lodge of Georgia issued a Warrant to Halo Lodge, No. 21, January 24, 1821; the Grand Lodge of Tennessee issued a Charter to Moulton Lodge, at Moulton, October 3, 1820; the Grand Lodge of Tennessee granted a dispensation to Russellville Lodge, October 3, 1820; a dispensation from the Grand Master of Tennessee was issued to Farrar Lodge, at Elyton, March 5, 1821; the Grand Lodge of North Carolina granted a Charter to St. Stephen's Lodge, at St. Stephen's, December 14, 1816; Washington Lodge and Tuscumbia Lodge were granted charters by the Grand Lodge of Tennessee.

Tuscumbia had never reported its work, and soon went out of existence.

Washington very soon gave up her Charter.

The name of Madison Lodge, No. 21, was changed to Helion; Alabama Lodge, No. 21, at Huntsville, was changed to Bethsaida; soon afterward a consolidation took place and these two and Helion and Bethsaida became Helion, No. 1. Of all the above lodges there only remain at the present time Rising Virtue, No. 4; Moulton, No. 6; and Farrar, No. 8.

The Grand Lodge was organized by the above - mentioned lodges and a constitution was adopted and signed June 15, 1821.

December 6, 1836, a quorum was not present; and after waiting for three days, those who were present declared the Grand Lodge extinct.

The representatives of the lodges present reorganized a Grand Lodge, a new constitution was adopted, new Grand Officers were elected, and the old warrants were re-granted.

Arkansas.

November 29, 1819, a dispensation for Arkansas Lodge, located at the Port of Arkansas, was issued by the Grand Lodge of Kentucky.

A Charter was granted, August 29, 1820, Robert Johnson being W. Master.

This lodge surrendered her Charter, August 28, 1822.

A dispensation to organize Washington Lodge at Fayetteville was issued by the Grand Master of the Grand Lodge of Tennessee, December 24, 1835; and it mas renewed, November 12, 1836. October 3, 1837, a Charter was granted, and the lodge received as a present a set of jewels.

A dispensation was granted from the same Grand Lodge for a lodge at Clarksville, October 5, 1838, to which a Charter was issued, October 12, 1839. The dispensation of Clarksville Lodge was received prior to the organization of the Grand Lodge of Arkansas, but the Charter was issued after that event.

This lodge continued under the constitution of the Grand Lodge of Tennessee until 1843, when it came under the Grand Lodge of Arkansas as No. 5. In 1845 it ceased to work and surrendered the Charter.

January 6, 1837, the Grand Lodge of Louisiana issued warrants to two lodges in Arkansas, viz.: Morning Star, at Arkansas Post, and Western Star, at Little Rock.

The seat of State Government having been changed to Little Rock, Morning Star Lodge gave up the Charter.

A dispensation was issued by the Grand Master of Alabama in 1838 to Mount Horeb Lodge in Washington.

November 21, 1838, a convention was held and representatives from Washington, Morning Star, Western Star, and Mount Horeb, U.D., were present at which a constitution was adopted and officers were elected and the Grand Lodge was duly constituted.

Wisconsin.

The history of Freemasonry in the territory now embraced in the State of Wisconsin dates from December 27, 1823.

The only known record of the first lodge in what is now Wisconsin is founded in an address delivered at Green Bay, December 17, 1854, by P.G.M. Henry S. Baird.

He says:

The first action had with a view to organize a lodge of Masons at Green Bay is found in proceedings of a meeting of the members of the Fraternity, held on the evening of the 27th day of December, A.D. 1823.

A committee was appointed to draft a petition to the Grand Lodge of the State of New York, praying for a dispensation to open and hold a Lodge of Free and Accepted Masons at Green Bay, then in the Territory of Michigan.

In due time the prayer of the petitioners was responded to, and a dispensation granted.

On September 2, 1824, the first regular Lodge of Free and Accepted Masons was opened and organized at Fort Howard, directly opposite to the city, under a dispensation from the M.W. Grand Master of the Grand Lodge of the State of New York.

The officers named in the dispensation were:

Robert Irwin, Sr., W. Master.

Benjamin Watson, S. Warden.

W. V. Wheaton, J. Warden.

On December 3, 1824, a regular Charter was granted by the M.W. Grand Lodge of New York.

Mineral Point Lodge, No. 1, was organized July 27, 1841, from the Grand Lodge of Missouri, under dispensation dated October 8, 1840, named "Melody" (for Bro. George H.C. Melody, P. Dep. Grand Master of Missouri) Lodge, No. 65 (now No. 2).

A dispensation was issued by Brother Joab[10] T. Bernard, Dep. Grand Master, January 10, 1843.

A Charter was granted by the Grand Lodge of Missouri, October 13, 1843.[11]

A preliminary meeting, having in contemplation the formation of a Masonic lodge, was held at the house of John Beavans, in the town of Platteville, in the month of January, A.D. 1843. MILWAUKEE LODGE, NO. 22 (NOW KILBOURN LODGE, No. 3)

---

[10] Incorrectly called in the record John.

[11] The present writer was S.G.D. of the Grand Lodge of Missouri at that time.

The first meeting of this lodge was held July 5, A.L. 5843, A.D. 1843.

Bro. Normand Hawley, representing the Grand Master of Illinois, presented the dispensation which he had been deputed to bring to them.

The exact date of the Charter of this lodge does not appear from the minutes.

In the proceedings of the Grand Lodge of Illinois, October 2, 1843, the committee on Returns and Work recommended granting a Charter to Milwaukee Lodge, No. 22, "when dues are paid; "and on the first day of November, 1843, the election of officers was held under the Charter, 1843.

ACTION RELATIVE TO THE FORMATION OF A GRAND LODGE, NOVEMBER 22, 1843.

The worshipful Master, Bro. Abram D. Smith, presented a communication from Melody Lodge, at Platteville, upon the subject of establishing a Grand Lodge in the Territory of Wisconsin, which was read, and the Master and Wardens were appointed a committee to correspond with Platteville and Mineral Point lodges upon the subject.

The Charter of Milwaukee Lodge, No. 3, is dated January 17, 1844.

MASONIC CONVENTION HELD AT MADISON ON THE 18TH DAY OF DECEMBER, A.D. 1843.

The following lodges were represented:
Milwaukee Lodge, at Milwaukee.
Mineral Lodge, at Mineral Point.
Melody Lodge, at Platteville.

Bro. Moses Meeker was called to the Chair, and Bro. Geo. W. Lakin was appointed Secretary.

On motion of Bro. Ben. C. Eastman, it was Ordered, That a committee consisting of two be appointed to receive and examine the credentials of the members of the convention.

The committee appointed to receive and examine the credentials of the members of the convention, being the legal representatives of the regularly constituted lodges of the Territory of Wisconsin, to take into consideration and determine upon the expediency of forming a Grand Lodge within the said Territory, have attended to the duty assigned them, and submit the following:

Your committee find that there are seven members of said convention representatives of the lodges aforesaid, to wit:

From Milwaukee, Mineral Point, and Melody lodges.

On motion of Bro. Ben. C. Eastman, it was

Ordered, That a committee of three be appointed to take into consideration the expediency of forming a Grand Lodge in the Territory of Wisconsin.

The Chair appointed Bros. Ben. C. Eastman, Dwight F. Lawton, and Geo. H. Walker said committee.

Bro. Ben. C. Eastman, from said committee, submitted the following:

REPORT.

The committee appointed to take into consideration the expediency of forming a Grand Lodge in the Territory, have attended to their duty, and ask leave to report the following preamble and resolutions:

Whereas, There are now, within the Territory of Wisconsin, three chartered lodges, all of which are in a prosperous and happy condition; and

Whereas, It is competent for that number of lodges to emerge from a state of dependency, become legally organized, and be hereafter established and known as a separate, distinct, and independent body, having its own jurisdiction and

Whereas, In the rapidly increasing population of our Territory, it is believed many more lodges will immediately spring into existence whereby the great principles of Masonry will be promulgated, if the facilities for obtaining dispensations and charters are increased as they will be by the organization of a Grand Lodge in Wisconsin; and

Whereas, The Great Lights of Masonry should not be hidden under a bushel, but should shine in the fullness of their strength, that none may want a guide for their faith and practice, and that their acts be squared by the precepts of the Great Architect of the Universe, and their desire be circumscribed by the principles of morality and their passions restrained in due bounds.

Therefore, be it

Resolved, That it is expedient to form a Grand Lodge in the Territory of Wisconsin.

On motion of Bro. John H. Rountree, the report of the committee was accepted, the preamble and resolutions adopted, and the committee discharged.

On motion of Bro. Dwight F. Lawton, it was

Ordered, That a committee of three be appointed to draft a constitution for a Grand Lodge, and that said committee be instructed to report at as early an hour as possible.

The Chair appointed Bros. Lawton, Meeker, and Lakin said committee.

The convention adjourned till 6 P.M.

Evening at 6 P.M. convention met.

Bro. Lawton, from the committee appointed to draft a constitution for a Grand Lodge, reported the draft of a constitution, which report was accepted and committee discharged.

On motion, the convention adjourned sine die.

The M.W. Grand Lodge of Free and Accepted Masons met in annual communication in the city of Madison, on Monday, December 18, A.D. 1843, A.L. 5843.

The Grand Lodge was opened in the third degree, in due and ancient form.

On motion of Bro. Meeker, the constitution reported in the convention was taken up, read, and adopted.

Bro. Merrill, from said committee, made the following:

REPORT.

The committee appointed to nominate officers for the Grand Lodge have attended to the duty assigned them, and report that they have nominated the following:

Benjamin T. Kavanaugh, G. Master.
Abram D. Sniith, D. G. Master.
Moses Meeker, S. G. Warden.
David Merrilly, J. G. Warden.
Thomas P. Burnett, Grand Treasurer.
Ben. C. Eastman, Grand Secretary.
Dwight F. Lawton, Grand Lecturer.

Which report was accepted, and the committee discharged.

On motion of Bro. Rountree, it was

Resolved, That the Grand Lodge do now proceed to the election of officers, and all the above-named Brethren were elected and installed.

Texas.

During the very first effort to establish a lodge in Texas, that country was a dependency of Mexico, and the Roman Catholic priesthood controlled the most of the population and were the open enemies of Freemasonry, and the American settlers were objects of suspicion.

In the winter of 1834-35 five Master Masons having made themselves known to each other as such, after many conferences and much deliberation, concluded to establish a lodge in Texas.

These were John H. Wharton, Asa Brigham, James A.E. Phelps, Alexander Russell, and Anson Jones; they fixed upon time and locality for their meeting to accomplish their desire.

Brother J. P. Caldwell subsequently joined them.

The town of Brazoria was selected for their meeting, and in a small grove of wild peach and laurel in a family burial-ground of General John Austin.

Here in a day of March, 1835, 10 A.M., "was held the first formal meeting of Masons in Texas." These six Brethren made arrangements to apply to the Grand Lodge of Louisiana for a dispensation to form and open a lodge to be called Holland Lodge.

A petition was drawn up and another Master Mason, Brother W.D.C. Hall, having signed it with the other six, it was forwarded to New Orleans.

The officers named were: Anson Jones, W. Master; Asa Brigham, Senior Warden, and J.P. Caldwell, Junior Warden.

This dispensation was granted, and Holland Lodge, No. 36, was started at Brazoria on December 27, 1835. In the second story of the old court-house was where the Communications were held.

In consequence of the difficulties with Mexico, which finally resulted in open hostilities, the succeeding war, and independence of the Republic of Texas, the lodge struggled on until February, 1836, the last conmmunication being held that month.

In March Brazoia was abandoned, and the dispensation was captured by Urrea, and with records, books, jewels, etc., was destroyed.

In October, 1837, the lodge was reopened in the city of Houston, a Warrant for it having been granted in the meantime, and the lodge is yet in existence.

Two other lodges, viz.: Milam, No. 40, at Nacogdoches, and McFarland, No. 41, at San Augustine, were warranted by the Grand Lodge of Louisiana.

These lodges, as also Holland Lodge, No. 36, sent delegates to a convention which met in Houston, and the Grand Lodge of the Republic at Texas was organized, December 20, 1837.

Brother Anson Jones was elccted Grand Master.

The three lodges surrendered their charters to the Grand Lodge of Louisiana, and received new charters from their own Grand Lodge.

Iowa.

The first dispensation for the organization of a lodge in the Territory of Iowa was issued November 20, 1840, to Des Moines Lodge, at Burlington, which was chartered October 20, 1841.

The second dispensation for a lodge was issued February 4, 1841, to Iowa Lodge, at Bloomington, Muscatine County, constituted February 4, 1841, and chartered October 20, 1841, as No. 42.

The third dispensation was dated October 10, 1842, to Dubuque Lodge, at Dubuque, and was chartered October 10, 1843.

The fourth was Iowa City Lodge, at Iowa City, County of Johnson, which was constituted October 10, 1842, by dispensation, and chartered October 10, 1843.

These lodges all derived their warrants from the Grand Lodge of Missouri, and the present writer, as an officer in that Grand Lodge, voted for all but the first one, but was a visitor in the Grand Lodge when the first one was chartered.

He made the personal acquaintance of Brother Theodore S. Parvin and the other representatives of those lodges at that time, and Brother Parvin and the writer are the only surviving members of that Grand Lodge since October, 1897.

These four lodges, by agreement, at a preliminary convention of their delegates, held at the communication of the Grand Lodge of Missouri, at St. Louis, October 11, 1843, met in convention at Iowa City, in Iowa Territory, January 2, 1844, and then and there organized the Grand Lodge of Iowa.

Delegates were present from the following other lodges in Iowa working under authority of the Grand Lodge of Illinois, viz.: Rising Sun, No. 12, at Montrose, Keokuk Lodge, at Keokuk, and Clinton Lodge, at Davenport.

The first under a Charter and the other two under dispensations.

These lodges were finally admitted to the Grand Lodge of Iowa.

January 3, 1844, the Grand Officers were elected.

Brother Oliver Cock was unanimously elected on the second ballot the Grand Master, and Brother Theodore Sutton Parvin unanimously elected Grand Secretary, which office he has filled, except when he was chosen Grand Master, ever since, now fifty-five years.

No Mason has a more extended reputation for abilities, so essential in the management of Masonic affairs, than has our illustrious Brother, who is so favorably known throughout the world of Masonry.

Oregon.

After the organization of Multnomab Lodge at Oregon City, a little more than two years elapsed before any additional lodges were established in Oregon.

Following the planting of this lodge, the Grand Lodge of California, on November 27, 1850, granted a Charter to Willamette Lodge, No. 11, at Portland.

This lodge was opened and constituted January 4, 1851. The Grard Lodge of California granted a Charter to Lafayette Lodge, of Oregon. This lodge was constituted and began work July 30, 1851. The establishment of this lodge gave to the Territory of Oregon the requisite number of lodges, under the common law of Masonry, to organize an independent Grand Lodge for the jurisdiction.

The opportunity was at once improved.

"The important question," says a distinguished Brother, recently deceased, "of having a Grand Lodge was agitated.

Consequently, on the 16th of August, A.L. 5851, A.D 1851, a convention of F. & A.

Masons of the Territory of Oregon was held at Oregon City to form a Grand Lodge.

Brother Berryman Jennings was elected Chairman and Bro. Benjamin Stark Secretary." The convention, after due consideration, resolved upon the wisdom and expediency of the "formation of a Grand Lodge." In pursuance of this action an address, giving official notice of the purpose in view, was prepared and sent out to the several lodges, requesting them to meet again in convention on the second Saturday in September following, to perfect the Grand Lodge organization.

In pursuance of this call, delegates from the several lodges assembled at Oregon City on September 13, 1851, and proceeded to the work in hand by the election of Bro. John Elliott Chairman, and Bro. W.S. Caldwell Secretary.

The three lodges, viz.: Multonomah, Willamette, and La Fayette, were duly represented.

Among the delegates present were those who were otherwise admitted to seats in the convention, viz.: Bros. J.C. Ainsworth, R.R. Thompson, Forbes Barclay, John Elliott, Lewis May, Benj. Stark, Wm.

M. Berry, D.D. Garrett, G.B. Coudy, B. Jennings, Robert Thompson, Amory Holbrook, and W.S. Caldwell.

On Monday, September 15th following, a constitution, through a committee, was reported and adopted, and the Grand Lodge of Oregon duly organized.

Bro. Berryman Jennings was elected and installed Grand Master, and Bro. Benj. Stark Grand Secretary.

The first lodge established under authority of the Grand Lodge of Oregon was organized at Salem, under the name of Salem Lodge, No. 4. The dispensation of this lodge was issued by the Deputy Grand Master, R.W. Bro. John Elliott, on October 4, 1851.

California.

The Grand Lodge of California was organized in the city of Sacramento, April 18, 1850.

The constituent lodges were California Lodge, No. 13, chartered by the Grand Lodge of the District of Columbia, located in San Francisco, November 9, 1848; Connecticut Lodge, No. 75, Sacramento City, chartered by the Grand Lodge of Connecticut, January 31, 1849; and Western Star Lodge, No. 98, from the Grand Lodge of Missouri, May 10, 1848; Benton City, Upper California.

Delegates were present from New Jersey Lodge, under dispensation from the Deputy Grand Master of the Grand Lodge of New jersey, dated March 1, 1849.

This lodge was opened in Sacramento City, December 4, 1849.

Credentials were presented by B.D. Hyam, from Benicia Lodge, at Benicia, but there being no dispensation or Charter or any other information of the existence of such a lodge, it was not recognized.

A constitution was adopted April 19th, and the Grand Officers were elected and duly installed.

Minnesota.

The first lodge organized in Minnesota was St. Paul's, No. 1, constituted by the Grand Lodge of Ohio, August 4, 1849; the second lodge was St. John's, No. 1, warranted October 12, 1850, by the Grand Lodge of Wisconsin; and the third was Cataract Lodge, No 168, founded by the Grand Lodge of Illinois, 1852.

These three lodges, by delegates, met in convention at the city of St. Paul, February 23, 1853, and constituted the Grand Lodge of the State of Minnesota.

New Mexico.

The Grand Lodge of Missouri issued warrants to the following lodges in New Mexico, viz.: Aztec Lodge, No. 108; Chapman Lodge, No. 95; and Montezuma Lodge, No. 109.

These lodges met in convention, August 6, 1877, at Santa Fe, for the purpose of discussing the question of forming a Grand Lodge.

Brother Simon B. Newcomb presided.

The committee on credentials found the representatives of the three above-mentioned lodges to be present.

The next day a constitution and by-laws were adopted, the Grand Officers were elected and installed, Brother Wm. W. Griffin being M.W. Grand Master, and David J. Miller R. W. Grand Secretary.

Washington.

The first steps of initiatory efforts toward Masonic organization and the formation of a Masonic lodge on the Pacific Coast, so far as any record has been shown or it is believed to exist, were taken jointly by three brother Master Masons, namely: Bros. Joseph Hull, William P. Dougherty, and Peter G. Stewart.

A petition was prepared and addressed to the Grand Lodge of Missouri praying that a Charter be granted to the petitioners, under the name of Multnomah Lodge.

The record of the Grand Lodge of Missouri reads as follows: "A charter was granted to Multnomah Lodge, No. 84, on the 19th day of October, 1846, locating the Lodge at Oregon City, Oregon Territory."

In his annual address to the Grand Lodge of Oregon, held June 13, 1853, M.W. Bro. Berryman Jennings, Grand Master, says:

"On the 25th day of November (1852) last, I granted a dispensation to sundry brethren residing at Olympia, Puget Sound, to open a Lodge under the name of Olympia Lodge, returnable at this Grand Communication, which return has been promptly made, through their Worshipful Master, Brother T.F. McElroy." Washington Territory was not organized until after this dispensation was issued and the lodge began work.

On Saturday evening, December 11, 1852, Olympia Lodge, U.D., held its first communication by virtue of Grand Lodge authority, and was thereunder duly organized, the following officers, members and Brethren being present, viz. : Bros. Thornton F. McElroy, W.M., James W. Wiley, S.W., and Michael T. Simmons, S.W.; also Bros. Smith Hays and Nicholas Delin of the original petitioners (Bros. Ira Ward and A.K.

Skidmore of said petitioners being absent); Bros. Fred A. Clark and Calvin H. Hale, visitors, were also present.

The Charter was granted to Olympia Lodge of Oregon, June 13th, and bears date June 15, 1853, and was designated as Olympia Lodge of Oregon, No. 5, of that grand jurisdiction.

The first meeting under the Charter was held on Saturday evening, July 24, 1853, at which time we may infer the lodge was regularly constituted, although the record is silent in this particular.

An election, however, was held that evening for new officers under the Charter, with the following result: Bros. T.F. McElroy, W.M.; B.F. Yantis, S. W.; M.T. Simmons, J.W.; B. Close, Sec.; Ira Ward, Treas., and Smith Hays, Tyler.

This was the first lodge established and constituted north of the Columbia River and west of the Rocky Mountains.

The records of Multnomah Lodge from its institution until 1868 were destroyed by fire, and the oldest record is the ledger dating from the year 1854.

Steilacoom Lodge, the second lodge established within the present jurisdictional limits of Washington, was organized U.D. in the year 1854. Since it first began work it has passed through several trying ordeals, some of which were of so serious a nature that its existence might well have been regarded as hopeless but for the pluck and Masonic energy of its membership.

The records of the Grand Lodge of Oregon, session of June, 1854, show that R.W. Dep. Grand Master J.C. Ainsworth, acting Grand Master, "granted a Dispensation to Brother W. H. Wallace and others to open a Lodge at Steilacoom, Washington Territory, under the name of Steilacoom Lodge."

The dispensation must have been granted during the latter part of January or some time in February, 1855.

During the summer or fall Of 1857, probably about September 1st, M.W. Bro. Ben. J. Stark, G.M. of Masons of Oregon, issued a dispensation for a new lodge at Grand Mound, Thurston County, Washington, named Grand Mound Lodge.

This lodge was chartered by the Grand Lodge of Oregon, July 12, or 15, 1858, under the name of Grand Mound Lodge, No. 21. On August 21, 1858, at its hall on Grand Mound Prairie, the lodge was duly constituted and its officers installed.

On September 19, 1868, after eleven years of hard struggling, in earnest and zealous efforts to build up and sustain the lodge, the

Brethren reluctantly felt it a duty to themselves and the Fraternity to surrender the Charter to the Grand Lodge.

In the annual address of M. W. Grand Master Benjamin J. Stark to the Grand Lodge of Oregon, July 13, 1858, among the seven dispensations he reported having granted during the year for the formation of new lodges is one "for Washington Territory."

On July 13, 1858, a Charter was granted by the Grand Lodge of Oregon to Washington Lodge, No. 22.

The Charter bears date the same as that of Grand Mound Lodge, namely, July 15, 1858.

In the foregoing references to the organization, severally, of Olympia, Steilacoom, Grand Mound, and Washington lodges, we find that they were the first organized Masonic bodies north of Columbia River.

On Monday, December 6, 1858, a little band of Freemasons, about one dozen in number, met at the Masonic hall, in the city of Olympia, Washington Territory.

Their declaration of purpose was to consider "the propriety of establishing a Grand Lodge of Free and Accepted Masons for said Territory."

This little band of Brethren in convention assembled resolved to proceed to the formation and organization of a Grand Lodge of Free and Accepted Masons for the Territory of Washington.

The convention was composed of delegates representing the four existing lodges in the Territory, viz.: Olympia Lodge, No. 5; Steilacoom Lodge, No. 8; Grand Mound Lodge, No. 21, and Washington Lodge, No. 22, together with all Past Masters by service, who were members of these lodges, and present during the sessions of the convention.

On the evening of December 8, 1858, a constitution, having been prepared by a committee appointed for that purpose, was submitted, duly considered and adopted, after which the Grand Officers were elected.

The convention, having completed its labors, was adjourned, sine die, on the morning of December 9th, whereupon the Most Worshipful Grand Lodge of Free and Accepted Masons of the Territory of Washington was opened in ample form, and was thus launched upon the sea of its sovereign existence.

The business transacted at this first session, though comparatively brief, was most important to the future interest and zeal of the Grand Lodge.

It related chiefly to formulating plans and adopting methods for placing the "machinery of Grand Lodge in Order," in furtherance of the important work before it.

We are indebted to the history of the Grand Lodge of Washington, by Bro. Grand Secretary Thomas M. Read, for the above sketch.

Kansas.

By reference to the proceedings of the Grand Lodge of Missouri the record will be found of the organization of the first three lodges in Kansas.

Dispensations for the formation of new lodges were issued:

August 4, 1854, to John W. Chivington and others, to open a lodge at the house of Mathew R. Walker, in Wyandotte Territory, to be called Kansas Lodge, by order of Most Worshipful Grand Master L.S. Cornwell.

October 6, 1854, to John W. Smith and others, to open a lodge at the town of Smithfield, Kansas Territory, to be called Smithfield Lodge, by order of R.W.N.B. Giddings, D.D.G. Master First Masonic District of Missouri.

December 30, 1854, to Richard R. Rees and others, to open a lodge at the town of Leavenworth, Kansas Territory, by order of R.W.D.P. Wallingford, D.G. Master of Missouri.[12]

At a meeting of delegates from several Masonic lodges in the Territory of Kansas, at the city of Leavenworth, on November 14, A.D. 1855, A.L. 5855.

Present: Bro. William P. Richardson of Smithton Lodge, No. 140, as proxy for W.M. Richard R. Rees, W.M. of Leavenworth Lodge, No. 150, and Bro. A. Payney, S.W. of Leavenworth Lodge, No. 150.

On motion of Bro. Rees, Bro. William P, Richardson was called to the Chair, and on motion, Bro. R.R. Rees acted as Secretary.

Bro. Rees moved, that as Wyandotte Lodge was not represented in this convention, that the convention adjourn until December 27th next, with a request that all the chartered lodges be represented; which motion was carried, and the convention adjourned.

The convention met in the office of A. and R.R. Rees, in the city of Leavenworth, pursuant to adjournment, December 27, 1855.

---

[12] Proceedings of Grand Lodge of Missouri, 1855, pp. 64, 65.

Present: Bro. John W. Smith, W. M. of Smithton Lodge, No. 140; Bro. R.R. Rees, W.M. of Leavenworth Lodge, No. 150; and Bros. C.T. Harrison, L.J. Eastin, J.J. Clarkson, G.W. Perkins, I.B. Donaldson, and Brother Kohn, Master Masons. Bro. J.W. Smith was called to the Chair, Bro. Rees acting as Secretary. Bro. Rees offered the following resolution, which was unanimously adopted:

Resolved, That we do proceed to organize a Grand Lodge for the Territory of Kansas, and that a copy of the proceedings of this convention be forwarded to Wyandotte Lodge with a request that they cooperate with us, and approve the proceedings of this convention; and that so soon as Wyandotte shall inform the Grand Master elect of their approval, and cooperation in the proceedings of this convention, that then, the Grand Master elect shall be installed as Grand Master and immediately issue a proclamation declaring this Grand Lodge fully organized.

On motion of Bro. Rees, the Chair appointed a committee of three to report a constitution and by-laws for the government of this Grand Lodge, which committee consisted of Bros. Rees, Eastin, and Harrison.

The committee appointed to report a constitution and code of bylaws made their report, which was adopted.

On motion of Bro. Rees, the convention adjourned, to meet at Masonic hall at early candle-light.

On motion of Bro. Rees, the constitution and by-laws adopted in convention are unanimously adopted as the constitution and by-laws of this Grand Lodge.

The Grand Lodge thereupon proceeded to the election of Grand Officers, which resulted in the election of Bro. Richard R. Rees as M.W.G.M.

On motion of Bro. Vanderslice, a committee consisting of Bros. Vanderslice, Walker, and Smith was appointed to report a constitution and code of bylaws for the government of this Grand Lodge.

The Grand Lodge was called from labor to refreshments until 7.30 P.M.

A committee appointed by the Grand Lodge of Kansas, at their convention held at Leavenworth City, on Monday, March 17, 1856, reported a constitution and by-laws for the government of said Grand Lodge which was adopted.

The Grand Lodge then proceeded to the election of Grand Officers for the ensuing year, which resulted in the election of Bro.

Richard R. Rees, Grand Master, who was then installed and who then installed all the other officers.

Nebraska.

The first lodge in the State of Nebraska was Nebraska Lodge, No. 184, at Belleville, Sarpy County, chartered by the Grand Lodge of Illinois, October 3, 1855.

The second lodge was Giddings Lodge, No. 156, at Nebraska City, Otoe County, chartered by the Grand Lodge of Missouri, May 28, 1856.

The third lodge was Capitol Lodge, No. 101, at Omaha City, Douglas County, chartered by the Grand Lodge of Iowa, June 3, 1857.

These three lodges, by their delegates, held a convention at Omaha City, September 23, 1857, and resolved to organize a Grand Lodge for the Territory of Nebraska.

The Grand Officers were elected, Bro. Robert C. Jordan being chosen Grand Master, who held that station until 1860.

We regret to record here that this "father of Nebraska Masonry" died January 9, 1899, aged seventy-four years.

Before closing this history of Nebraska, intelligence was received of the sad ending of the life of another distinguished brother, William R. Bowen, the Grand Secretary of the Grand Lodge, Grand Chapter, and Grand Recorder of the Grand Commandery, who, like Brother Jordan, had been called the father of Nebraska Masonry.

These remarks are due, because of the writer's personal knowledge of, and intimate association with, both of these Brethren, not only in the above grand bodies, but also in the Supreme Council of the A.'.A.'.A.'.S.'. Rite, of which Bro.' Jordan was the Active Member for Nebraska up to the date of his death, and Bro.'.Bowen was an Emeritus, having retired from the Active list several years since.

Indian Territory.

The first lodge organized in the Indian Territory was Flint Lodge, in the "Cherokee Nation," which received a Charter from the Grand Lodge of Arkansas, dated November 9, 1853.

The second lodge was called Muskogee, and subsequently named Eufala, in the "Creek Nation," and received a dispensation, supposedly, from the Grand Master of Arkansas in 1855; and a Charter was granted, November 7, 1855.

During the war of 1861-65 it ceased its labors, and its Charter was arrested November 6, 1867.

Early in 1874 the Grand Master of Arkansas revived the lodge; it remained on the registry of that Grand Lodge nearly two years, until that Grand Lodge recognized the Grand Lodge of Indian Territory.

Doaksville Lodge received a dispensation from the Grand Lodge of Arkansas, December 23, 1870, and was chartered November 8, 1871. Caddo Lodge received a dispensation, August 26, 1873, from the Grand Lodge of Arkansas, and was chartered October 14, 1873.

These two were in the "Choctaw Nation."

Muskogee, Doaksville, and Caddo lodges met in convention, by their delegates, October 5, 1874, and decided to form a Grand Lodge for the Indian Territory. A constitution was adopted, Grand Officers were chosen and installed, and the Grand Lodge was constituted, October 6, 1874.

Three other lodges were in existence when the Grand Lodge was constituted, viz.: Oklahoma, in the "Choctaw Nation," which had been chartered by the Grand Lodge of Arkansas, November 18, 1868.

This lodge, as soon as the Grand Lodge was started, sent in her Charter and had it endorsed; it then came under that constitution.

Flint Lodge, already described, and Alpha Lodge, also in the "Cherokee Nation," which had received a dispensation from Kansas, May 18, 1872, and a Charter, October 17, 1872, declined joining the New Grand Lodge, and adhered to the Grand Lodges from which they had received their warrants.

The Grand Lodges of Arkansas and Kansas for some time refused to recognize the Grand Lodge of Indian Territory.

In 1876 the latter Grand Lodge arrested the charters of the two delinquent lodges.

The Grand Lodge of Kansas sustained her daughter lodge and still refused to acknowledge the New Grand Lodge.

The issue continued until the Grand Lodge of Indian Territory rescinded her action of 1876.

Soon thereafter Flint Lodge surrendered, and Alpha Lodge followed her in October, 1878, after the desired action of the Grand Lodge of Kansas had been obtained.

Other lodges subsequently had been chartered by the New Grand Lodge - two in the Cherokee, two in the Choctaw, and two in the Chickasaw nations.

Colorado.

The first lodges in Colorado were Golden City Lodge, at Golden City, chartered by the Grand Lodge of Kansas, October 17,

1860; Summit Lodge, at Parkville, chartered by the Grand Lodge of Nebraska, June 5, 1861; and Rocky Mountain Lodge, at Gold Hill, June 5, 1861, by the same Grand Lodge.

August 2, 1861, the above-mentioned lodges met, by their delegates, in convention at Golden City.

They elected and installed their Grand Officers and constituted the Grand Lodge of Colorado, and declared it to be regularly organized.

A constitution was adopted.

The Grand Lodge of Kansas, October 15, 1867, chartered Nevada Lodge, in Colorado, it seems without the knowledge of the formation of the Grand Lodge of Colorado. (How this could lave occurred we can scarcely conceive, as six years had elapsed.) This lodge, not having done any Masonic work under the Charter, was permitted to surrender the Charter and take anew one from the Grand Lodge of Colorado.

Nevada.

Carson Lodge, at Carson City, was chartered May 15, 1862; Washoe Lodge, at Washoe City, and Virginia City Lodge, at Virginia City; both chartered May 14, 1863; Silver City Lodge, changed afterward to Amity, at Silver City, chartered May 15 1863; Silver Star Lodge, at Gold Hill, Esmeralda Lodge, at Aurora, and Escurial Lodge, at Virginia, all three chartered October 13, 1864; and Lander Lodge, at Austin, chartered October 14, 1864. All of these eight lodges recoved their charters from the Grand Lodge of California.

A convention was called to meet January 16, 1865, which was accordingly done and six lodges were represented the first day; the next day another lodge was represented.

Lander Lodge, of the above list, was the only lodge which did not appear in the convention.

A constitution was adopted. The Grand Officers were elected and installed January 17, 1865.

The old charters were endorsed for present use. Lander Lodge, although unrepresented in the convention and organization, presumed herself to be a part of the Grand Lodge, and under its jurisdiction made the returns to the Grand Lodge with the other lodges.

The first annual grand communication was held October 10, 1865.

Dakota.

The first lodge organized in Dakota was St. John's Lodge, at Yankton, which received from the Grand Lodge of Iowa, December 5, 1862, a dispensation, and afterward a Charter, dated June 3, 1863; Incense Lodge, at Vermillion, received a dispensation, January 14, 1869, and a Charter, June 2, 1869; Elk Point Lodge, at Elk Point, received a dispensation, March 23, 1870, and a Charter, June 8, 1871; Minnehaha Lodge, at Sioux Falls, received a dispensation, July 13, 1873, and a Charter, June 3, 1874; Silver Star Lodge, at Canton, received a dispensation, February 6, 1875, and a Charter, June 2, 1875; and Mount Zion Lodge, at Springfield, received a dispensation, February 16, 1875, and a Charter, June 2, 1875. All of the above warrants were granted by authority of the Grand Lodge of Iowa.

A dispensation was issued by the Grand Master of Minnesota, November 22, 1872, for Shiloh Lodge, at Fargo, and a Charter was issued January 14, 1874.

He also issued a dispensation to Bismarck Lodge in 1874, and again in 1875, and on January 12, 1876, the lodge received a Charter.

June 21, 1875, a convention was held of the representatives of St. John's, Incense, Elk Point, Minnehaha, and Silver Star lodges.

Those of Mt. Zion Lodge, U.D., were present but did not participate in the proceedings, the lodge not having a Charter. A constitution was adopted and they elected their Grand Officers.

July 21, 1875, convention met again and the Grand Officers were installed in public, by Illustrious Brother Theodore S. Parvin, P.G. Master and Grand Secretary of the Grand Lodge of Iowa.

This Grand Lodge continued until the session of June 11-13, 1889, when by Act of Congress, approved February 22, 1889, the division of the Territory of Dakota into North and South Dakota was likely to be accomplished within a few months.

The report of a committee on division of the Grand Lodge was adopted, and certain lodges located in North Dakota were permitted to organize a Grand Lodge of North Dakota, which will be stated under that designation.

The name of "Dakota" was changed to "South Dakota" at the sixteenth communication of the Grand Lodge, held June 10, 1890, in Madison.

South Dakota is the designation of the original Grand Lodge of Dakota.

North Dakota.

So soon as it was determined by the Grand Lodge of Dakota, at its session, held June 11-13, 1889, that there should be a division of the Grand Lodge of Dakota to correspond with the political division of the Territory into North and South Dakota, a convention was held, June 12, 1889, at the city of Mitchell, where the Grand Lodge was in session, and the following lodges of North Dakota were represented, viz.:

Shiloh, No. 8; Pembina, No. 10; Casselton, No. 12; Acacia, No. 15; Bismarck, No. 16; Jamestown, No. 19; Valley City, No. 21; Mandan, No. 23; Cereal, No. 29; Hillsboro, No. 32; Crescent, No. 36; Cheyenne Valley, No. 41; Ellendale, No. 49; Sanborn, No. 51; Wahpeton, No. 58; North Star, No. 59; Minto, No. 60; Mackey, No. 63; Goase River, No. 64; Hiram, No. 74; Minnewaukan, No. 75; Tongue River, NO. 78; Bathgate, No. 80; Euclid, No. 84; Anchor, No. 88; Golden Valley, No. 90; Occidental, No. 99.

The convention resolved that it was expedient to organize a Grand Lodge for North Dakota.

A constitution and by-laws were adopted.

June 13th, the first session of the Grand Lodge was held in the city of Mitchell.

The elected and appointed officers were present and representatives of the above twenty lodges.

The Grand Lodge of North Dakota has continued to keep pace with the other Western Grand Lodges.

Idaho.

In 1863 a meeting of Masons was held in Idaho City, Boise County, and it was resolved to apply to the Grand Master of Oregon for a dispensation to organize a lodge, which was granted July 7, 1863, and on June 21, 1864, a charter was granted to Idaho Lodge, No. 35.

The next lodge was in Boise City, No. 37, April 1, 1865, under dispensation from the Grand Lodge of Oregon.

At a communication held in June, 1865, it was resolved to apply for a Charter, which was granted to Boise City Lodge, No. 37, June 20, 1865.

Placer Lodge, No. 38, was the third lodge organized under Warrant from the Grand Lodge of Oregon, June 20, 1865. Pioneer Lodge, No. 12, recoved her Warrant from the Grand Lodge of the Territory of Washington, June 7, 1867. Owyhee Lodge received a dispensation from the Grand Lodge of Oregon, July 21, 1866.

The above four chartered lodges held a Convention in Idaho City, December 16, 1867.

Owyhee Lodge, U.D., from courtesy, was admitted and permitted to vote. The convention decided to organize a Grand Lodge.

December 17, 1867, a full corps of Grand Officers was elected and installed.

Constitution of Grand Lodge of Oregon was adopted temporarily.

December 17th, Grand Lodge was opened in ample form and so has continued to present time.[13]

Montana.

At the burial of a Mason in the Territory of Montana was the first gathering of Masons, which led to an effort to organize a lodge by an application to the Grand Master of Nebraska, who issued a dispensation, April 27, 1863, to form a lodge at Bannock, which was in Dakota, but supposed to be in Idaho.

This dispensation was renewed on June 24, 1863, and authorized again on June 24, 1864, and finally, when it arrived at the place, the members had been dispersed by removal of residence and no lodge was ever opened.

The lodge Virginia City, No. 43, received a Charter dated December 26, 1864, from the Grand Lodge of Kansas.

A dispensation was received from the Grand Lodge of Colorado dated April 4, 1865, for Montana Lodge, No. 9, at Virginia City.

Helena Lodge, No. 10, received a dispensation from the same Grand Lodge and was organized August 17, 1865.

Both of these lodges received charters granted November 7, 1865, from the Grand Lodge of Colorado.

A convention of the representatives of the above lodges was held January 24, 1866.

After proper investigation as to the membership of the convention, it was decided to form a Grand Lodge and the convention closed.

The officers of the three lodges then opened a Grand Lodge in due form.

A constitution was adopted and the Grand Officers were elected.

---

[13] From proceedings of Grand Lodge of Idaho, September, 1883.

January 26, 1866, the Grand Officers were regularly installed and at the same time charters were issued to the lodges and returns were made of one hundred and five members.

West Virginia.

In consequence of the Civil War, from 1861 to 1865 the affairs of Masonry, in common with all civil matters in Virginia and West Virginia, which latter had been separated from the parent State, were in utter confusion.

Many of the lodges, in West Virginia had ceased to meet, some had lost their charters and other properties.

After due consideration of the condition of things, in response to a circular from Fairmont Lodge, No. 9, which had heen sent throughout the State, a convention was held, December 28, 1863, at Grafton, which was held during a period of great excitement, in consequence of some of the delegates having been prevented from attending, by the movements of the war having again disturbed the condition of the State.

After two adjournments the convention finally met, June 24, 1864, in Fairmont.

Eight of the working lodges out of thirteen in the State were represented.

Grand Officers were elected and a day selected for their installation, but as the convention adjourned sine die the Grand Officers decided that no further action could be had under a misapprehension of an informality in their proceedings.

A new convention was called to meet April 12, 1865.

The lodges represented were those at the prior convention, and were as follows, viz.: Wellsburg, No. 108; Wheeling, No. 128; Ohio, No. 101; Marshall Union, No. 37; Cameron, No. 180; Morgantown, No. 93; Fairmont, No. 9; Fetterman, No. 170.

Grand Officers were again elected, and May 10th[14] selected for their installation.

The convention met on that day.

One other lodge, Mt. Olivet, No. 113, in addition to the eight, was represented, The convention closed and a Grand Lodge was opened.

The Grand Officers were installed.

---

[14] The record, page 13, says 11th, which is an error.

The old charters were ordered to be endorsed under the seal of the Grand Lodge, and to be retained until new ones could be prepared and issued.

Utah.

"Through much tribulation ye shall enter into" - Masonry.

A dispensation was issued, February 4, 1866, by the Grand Master of Nevada for the organization of Mt. Moriah Lodge at Salt Lake City.

The lodge duly organized, but very soon the treatment by one of the lodges of Masons of the Mormon faith became an issue, which was submitted to the Grand Master of Nevada, who accordingly issued an edict forbidding the admission, as visitors and the affiliation, of Mormons claiming to be Masons; and also the reception of their petitions for the degrees.

The lodge demurred to this decree, but submitted to the order of the Grand Master.

A petition, however, was sent to the Grand Master to modify the decree, so that Mormons not polygamists would be exempted from the decree.

The dispensation of the lodge was returned, and a Charter asked for.

The Grand Lodge approved of the edict of the Grand Master, and, declining to grant a Charter, renewed the dispensation.

The lodge, although "worse than sorrow-stricken," still continued to work for another year.

The lodge then petitioned for a Charter, with the condition that if they could not have a Charter unrestricted by the edict, they declined having a Charter.

The surrender of the dispensation was promptly accepted by the Grand Lodge.

The members then presented their petition to the Grand Lodge of Montana, October 8, 1887, with a statement of the circumstances of their relation with the Grand Lodge of Nevada.

The Grand Lodge of Montana declared, that the assumption of the petitions that the Grand Lodge of Nevada did not possess the power to decide who are not proper persons to be admitted into its subordinate lodges, was "subversive of the principles of Masonry." The petition for a Charter was rejected, and they were referred to the Grand Lodge of Nevada for a redress of their alleged grievances.

The lodge applied then to the Grand Master of the Grand Lodge of Kansas, who issued a dispensation, November 25, 1867, and on October 21, 1868, a Charter was granted by the Grand Lodge.

A convention was held at Salt Lake City, January 16, 1872, by the representatives of the three lodges located in that city, viz.:

Wasatch Lodge, chartered by the Grand Lodge of Montana, October 7, 1867; Mount Moriah Lodge, chartered by the Grand Lodge of Kansas, October 21, 1868; Argenta Lodge, chartered by the Grand Lodge of Colorado, September 26, 1871.

It was decided, by unanimous vote, to organize a Grand Lodge for Utah.

The Grand Officers were chosen and installed, and the Grand Lodge was duly constituted.

In consequence of the Mormon Church being in their midst, difficulties at once arose in one of the lodges.

A member joined the Mormons, and upon trial by regular process he was expelled, and the Grand Lodge affirmed the expulsion.

This matter drew the attention of other Grand Lodges, who took formal action upon it; and the course of the Grand Lodge of Utah was nearly, if not unanimously, sustained.

Arizona.

Aztlan Lodge, at Prescott, was chartered by the Grand Lodge of California, October 11, 1866; which also chartered Arizona Lodge, No. 257, at Phoenix, October 16, 1879, and Tucson Lodge, No. 263, at Tucson, October 15, 1881.

A dispensation was issued to Solomon Lodge, at Tombstone, June 4, 1881, which was continued at the next communication of the Grand Lodge of California, October 1, 1882.

White Mountain Lodge, No. 5, at Globe, received a Charter from the Grand Lodge of New Mexico dated January 18, 1881.

The representatives of Arizona Lodge, No. 257, Tucson Lodge, No. 263, and White Mountain Lodge, No. 5, held a convention, March 23, 1882, at Tucson, and the representatives of Solomon Lodge, U.D., were invited "to take part in the deliberations of the Convention." The convention adopted a constitution.

A lodge of Master Masons was then opened, and the Grand Officers were elected.

On March 25th the Grand Officers were installed and the convention closed, and the Grand Lodge was duly opened. The charters of the lodges were properly endorsed and returned to them as the authority under which they continued their existence.

Solomon Lodge, U.D., received her Charter under the name of King Solomon, No. 5. Aztlan Lodge had her Charter endorsed, and she made her returns.

These five lodges had a membership of two hundred and seventy-four.

Wyoming.

Cheyenne Lodge, No. 16, at Cheyenne, was chartered by the Grand Lodge of Colorado, October 7, 1868.

Laramie Lodge, No. 18, at Laramie City, received a dispensation from the same Grand Lodge, January 31, 1870, and a Charter, September 28, 1870.

Evanston Lodge, No. 24, at Evanston, recoved a dispensation from the same Grand Lodge, September 8, 1873, and a Charter, September 30, 1874.

Wyoming Lodge, No. 28, at South Pass City, had a dispensation issued to her by the Grand Lodge of Nebraska, November 20, 1869, and a Charter, June 23, 1870.

The representatives of these four lodges met in convention December 15, 1874, at Laramie City, and proceeded to organize a Grand Lodge for Wyoming by adopting a constitution, electing and installing their Grand Officers on the 16th.

The four lodges then had a membership of two hundred and fifty.

The first annual communication was held October 12, 1875, and the Grand Lodge has continued to hold its annual communications, and from the tabular statement at the conclusion of this chapter will be found the number of members.

Oklahoma.

At the eighteenth annual communication of the Grand Lodge of Indian Territory, under which Grand Lodge all the then existing lodges in Oklahoma Territory held their lodge warrants, a paper was presented to the Grand Lodge from the "members and representatives of the various Lodges of Masons in the Territory of Oklahoma organized and bring within the jurisdiction of the Grand Lodge of Indian Territory, respectfully ask your consent and the consent of said Grand Lodge to the formation and organization by the said Oklahoma Lodges of a separate and independent Grand Lodge within and for said

Oklahoma Territory to be known as the 'Grand Lodge of Oklahoma' and to have and possess hereafter exclusive Masonic jurisdiction and authority as the Grand Lodge within and for the said Territory of Oklahoma.

"Dated at Tahlequah, I.T., August 16, 1892."

This was signed by the representatives of the following lodges: Guthrie Lodge, No. 35; North Canadian Lodge, No. 36; Edmond Lodge, No. 37.

This was referred to a committee, and upon a favorable report, the petition was granted and suitable arrangements were made for holding a convention of all the lodges in the new Territory, at which the Grand Master of the Grand Lodge was to preside and install the newly elected Grand Officers and formally proclaim by authority of that Grand Lodge "that the Grand Lodge of Oklahoma is legally organized," etc.

On motion of Rev. Bro. R.W. Hill the Grand Lodge unanimously voted a set of Grand Lodge jewels to the new Grand Lodge.

We have not been able to get a copy of the proceedings of the convention which was held November 10, 1892, but have before us the proceedings of the first annual communication held at El Reno, Oklahoma Territory, February 14, 1893, when there were represented the following lodges, viz.:

Anadarko, No. 1, at Oklahoma City; Guthrie, No. 2, at Guthrie; Oklahoma, No. 3, at Oklahoma City; Edmond No. 4, at Edmond; Norman, No. 5, at Norman; Frontier, No. 6, at Stillwater; El Reno, No. 7, at El Reno; Kingfisher, No. 8, at Kingfisher; Coronado, No. 9, at Hennessy; Chandler, No. 10, at Chandler; Crescent, No. 11, at Crescent City; Mulhall, U.D., at Mulhall.

Alaska.

We have received the information that the Grand Master of Washington Territory issued a dispensation for a lodge to be organized in Sitka, Alaska, April 14, 1868.

This dispensation was continued September 17, 1868, and finally revoked October 18, 1872.

We have no further information as to any lodges since that time.

There is no doubt that very soon lodges will be formed in several of the new towns which have sprung up in the gold regions, so soon as the population shall have become more stable and permanently settled.

TABLE SHOWING THE NUMBER OF GRAND LODGES IN THE UNITED STATES; AND NUMBER OF MEMBERS IN EACH, FOR THE YEAR 1908.

No.	Names of Grand Lodges	Date of Formation.	Membership.
1	Alabama	June 14, 1821.	19,966
2	Arizona	March 25, 1882	1,394
3	Arkansas	February 22, 1832	18,293
4	California	April 18, 1850	36,126
5	Colorado	August 2, 1861	12,226
6	Connecticut	July 8, 1789	20,752
	Dakota Territory	July 21, 1875	Extinct.
7	Delaware	June 6, 1806	2,888
8	District of Columbia	December 11, 1810	7,999
9	Florida	July 6, 1830	7,228
10	Georgia	December 16, 1786	28,420
11	Idaho	December 17, 1867	2,395
12	Illinois	April 6, 1840	85,683
13	Indiana	January 13, 1818	47,353
14	Indian Territory	October 6, 1874	8,476
15	Iowa	January 2, 1844	37,838
16	Kansas	March 17, 1856	28,764

17	Kentucky	October 16, 1800	30,600
18	Louisiana	July 11, 1812	10,584
19	Maine	June 1, 1820	26,530
20	Maryland	April 17, 1787	12,310
21	Massachusetts	July 30, 1733	51,825
22	Michigan	June 24, 1826	56,010
23	Minnesota	February 23, 1853	22,014
24	Mississippi	July 27, 1818	14,371
25	Missouri	April 23, 1821	45,348
26	Montana	January 26, 1866	4,421
27	Nebraska	September 23, 1857	15,728
28	Nevada	January 17, 1865	1,241
29	New Hampshire	July 8, 1789	9,727
30	New Jersey	December 18, 1786	26,595
31	New Mexico	August 7, 1877	1,590
32	New York	September 5, 1781	152,928
33	North Carolina	December 9, 1787	16,835
34	North Dakota	June 13, 1889	5,945
35	Ohio	January 5, 1809	68,679
36	Oklahoma	October, 1892	7,978

37	Oregon	August 16, 1851	8,085
38	Pennsylvania	September 26, 1786	75,273
39	Rhode Island	June 21, 1791	6,719
40	South Carolina	February 5, 1787	10,403
41	South Dakota	June 21, 1875	6,675
42	Tennessee	December 27, 1813	20,986
43	Texas	December 20, 1837	41,736
44	Utah	January 1, 1872	1,343
45	Vermont	October 15, 1794	12,078
46	Virginia	October 13, 1777	17,644
47	Washington	December 8, 1858	10,903
48	West Virginia	May 11, 1865	1,778
49	Wisconsin	December 18, 1843	22,974
50	Wyoming	December 5, 1874	2,102

CHAPTER LVI

HISTORY OF THE INTRODUCTION OF FREEMASONRY INTO EACH STATE AND TERRITORY OF THE UNITED STATES

Royal Arch Masonry.

ON Chapter XLIX., Dr. A. G. Mackey, having, in a very elaborate and satisfactory manner, given the history of the introduction of Royal Arch Masonry into America; and in Chapter L., the organization of the General Grand Chapter in the United States, it is quite unnecessary for the present writer to make any preface to the details of the organization of the particular Chapters and the Grand Chapters in the several Grand jurisdictions.

We shall, therefore, proceed at once to that work, and in an alphabetical arrangement, for a better reference to any special jurisdiction when required.
Alabama.

Prior to May, 1823, there were four chapters in Alabama having been chartered by the General Grand Chapter.

A convention of the delegates of these chapters was held in Mobile in May and June, 1823, and it was decided to form a Grand Chapter for the State.

The junior Chapter, Monroe, having taken exceptions, referred the matter to the General Grand Chapter at its session, September 16, 1826, when the following was adopted:

"Resolved, That the formation of a Grand Chapter for the State of Alabama, in May, 1823," prior to the expiration of one year from the establishment of the junior chapter in such State, "was prohibited by the 11th section of the 2d Article of the General Grand

Constitution, and that therefore this General Grand Chapter cannot ratify or approve of the proceedings of the convention held at Mobile on the third Monday of May, 1823, or recognize the body claiming to be considered the Grand Chapter of Alabama"

A recommendation was, however, made to the four chapters to proceed to form a Grand Chapter.

On June 2, 1827, the Grand Chapter was reorganized, and met in December following, and annually until 1830, when it ceased to meet.

December, 1837, the delegates from the several chapters met and reorganized the Grand Chapter, and it has continued as a constituent of the General Grand Chapter.

Arizona.

Pursuant to an invitation from Companion Past High-Priest George J.

Roskruge of Tucson Chapter, No. 3, a convention of Royal Arch Masons met in the hall of Tucson Lodge, No. 4, F. & A. M., in Tucson, County of Pima, for the purpose of taking steps to organize a Grand Chapter of Royal Arch Masons for the Territory of Arizona, November 13, 1889.

The convention was called to order by Companion Past High-Priest Martin W. Kales of Arizona Chapter, No. 1. Companion George J. Roskruge of Tucson Chapter 3 was chosen Chairman of the convention and Companion Frank Baxter was elected Secretary.

A committee on credentials was appointed and reported the following chapters as being represented, viz. Date of Charter August 24, 1880. Arizona Chapter, No. 1, located at Phoenix, Maricopa County.

August 15, 1883. Prescott Chapter, No. 2, located at Prescott, Yarapai County.

Tucson Chapter, No. 3, located at Tucson, Pima County.

Cochise Chapter, NO. 4, located at Tombstone, Cochise County.

Nov. 22, 1889. Flagstaff Chapter, No. 5, located at Flagstaff, Coconino County.

A committee was appointed on Constitution and By-Laws, and the convention took a recess; and on resuming labor the committee reported a Constitution and By-Laws, which were adopted.

The convention then elected their officers; Martin W. Kales was chosen Grand High-Priest, and Gcorge J. Roskruge Grand Secretary.

The convention then adjourned subject to a call from the Grand Secretary.

November 12, 1890, the convention met and Companion George J. Roskruge presided.

The same chapters, as before, were represented, and there were also present a number of Past High-Priests and Past Grand High-Priests, and Companion Titus of California, all of whom were invited to seats (without votes).

The President stated the object of the convention and read his Warrant as Deputy of the General Grand High-Priest of the General Grand Chapter of the United States, dated November 1, 1890.

On motion, the constitution, as adopted at the former convention, was amended, to conform to the recommendation of the General Grand High-Priest.

The convention then adjourned, that the Grand Chapter of Royal Arch Masons of Arizona might be opened in ample form.

The first annual convocation was then opened (November 12, 1890) at 8 P.M., George J. Roskruge, Grand High-Priest, presiding, and Morris Goldwater, Grand Secretary.

The convention then proceeded to elect the Grand Officers, and Martin W. Kales was elected Grand High-Priest, and George James Roskruge was elected Grand Secretary.

Companion Roskruge acting as Deputy General Grand High.

Priest of the United States constituted the Grand Chapter of Arizona and installed the officers in accordance with the dispensation granted by the General Grand High-Priest, David F. Day.

On the following day (November 13, 1890) a convention of Anointed High-Priests was organized and officers were elected.

Eight Past High-Priests were anointed.

Arkansas.

Charters were granted by the General Grand Chapter of the United States to three chapters in Arkansas, the first being under date of September 17, 1841.

The Grand Chapter was organized at a convention held April 28, 1851, and Companion Elbert H. English was the first Grand High-Priest.

When the General Grand Chapter of the United States held its convocation at Nashville, Tenn., on November 24, 1874, Companion English was elected General Grand High-Priest.

His death occurred September 1, 1884.

In the years 1853 and 1854, Companion Albert Pike was the Grand High-Priest.

California.

The first dispensation to organize a chapter of Royal Arch Masons in California was issued May 9, 1850, to San Francisco Chapter, No. 1, and a Charter was granted September 13th.

Charters were issued to Sonora, No. 2, and Sacramento, No. 3, September 17, 1853. These three chapters sent delegates to a convention held May 6, 1854, at Sacramento, where measures were taken to organize a Grand Chapter, and after three days' session adjourned to meet at San Francisco, July 18, 1854, where the organization and constitution were fully completed by the installation of the Grand Officers.

Colorado.

Central City Chapter, No. 1, in Central City, was the first chapter to which a dispensation, dated March 23, 1863, was issued in Colorado, which was granted by the General Grand King.

The Deputy General Grand High-Priest granted a dispensation to Denver Chapter, No. 2, April, 1863.

These two chapters had their charters granted at the following session of the General Grand Chapter, September, 1865.

A dispensation was issued to organize Pueblo Chapter, No. , at Pueblo, May 24, 1871, and a Charter for the same was issued September 20, 1871.

November 25, 1874, charters were issued to Georgetown, No. 4, and Golden, No. 5.

A convention was held at Denver City by the authority of Elbert H. English, M.E. General Grand High-Priest, May 11, 1875, and the Grand Chapter of Colorado was regularly constituted.

Connecticut.

Six members of Saint John's Lodge, No. 2, located in the town of Middletown, Conn., having received and been "duly initiated into the most sublime degree of an Excellent, Superexcellent, and Royal Arch Mason in regular constituted Royal Arch Chapters," and proving each other, they "duly opened and held the first regular Grand Royal Arch Chapter."[15] They elected their officers. Their first meeting was held September 12, 1783.

---

[15] At that day the word "Grand" was taken from the A. A. A. R., where all the bodies were termed Grand.-EDITOR.

The "Mother-Chapter," or Washington Chapter of Royal Arch Masons of the City of New York, granted the following charters in Connecticut: Hiram, No. 1, in Newtown, April 29, 1791; Franklin, No. 2, New Haven, May 20, 1795; Franklin, No. 4, Norwich, March 15, 1796, and Solomon, No. 5, Derby, March 15, 1796.

Vanden Broeck also No. 5, received its Charter from the Grand Chapter of New York, dated April 6, 1796; it is said, however, that the first record was dated December 24, 1795.

A convention Nyas held by the delegates of these six chapters, in Hartford, May 17, 1798, which organized the Grand Chapter of Connecticut.

Half-yearly convocations were held until May, 1819, when the constitution was changed to annual convocations and specials when required.

When the convention to form a Grand Chapter met in Hartford, Conn., January 24, A.L. 5798, "agreeable to the recommendation of a Convention of Committees assembled at Boston, in the State of Massachusetts, in October, 1797," there were present: from Connecticut, representatives of Solomon Chapter of Derby, instituted 5794; Franklin Chapter, No. 4, Norwich, and Franklin Chapter, No. 5, New Haven.[16] Ephraim Kirby, of Litchfield, was chosen the first General Grand High-Priest.

In examining the records of the first chapters prior to the organization of the General Grand Chapter of 1797, we notice the designation of the officers as being somewhat different from the same officers at a more recent date.

In Hiram Chapter of Connecticut the officers were "High-Priest, King, Scribe, Zerubbabel a Royal Arch Captain, three Grand Masters, a Treasurer, a Secretary, an Architect, a Clothier, and a Tyler." It was required that the "High-Priest should preside, direct the business, and occasionally to give a lecture." Now it is "to read and expound the law." The Scribe's duty was to "cause the Secretary to enter, in a fair and regular manner, the proceedings of the chapter," and "to summons the members for attendance at every regular and special meeting... and also to administer the obligation." It was the duty of Zerubbabel "to superintend the arrangements of the Chapter"; of the Royal Arch Captain, "to keep watch at the Sanctuary"; of the three Grand Masters,

---

[16] Compendium, Genl. Gr. Ch., p. 8.

"to watch the Veils"; of the Clothier, "to provide and take care of the Clothing"; of the Architect, "to provide and take care of the furniture."[17]

In the English Royal Arch, Zerubbabel is the first Principal and in the present American Royal Arch, Zerubbabel is the Second Principal, and designated King, which designation, in our judgment, is a misnomer, as he never was a King, but was called "Tirshatha," which was an office of Governor under the King of Persia, and was, in reality, in the construction of the second Temple, subordinate to the High-Priest, who had entire management of that work.

Zerubbabel soon retired and returned to Babylon, and the Temple was finally completed by a High-Priest.

Dakota.

In 1883 eight chapters had, at different times, been chartered by the General Grand Chapter of the United States, viz. -. Yankton, No. 1, at Yankton; dispensation, April 15, 1876 chartered, August 24, 1880. Sioux Falls, No. 2, at Sioux Falls; chartered, August 27, 1880. Dakota, No. 3, at Deadwood; chartered, August 27, 1880.

Siroc, No. 4, at Canton; chartered, August 15, 1883.
Pembina, No. 5, at Pembina.
Missouri, No. 6, at Bismarck.
Casselton, No. 7, at Casselton.
Corinthian, No. 8, at Grand Forks.

A convention was held at Aberdeen, June 10, 1884, at which the following chapters were represented: Nos. 1, 2, 3, 4, 6, and 7 of the above list.

When it was agreed to petition the General Grand High-Priest to grant a Warrant to organize a Grand Chapter for Dakota, five chapters voted for it and No. 7 against, and finally agreed, as also did Keystone chapter, No. 11, under dispensation.

A convention met February 25, 1885, pursuant to a call made January 8, 1885 at Sioux FaHs.

Companion William Blatt was chosen Chairman, and the following chapters were reported as being duly represented, viz.: Nos. 1, 2, 3, 4, and 7 of the above list, and Cheyenne, No. 9, U, D., at Valley City; Huron, No. 10, U.D., at Huron; Keystone, No. 11, U.D., at Fargo; Watertown, No. 12, U.D., at Watertown; Jamestown, No. 13, U.D., at Jamestown, Aberdeen, No. 14, U.D., at Aberdeen.

The first annual convocation was held June 8, 1885.

---

[17] Capitular Degrees, " Hist. Masonry and Con. Orders," p. 606.

Charters were granted to Corinthian, No. 8; Huron, No. 10; Watertown, No. 12; Jamestown, No. 13; Aberdeen, No. 14; Millbank, No. 15; and dispensations were litf to Denver, Brookings; Flandreau; Redfield.

Chapters which were not represented were: Pembina, No. 5, at Pembina; Missouri, No. 6, at Bismarck, and Millbank, U.D., at Millbank.

The Grand Chapter of Dakota continued to prosper until the division of the State, by Act of Congress, February 22, 1889, into North and South Dakota.

When, on January 6, 1890, a convention was held in Yankton, S. D., and the representatives of the chapters located in South Dakota held a convention, and by the consent of the Grand Chapter of Dakota they organized the Grand Chapter of South Dakota, January 6, 1890, under the constitution of the General Grand Chapter.

Delaware.

The early history of the innoduction of Royal Arch Masonry into the State of Delaware is very uncertain.

We have no records to refer to.

It is said that a Grand Chapter was formed on June 19, 1818.

By what authority we can not ascertain; the "compendium" is silent upon Delaware.

In the Proceedings of the General Grand Chapter of the Twenty-first Triennial Convocation, held in Baltimore, September 19, 1871, we find the General Grand High-Priest's reference to the State of Delaware,' as follows:

"Among the first to demand my attention was to examine into the condition of the Grand Chapter of Delaware, and if found to be a legal Grand Chapter, to have the same enrolled under the jurisdiction of the General Grand Chapter, as requested by the companions in Delaware.

Having been solicited to visit Wilmington, for the purpose of instituting St. John's Chapter, which had been chartered by this Body at its last convocation (1868), I did so on the 19th of October, 1868, and having instituted said chapter, embraced that opportunity to fully investigate the condition of Royal Arch Masonry in the State, and for that purpose I held interviews with some of the most prominent Royal Arch Masons in the jurisdiction.

From those companions, and from the records, I ascertained that there had existed in Delaware no regular Grand Chapter since the year 1856, at which time the original Grand Chapter ceased to meet and elect Grand Officers. I ascertained that there had been a 'Convocation of Royal Arch Masons' at Dover in 1859, at which meeting but one chapter, of the three then existing in that State, was legally represented. At that irregular 'Convocation' an election was had, Companion GEO. W. CHAYTOR being elected Grand High Priest.

"No other convocation of the (so-called) Grand Chapter was held until January, 1868, a period of nine years.

During this time, Companion Chaytor claimed to be the Grand High-Priest, but he[18] proceedings Genl. Gr. Ch. U.S., 1871, P.10. refused persistently to assemble the Craft in Grand Convocation.

Some three or four years subsequent to the meeting of 1859, a difficulty having aisen between Companion Chaytor and the other members of Washington and Lafayette Chapter, No. 1, of which he was then High-Priest, he, in his capacity of Grand High-Priest, declared the said chapter suspended, thereby placing himself in the anomalous position of a self-suspended Royal Arch Mason; that is, provided he possessed any powers as Grand High-Priest.

"At the meeting in January, 1868, there was simply an assemblage of Royal Arch Masons, no one of whom claimed to act in a representative capacity.

Companion Chaytor was present, but he refused to open a Grand Chapter, giving as a reason, that his chapter was under a suspension, and therefore there were but two chapters left in the State.

Thereupon the assemblage resolved itself into a 'Royal Arch Convention,' and proceeded to elect Grand Officers and to adopt a constitution.

And this was the body which made application to the last Convocation of the General Grand Chapter, to be recognized as the Grand Chapter of the State of Delaware.

"With these facts before me, there was but one conclusion to which I could legitimately arrive.

Accordingly, on the 20th of October 1868, I issued an edict, declaring that any legal existence heretofore attaching to a Grand Royal Arch Chapter of the State of Delaware had ceased; that said State Grand Chapter no longer existed; and that the several chapters heretofore holding under it had become dormant for non-use and for other reasons.

---

[18] It will be observed that there was but one degree.-EDITOR.

And that, by the fact of the cessation of the Grand Chapter of the State of Delaware, all semblance of lawful governmental authority in that State had ceased, and the territory had become litfore vacant; and therefore the authority of the General Grand Chapter of the United States did, of right, obtain, and was in full force and effect, in said State of Delaware.

Thereupon, I did order and direct, that the three Chapters which had formerly held under the Grand Chapter of Delaware, should be received and recognized as lawful Royal Arch Chapters, under the jurisdiction of the General Grand Chapter, and with authority to resume and continue work under the warrants then held by them, until the pleasure of the General Grand Chapter was made known, or a State Grand Chapter was formed.

"On the 9th day of January, 1869, upon application duly made, and under the power and authority vested in me by the Constitution of the General Grand Chapter, I issued an edict granting permission for the formation of a Grand Chapter of Royal Arch Masons of the State of Delaware."

January 20, 1869, the legal representatives of four chapters in Delaware met in convention at Dover and organized a Grand Chapter for the State and adopted their constitution.

The General Grand High-Priest, Dr. James M. Austin, was present and installed the Grand Officers; and he officially received and welcomed the said Grand Body into the family of Grand Chapters; and on January 30, 1869, by special edict, he ordered and directed that Grand Chapter to be enrolled under the jurisdiction of the General Grand Chapter of the United States.

District of Columbia.

The very first intimation we have of the Royal Arch degree in the District of Columbia, we find in the old record-book of the "Excellent, Superexcellent, Royal Arch Encampment," under the Charter of Federal Lodge, No. 15, F.A.A.M., under the jurisdiction of the Grand Lodge of Maryland, which is referred to in Chapter LIL.

We make the following extracts from that first "Encampment": "At a meeting of the Royal Arch Encampment, held in the Lodge, No. 15 (Federal Lodge), on Monday, December '4th, A. L. 5795. Present:

Rev. George Ralph, John Bradford, Robert Brown, C. Worthy Stephenson Dennis Dulancy, Thomas Wilson, David Cummings, James Sweeney.

Whereas, It appears to be the desire of several Brethren of this Lodge that a Royal Arch Encampment should be established in this city, therefore,

"Resolved, That a committee be appointed of the following Brethren, viz.: Brothers Ralph, Wilson, and Dulancy, to procure every necessary apparatus, and to adjust the necessary fees and expenses of admission to this Degree.

"Resolved, That the Brethren who wish to join this Encampment be requested to subscribe to a paper instrument, handed to them by Bro. Sweeney previous to the foregoing Committee proceeding in the calculation in the expenses of our Robes, Veils,[19] Furniture, &c.

The Committee to meet on Wednesday evening, at 4 o'clock p.m. and general meeting of the Royal Arch Masons to meet at 6 o'clock previously the same evening." The meeting then adjourned. December 16, 1795. Present as at last meeting except Bro. Stephenson.

The Committee appointed at the last meeting made their report: which was that twenty-three pounds and one shilling is indispensably necessary to provide the materials to prepare them and to arrange the Lodge room previous to the formation of a Royal Arch Encampment) &c., &c., which was agreed to.

At a meeting held June 17, 5797, it was announced by a letter from Comp. Sweeney that a Royal Arch Grand Lodge is about to be formed for the State of Maryland to meet at Baltimore June 24th.

A circular letter was received from George L. Gray, No. 5 Market St., Baltimore, giving information of the establishment of a Grand Chapter in the city of Baltimore.

This chapter or encampment held its meetings until February, 5799, when it "resolved that the Royal Arch Encampment be broke up!" and a committee was appointed to settle up its affairs and everyone to receive his dividend.

To show who were the officers and their titles we give the following list:

M.W. James Hoban, High-Pricst.
R.W. John Carter, Captain-General.
R.W. Robert Brown, 1st Grand Master.
R.W. Redmond Purcell, 2d Grand Master.
R.W. Peter Lenox, 3d Grand Master.
John Hanley, Treasurer.

---

[19] Robes and Veils are here specified for the first time, we believe.-EDITOR.

Patrick Hearly, Secretary.

John Lenox, Tyler.

The second record-book begins as follows

At a meeting of the Royal Arch Chapter at their Lodge room on Saturday evening, December 1, 1804, the following Companions present:

Phil P. Eckel, High-Priest, p. t.[20]

Charles Jones, Captain-General.

Benj. King, 1st Grand Master.

C. M. Laughlan, 2d Grand Master.

Bern'd Doland, 3d Grand Master.

John Davis, Grand Scribe.[21]

Visitors, John Scott, John Carter.

The degree of Excellent, Superexcellent, Royal Arch was conferred upon several Brethren, ten dollars being the fee.

On Sunday, December 14, 1806, a meeting is recorded, and they adopted the following:

"Resolved, That this Chapter concur with the resolution passed by Concordia R. A. Chapter as far as respects a Grand Royal Arch Chapter and that a Committee be appointed to meet in Grand Convention at the City of Washington on the third Wednesday in January next (1807) any Committees which may be appointed for the purpose aforesaid.

"February 14, 1807. Ordered that this Chapter be represented at the next Royal Arch Chapter to be held at Baltimore, in the State of Maryland, on the second Thursday of May next, by the Officers fixed on by the Constitution of the Grand Chapter.

"Resolved, That that part of the Constitution which states that the High-Priest and King are the proper representatives be altered so as to add, 'unless ordered by the Chapter.'

"Resolved, That the Treasurer do pay into the hands of the Treasurer of the Grand R.A. Chapter $10, for the purpose of obtaining our Warrant[22] and also other Contingent expenses relative thereto."

February 7, 1807, was adopted the following:

"Resolved, That in future the following sums shall be paid by Candidates for the following degrees, namely, for Past Master $2, for

---

[20] Title of Grand Scribe unknown in the first Encampment.-EDITOR.

[21] This seems to indicate that there was no Warrant prior to this date.

[22] Philip P. Eckel was a distinguished member of a chapter in Baltimore.-EDITOR.

Mark Master $3, and for the degree of Excellent, Superexcellent, Royal Arch $10."

At this time it was

"Resolved, That this Chapter shall hereafter be entitled and known by the name of the Royal Arch Union Chapter."

This record-book terminates August 20, 5808, giving no intimation of any cause whatever why the chapter should not have continued its sessions.

At the meeting previous to the above date all the officers had been elected and installed.

A dispensation had been Isued by the General Grand High-Priest to the several chapters in the District of Columbia to organize a Grand Chapter August 30, 1822, and the report of the committee was adopted recommending the adoption of the resolution above quoted.[23]

This Grand Chapter continued in existence from February 10, 1824, to January 8th, 1833, being composed of the following chapters, viz.: Federal Chapter, No. 3; Union Chapter, No. 4; Potomac Chapter, No. 8.

Several conventions were held from time to time, however, between May 11, 1822, and February 10, 1824, at which latter date the delegates of the several chapters of Royal Arch Masons of the District of Columbia met in General Convention and the following chapters were properly represented: Federal Chapter, No. 3; Union Chapter, No. 4; Brooke Chapter, No. 6, of Alexandria, Va., and Potomac Chapter, No. 8, of Georgetown.

The convention was duly organized, and the Grand Officers were elected and a constitution which had been regularly formulated and adopted at a former convention was adopted.

In the evening of the same day (Tuesday, February 10, 1824) the Grand Royal Arch Chapter for the District of Columbia was opened in ample form, and the convention was accordingly dissolved.

The Grand Officers were duly installed by Comp'n John B. Hammett, a Past Grand High-Priest.

At a meeting of the Grand Chapter held March 9, 1824, the following communication was received and read and laid on the table:

"GEORGETOWN, February 11, 1824, POTOMAC ROYAL ARCH CHAPTER, No. 8.

"Resolved Unanimously, That we deem it inexpedient to separate from the Grand Chapter of the State of Maryland and District

---

[23] Pro. Gen. Gr. Ch., 1826, P. 77.

of Columbia and that we will not avail ourselves of the permission and authority granted by a resolution past said Grand Chapter at their last Communication. (Extracts from the Minute.) EDW. DEEBLE, Scribe."

Previous to the closing of the convention the numbers of the chapters were arranged as follows: Federal, No. 1; Union, No. 2; Brooke, No. 3; Potomac, No. 4, and that charters to these should be made accordingly.

At the semi-annual meeting we find No. 1 to be designated as Washington Royal Arch Chapter, No. 1." This change was made by that chapter at a meeting held February 23, 1824.

The Grand Chapter continued to exist until its annual communication, held January 8, 1833, which is the last record in the book.

Potomac Chapter, No. 4, never united with this Grand Chapter, but held under her old Charter.

At the annual meeting of the Grand Chapter, held January 9, 1827, a petition was received from Comp. P. Mauro, on behalf of himself and thirteen other Companions requesting a dispensation or Charter be granted to them for a chapter under the title of Temple Chapter, No. 4, which was unanimously granted.

At an adjourned convocation, held March 14, 1827, after installation of the Grand Officers, the officers elect of Temple Chapter, No. 4, were installed by the Grand High-Priest.

This Grand Chapter closed its existence after the annual convocation January 8, 1833, as no meeting was recorded in the old book after that date, if any were held at all.

We must now refer to the proceedings of the General Grand Chapter and at the eleventh meeting, held September 14, 1841, we find that a resolution was adopted authorizing the Deputy General Grand High-Priest to take the necessary steps to place all chapters of Royal Arch Masons in that part of the District of Columbia, formerly belonging to the State of Maryland, under the jurisdiction of the Grand Chapter of Maryland.[24] At the next meeting, held September 10, 1844, that officer reported that the resolution above referred to had been duly enforced and confirmed by the Grand Chapter of the State of Maryland; and that Grand Chapter has assumed and now holds jurisdiction over that portion of the District of Columbia lying within the limits of the State, that at present Maryland has two chapters at work therein.[25] These two chapters were, Columbia No. 15, and Washington No. 16.

---

[24] 1841, p. 165.
[25] 1844, p. 181.

The chapters in the District of Columbia remained attached to and under the Grand Chapter of Maryland which on September 10, 1844, was changed to Maryland and District of Columbia, until the year 1867, when steps were taken by the four chapters in the District of Columbia to reorganize a Grand Chapter.

These were: Columbia, No. 15; Washington, No. 16; Mount Vernon, No. 20; and Potomac, No. 8. After many preliminary conventions, and surmounting technical difficulties and bitter hostilities to their efforts, the General Grand High-Priest, John L. Lewis, gave his consent by telegram first, which was followed by his official letter.

Companion Albert G. Mackey, Past General Grand High-Priest, was invited to come from Charleston, S.C., to constitute the Grand Chapter and install the Grand Officers, which ceremonies took place in Washington at the Opera-house, May 23, 18767. The Grand Chapter was successfully launched, but soon encountered quicksand and shoals.

The enemies of the Grand Chapter did not hesitate to take the most unmasonic measures to stop the progress of Royal Arch Masonry in the District of Columbia; a self-constituted committee of four visited the General Grand High-Priest at his home in New York and by a tissue of falsehoods and a well-concocted false statement, induced that officer to recall his permission, long after the Grand Chapter had successfully entered upon a very prosperous course.

Two constituent chapters had been chartered to take the place of Potomac Chapter, which withdrew from the Grand Chapter and, as in 1824, decided to remain with the Grand Chapter in Maryland.

The General Grand High-Priest issued his edict, requiring the chapters in the District of Columbia to disband the new Grand Chapter, and return to their allegiance to the Grand Chapter of Maryland and District of Columbia.

This not being complied with, he at once issued another edict, and expelled every Royal Mason belonging to the chapters in the District except those four and the members of Potomac Chapter.

Thus matters remained.

The Companions in Washington went along about their business of Masonry and a wonderful prosperity followed them.

When the General Grand Chapter met in St. Louis in 1868, the Grand Chapter of the District was sustained in her action and admitted to the General Grand Chapter.

We have kindly omitted all personalities in this veritable history, because nearly every prominent Companion in this contest has gone to his reward, and we say, as all interested should, Pax Vobiscum.

The General Grand Chapter permitted Potomac Chapter, No. 8, to retain her place under the Grand Chapter of Maryland, but decided that the whole territory of the District was in the jurisdiction of the Grand Chapter of the District of Columbia, and she could not receive any petitions for the degrees.

This continued for a few months, when Potomac finally asked to be admitted among the faithful, which was readily granted, and since that time there has been no more faithful members of the Grand Chapter than the Companions of Old Potomac, No. 8, and universally esteemed and beloved.

The Grand Chapter of the District of Columbia has increased since May 7, 1867, from three chapters with 498 members, to eleven chapters and 2,204 members in 1898.

Florida.

In the "Compendium" giving the proceedings of the General Grand Chapter for the sixth meeting of that body, September 14, 1826, the General Grand High-Priest, DeWitt Clinton, reported that he had granted dispensations for a Mark Lodge in St. Augustine and also one in St. Francisville in Florida.[26]

The Grand Chapter of Virginia had chartered two chapters in Florida, viz.: Magnolia, No. 16, at Appalachicola, and Florida, No. 32, at Tallahassee.

There was a chapter at St. Augustine chartered by the Grand Chapter of South Carolina.

We find in the "Compendium" in the proceedings for the thirteenth meeting of the General Grand Chapter, held September 14, 1847, the following in the report of the General Grand Secretary:[27]

"On the 11th day of January last (1847), three chapters of Royal Arch Masons in the State of Florida, by their delegates, met in Convention and resolved to form a Grand Chapter for that State.

They therefore proceeded to frame a Constitution and enact bylaws; and on the 21st of the same month they elected officers and organized a Grand Chapter; and among their proceedings it will be found that they desire to place their Grand Chapter under your jurisdiction.

---

[26] "Compendium," 1826, P. 73.
[27] Ibid., 1847, P. 140.

On receipt of the copy of their Constitution and letter accompanying it, I immediately acknowledged the same, and requested their Grand Secretary to inform me from what Grand Chapter the several Chapters in the State received their respective charters, and the time when each was issued.

To this letter, as yet, I have received no answer."

The next notice of Florida we find in the proceedings of the same meeting,[28] where a committee on General Grand Secretary's report say :

"That it appears from documents referred to your committee, a Convention of delegates from the Royal Arch Chapters in the State of Florida, assembled in Tallahassee, in the month of January, 1847, at which time the following preamble and resolutions were adopted" (which we omit).

The committee say:

"In the published proceedings of said Grand Chapter we find the adopted Constitution, and the following resolutions: "Resolved, That the Grand Chapter of Florida, duly appreciating the advantages of a Masonic head and paramount authority, are disposed to come under the jurisdiction of the General Grand Chapter of the United States.

"Resolved, That the Grand Secretary communicate the same to the General Grand Secretary of the General Grand Chapter."

Among the comments of the committee they say: "It is to be regretted that the Grand Secretary did not furnish that precise information of the origin of the several chapters which composed the convention as would have enabled your committee to report in such a manner as to recommend to this General Grand Chapter the incorporation of that Grand Chapter under your jurisdiction at the present time," etc.

Some objections were also made to several sections of their constitution; they recommended certain resolutions aiming to overcome the objections, and thereby to admit the Grand Chapter to her proper place as a constituent of this General Grand Chapter.

The Grand Chapter of Florida did not understand the motive of the action of the General Grand Chapter and did not comply with the request for explanations.

At the sixteenth meeting of the General Grand Chapter held in 1856 the General Grand High-Priest was authorized to recognize the

---

[28] "Compendium," pp. 158, 159, 161, 171.

Grand Chapter of Florida and place it in the same position as the other Grand Chapters, at its request.

The war period of 1861 to 1865 prevented the accomplishment of this arrangement until January 13, 1869, when the Grand Chapter of Florida accepted the invitation by passing the following:

"Resolved, That this Grand Chapter accept such invitation in a true Masonic spirit and will hereafter bear allegiance and support to the said General Grand Chapter."

Georgia.

The office of the Grand Secretary of the Grand Chapter of Georgia can not furnish any information as to when Royal Arch Masonry was introduced into that jurisdiction.

The first notice of Georgia in the proceedings of the General Grand Chapter is at the third septennial meeting, January 9, 1806, and is a Warrant to Georgia (Chapter at Savannah.

At the fourth meeting, beld June 6, 1816 (special), Union Chapter, at Louisville, received a Warrant.

At the fifth regular meeting, Augusta Chapter received a Warrant.[29] At the tenth meeting, held September 11, 1838, a dispensation was granted to a chapter at Macon.[30]

The next notice of Georgia in the proceedings of the General Grand Chapter is at the sixth meeting, in 1826. "That charters have been granted to Mechanic's Chapter, at Lexington, Georgia, on the 10th June, 1820; to Webb Chapter, at Sparta, Georgia, on 16th November, 1821; by the Deputy General Grand High-Priest, Henry Fowle."[31] At the same meeting we find the following: "That Grand Royal Arch Chapters have been legally and constitutionally formed, since the last meeting of this Body, within and for the States of Maine, New Hampshire, New Jersey, Georgia, and Tennessee, with the consent of one of the General Grand Officers."[32]

At the thirteenth meeting of the General Grand Chapter, held September 14, 1847, the General Grand Secretary reports as follows:[33] "Within the last few days, however, on examination of the old files of papers, I found a printed paper, to which the name of one of the General Grand Secretaries is affixed, giving a list of the Grand Chapters

---

[29] "Compendium," pp. 36, 46, 56.
[30] Ibid., pp. 103, 106.
[31] Ibid., p. 72.
[32] Ibid., p. 76.
[33] Ibid., pp. 140, 141.

under the jurisdiction of the General Grand Chapter, and therein appears the name of the Grand Chapter of Georgia.

"It would seem that this is a good evidence of that Grand Chapter having been recognized, and that if so, it should be, in some way, made to appear upon the record."

The report of the committee on the last item as found at the same meeting, was that they did find documentary evidence in the hands of the General Grand Secretary sufficient to prove that the Grand Chapter of Georgia was a constituent of the General Grand Chapter, although said Grand Chapter had not been represented, or made returns to that body since 1822.

The above statement of facts is not very flattering to the officers of the General Grand Chapter, whose duty it evidently was to know from the records and registers who were the constituents of that Grand Body.

Such remissness and want of knowledge in regard to the very vital affairs show gross neglect of duty and want of care in the management of so important a body of Masons as the General Grand Chapter.

Idaho.

The Grand Chapter of Oregon granted a Charter to Idaho Chapter, in Idaho City, June 18, 1867, being under the impression that the General Grand Chapter had ceased to exist.

This chapter was constituted August 18, 1867.

At the twentieth session of the General Grand Chapter, held September 18, 1868, the General Grand Chapter adopted a report, which included "good faith" of the petitioners, healing 61 those who had been exalted in the chapter, and granting a Charter to Idaho Chapter, No. 1, Idaho City, on September 18, 1868. The General Grand Chapter issued warrants to other chapters in Idaho, viz. : February 14, 1870, a dispensation to Cyrus, No. 2, at Silver City, then in Dakota; March 30, 1870, a dispensation to Boise, No. 3, at Boise City; charters were issued to these two September 20, 1871.[34]

In the proceedings of the General Grand Chapter for August 25, 1880, on petition of Comp. C.P. Coburn and others of Lewiston, Nez Perce County, Idaho, a Charter was granted, August 27, 1880, to Lewiston Chapter, No. 4.[35]

---

[34] "Pro. Gen. Gr. Ch. For 1871," p. 33.
[35] Ibid., p. 8t.

At the twenty-sixth triennial, held October 1, 1886, Alturas Chapter, No. 5, at Harley, Dak., was granted a Charter.[36]

Pocatello, No. 6, at Pocatello, received a dispensation dated May 28, 1889, and a Charter November 22, 1889; Moscow Chapter, at Moscow, received a Charter July 23, 1891; Fayette Chapter. No. 8, at Fayette, received a Charter August 24, 1894.

Illinois.

The Deputy General Grand High-Priest, Joseph K. Stapleton, gave a dispensation to Springfield Chapter, in Springfield, July 19, 1841;[37] and at the eleventh triennial meeting of the General Grand Chapter, held September 14, 1841, a Charter was granted on the 17th.[38]

At the twelfth triennial session, September 10, 1844, the Deputy General Grand High-Priest reported having issued a dispensation for Lafayette Chapter, in Chicago, dated July 2, 1844.[39]

At the thirteenth triennial session, September 14, 1847, he reported having issued litforens to Jacksonville Chapter, No. 3, at Jacksonville and Shawneetown Chapter, No. 6, at Shawneetown, since the session of 1844, and a Charter to Lafayette Chapter, in Chicago.[40]

The General Grand Scribe Ezra S. Barnum reported having issued dispensations on March 10, 1846, to open Horeb Chapter, No. 4, at Henderson, and April 1, 1846, to open Quincy Chapter, No. 5, at Quincy.

At the fourteenth triennial session, September 10, 1850, several of the chapters working under dispensations having applied for charters were refused because they had failed to send up the records of their proceedings, and therefore the committee was unable to say whether their doings had been regular or not.

Among these were the chapters Reynolds, Stapleton, Springfield, and Quincy, and recommended that their dispensations be continued in force until next triennial meeting.[41]

At the same session (fourteenth) the Deputy General Grand High-Priest reported having issued dispensations for the formation of Howard Chapter, on July 28, 1848, and Stapleton Chapter, June 28, 1849.

---

[36] Ibid., p. 125
[37] "Compendium," p. 110
[38] Ibid., p. 111.
[39] Ibid., p. 122.
[40] Ibid., p. 145.
[41] Ibid., p. 201.

The General Grand King reported that since the last triennial he had granted a dispensation to a chapter to be held in Cambridge in the County of Henry, Ill., to be called Reynolds Chapter, No.-,[42] dated March 2, 1850.

The General Grand Scribe reported that since the last triennial he had granted a dispensation to open a chapter of Royal Arch Masons at Rock Island, Ill., August 1, 1849,[43] to be called Barrett.

At the thirteenth triennial meeting the General Grand King reported that he had granted authority to seven chapters in Illinois to organize a Grand Chapter.

April 10, 1850, a convention of the representatives of six of these chapters was held, and having the authority of the General Grand King, a Grand Chapter for the State of Illinois was organized."[44]

Indian Territory.

A convention of three chartered chapters, Indian, No. 1; Oklahoma, No. 2, and Muskogee, No. 3, was held by their representatives, October 15, 1889; organized and made application to the General Grand High-Priest for authority to constitute a Grand Chapter for Indian Territory, which was refused.

Subsequently the succeeding General Grand High-Priest, David F. Day, at the general grand convocation, held at Atlanta, Ga., November 22, 1889, granted their request, and on February 15, 1890, the Grand Chapter was constitutionally instituted.

At the second annual convocation, held at Oklahoma, August 20, 1891, seven chapters were represented.

Indiana.

The first record evidence of the establishment of Royal Arch Masonry in the State of Indiana is found in the proceedings of the General Grand Chapter at the sixth meeting, held September 14, 1826, where under the report of a committee on the papers and proceedings of the General Grand Officers they say : "That a Charter had been granted to Vincennes Chapter, at Vincennes, State of Indiana, on 13th May, 1820; to Jennings Mark Lodge, at Vevay, Indiana, on 4th May, 1821, by the General Grand King, John Snow."[45]

---

[42] "Compendium," p. 182.
[43] Ibid., p. 184.
[44] Ibid., p. 183.
[45] Ibid., p. 73.

September 14, 1838, the committee on the doings of General Grand Officers reported a dispensation having been granted by M.E. Companion Stapleton for a chapter at Richmond, Ind., and recommended a Charter for that chapter (September 14, 1838).

This Chapter was named King Solomon.

At the eleventh meeting, held September 14, 1841, the Committee on Warrants recommended a Charter to be issued to Logan Chapter, Logansport; the dispensation of this chapter was dated March 12, 1839.

At the twelfth meeting, held September 10, 1844, the following statements were made by the General Grand Secretary:[46] "By the records of the proceedings of the General Grand Chapter in 1819, it appears that the Committee to whom was referred the subject matter of dispensations granted by the General Grand Officers during the previous recess had heard that the then late Deputy General Grand High-Priest had granted dispensations for charters at Madison, and at Brookville, in Indiana; but there being no further evidence of their existence before the General Grand Chapter, no ratification of these acts was passed, nor were their charters ordered; although several charters were at that time ordered for other chapters holding dispensations under authority of other General Grand Officers.

Consequently, Madison and Brookville Chapters ceased to exist as legally constituted Masonic Bodies at that time.

It appears, however, from the herewith accompanying papers, that Madison Chapter continued its labors for many years; and there having been another chapter established at Vincennes, in that State, in 1823, it is said a Grand Chapter was organized with the approbation of M.E. Comp. John Snow, General Grand King. No documentary evidence of that authority, however, or even records of the proceedings of that Grand Chapter are known to exist.

Nor does it appear of record that the General Grand Chapter was ever advised of the existence of such an institution....."

On the true position of these things being made known to the Companions at Madison, in the proper spirit of Masonry they immediately suspended all work, closed their chapter, and determined to lay their case before the General Grand Chapter, which was done by their High-Priest, M.E. Joseph G. Norwood, in a very frank, perspicuous, and able manner, presented amongst the documents, accompanied by

---

[46] "Compendium," p. 116.

their dispensation, their return for 1842 to the present time (September 10, 1844), and the payment of such dues as have accrued within that time.

No return had been made from 1819 to 1842.

Their irregularities were evidently the result of mistakes as to the extent of power given by their dispensation, and they asked that their acts may be made lawful by the General Grand Chapter and that all dues up to 1842 be remitted, and asked for a Charter.[47] This was duly granted, September 12, 1844,[48] and all dues remitted up to 1842.

The past work was pronounced illegal, and authority was given to heal all who had received degrees in it.

At the twelfth meeting above mentioned (1844), the Deputy General Grand High-Priest reported having issued a dispensation to Lafayette Chapter, No. 3, at Lafayette, August 17, 1843;[49] a Charter was granted to this chapter, September 11, 1844; at this meeting permission was granted by the General Grand Chapter for a convention to assemble, dated November 18, 1845, and the Grand Chapter of Indiana was duly constituted December 25, 1845.

Iowa.

At the thirteenth ineedng of the General Grand Chapter, held September 14, 1847, the Deputy General Grand High-Priest reported that since the triennial session, in 1844, he had litfore the consecration, by proxy, of Iowa Chapter, at Burlington, Ia., and also Iowa City Chapter, at Iowa City.

He had also issued a dispensation to form Dubuque Chapter, No. 3, at Dubuque, Ia.[50] Charter to the same was dated September 17, 1847.

Dispensation to Iowa Chapter, No. 1, was dated August 24, 1843.[51]

Charter to the same was dated September 11, 1844.

Dispensation to Iowa City Chapter, No. 2, was dated March 19, 1844.[52] Charter to the same was dated September 17, 1847.

At the fifteenth meeting of the General Grand Chapter, held September 17, 1853, Washington Chapter, No. 4, at Muscatine, Ia., was

---

[47] "Compendium," p. 117.
[48] Ibid.,
[49] Ibid., p. 121.
[50] Ibid., p. 145.
[51] Ibid., p. 121
[52] Ibid., p. 122.

chartered, dated September 17, 1853.[53] A dispensation had been issued to McCord Chapter, No. 5, at Fairfield, probably in March, 1853.

The Deputy General Grand High-Priest, Joseph K. Stapleton, having died very soon thereafter, no report was made.[54] That chapter received a Charter from the Grand Chapter of Iowa after it was constituted, dated June 14, 1854.

A convention of the above-narmed chapters, by their delegates, was held at Mount Pleasant, June 8, 1854, by the authority of the General Grand Scribe, A.V. Rowe.[55]

The history of Capitular Masonry in Iowa would not be completed were we to omit one of those peculiar episodes which, with cyclonic force, carries away before it all the valuable works of the good and great Masonic Architects, who have labored so hard, and industriously, in the erection of Masonic temples, and which we quote from Companion A.F. Chapman's history of Capitular Masonry in the History of Masonry and Concordant Orders:

"Within about two years after being organized, the usefulness of the General Grand Chapter came under discussion.

The Grand High Priests early gave emphasis to this negative feeling.

In 1857 the delegates to the next session of the General Grand Chapter were instructed to vote for its dissolution.

This was re-enforced in 1858.

The Grand Chapter asserted its sovereignty and independent right to organize chapters in Nebraska or elsewhere, where no Grand Chapter existed, and finally, on August 16, 1860, the resolution declaring the

"'Grand Chapter sovereign and independent, and in no manner whatever subject to the General Grand Chapter of the United States, and this Grand Chapter is forever absolved from all connection therewith,' was passed by a vote of twenty-eight ayes to fifteen nays.

"This condition continued for nine years, when, at the triennial convocation, September, 1871, the General Grand High Priest reported that, under date of October 26, 1869, he had 'received official notice that the Grand Chapter of Iowa had rescinded the act of secession passed in 1860, and had directed that the O.'.B.'. of allegiance should be administered to all the members of chapters in that jurisdiction, and that

---

[53] Ibid., p. 259.
[54] Proceedings, 1856, p. 361.
[55] Proceedings, 1856, p. 376.

hereafter it would be administered to candidates receiving the Royal Arch degree.'[56]

"This Grand Chapter has been represented in the General Grand Chapter since 1871.

"Robert Farmer Bower of Iowa Grand Chapter was chosen General Grand High Priest in 1880, and died before his term was out."

The first dispensation was issued to Leavenworth Chapter, No. 1, at Leavenworth, January 24, 1857; to Washington Chapter, at Atchison, May 18, 1859. These two dispensations were reported by the General Grand High-Priest at the seventeenth meeting of the General Grand Chapter, held September, 1859, and at this meeting a Charter was granted to Washington Chapter, No. 2, September 14, 1859.

In the proceedings of the special convocation of the General Grand Chapter called by Comp. Albert G. Mackey, General Grand High-Priest, which assembled in Columbus, O., September 7, 1865, Washington Chapter, No. 1, of Kansas is reported present by Jacob Saqui, H.P.[57] At the triennial communication held next day, September 8th, at the same place, the Deputy General Grand High-Priest reported that he had renewed the dispensation of Leavenworth Chapter in May, 1863.[58] On September 8, 1865, a Charter was granted,[59] and also a Charter was granted to Fort Scott Chapter, the General Grand Secretary having reported that a dispensation had been issued to the chapter.[60]

By permission of the Deputy General Grand High-Priest a convention of the delegates of the several chapters was held January, 1866, and on February 23, 1866, a Grand Royal Arch Chapter was duly organized and constituted.

Kentucky.

In the proceedings of the General Grand Chapter at the fifth regular meeting, September 9, 1819, the proceedings of the Grand Chapter of Kentucky were presented and read, and a resolution was passed, viz.: "Whereas, It has been communicated to the General Grand Chapter that several Warrants of Constitution were granted since the last communication authorizing the opening and holding of Royal Arch Chapters in Lexington, Frankfort, and Shelbyville, in the State of

---

[56] "History of Masonry," p. 613.
Kansas.
[57] Proceedings of the General Grand Chapter, 1862-65, p. 7
[58] Ibid., p. 23.
[59] Ibid., p. 31.
[60] Ibid., p. 27.

Kentucky, by our late Most Excellent Companion, Thomas Smith Webb, and that said Chapters having been constitutionally in operation for the space of more than one year, did form themselves into a Grand Chapter for said State under the jurisdiction of this body, and have been regularly organized as such, by M.E. Companions De Witt Clinton, General Grand High Priest, and Thomas Smith Webb, late Deputy General Grand High Priest.

"Resolved, Therefore, that this General Grand Chapter approves and recognizes the formation of said Grand Chapter for said State of Kentucky."[61]

The dispensations for the above-mentioned three chapters had been issued by Companion Thomas Smith Webb, Deputy General Grand High-Priest, October 16, 1816.

In the proceedings of the Grand Chapter of Kentucky will be found the correspondence in reference to the formation and constituting of the Grand Chapter, and also the recognition by the Deputy General Grand High-Priest, dated December 12, 1817, at Worthington, O., and by DeWitt Clinton, M. Ex. General Grand High-Priest, December 30, 1817.

At the annual convocation of the Grand Chapter, held in Lexington, September 5, 1825, the Grand Chapter adopted certain resolutions, to petition the General Grand Chapter, and to address letters to the other Grand Chapters on the propriety of dissolving the General Grand Chapter.[62] The memorial was issued, and it is found in the proceedings of the General Grand Chapter for the sixth meeting, September 4, A.L. 5826.[63] This memorial was referred to an appropriate committee, which reported, giving a statement as to how the several Grand Chapters had acted upon the question showing, that "as a majority of the Grand Chapters of the Several States dissented from the resolution of the Grand Chapter of Kentucky, it is not expedient for the General Grand Chapter to take any further measures on the subject." This was after some consideration referred to a committee of the whole.

That committee after having deliberately considered and discussed the report, it was agreed to report the same without amendment to the General Grand Chapter, which body decided by a vote of yeas 47, noes 2, to agree to the report of the committee.[64]

---

[61] "Compendium," p. 52.
[62] Ibid., p. 62.
[63] Ibid., pp. 52-69.
[64] Ibid., p. 71.

Very properly, the Grand Chapter of Kentucky appeared to be contented with this decision.

The report of the General Grand Secretary at the triennial session, Proceedings, 1874, p. 17.

September, 1859, shows that the Grand Chapter of Kentucky had adopted resolutions of withdrawal from the General Grand Body.

At the twenty-second triennial convocation, held November 24, 1871 the General Grand High-Priest, in his address, stated "That the Grand Chapter of Kentucky has rescinded her resolutions of withdrawal and has renewed her allegiance.

Her representatives are here with us," etc.

She has remained in true allegiance ever since.

Louisiana.

The first reference we find in the proceedings of the General Grand Chapter to Royal Arch Masonry in Louisiana, is at the twelfth meeting, held September 10, 1844, wherein is a report on the appeal of C.D. Lehman, of New Orleans, from a judgment of the so-called Grand Chapter of Louisiana.

Difficulties had occurred between the officers and members of Holland chapter, No. 9, in New Orleans.

From the documents presented the committee learned "that a Grand Chapter of Louisiana was organized in 1813, by the 'Royal Lodges' Concordia and Perseverance, and such Officers and Members of the Grand Lodge of the State as were Royal Arch Masons." Note, these lodges were originally organized in the Island of San Domingo, under charters from the Grand Lodge of Pennsylvania, with powers to confer all the degrees from Entered Apprentice to Royal Arch inclusive.

When the revolution occurred in San Domingo, many of the members of these lodges made their escape and stopped for a while in Cuba, but finally settled in New Orleans, and having retained their charters, resumed labor in that city.[65]

The Grand Chapter formed in the manner above stated was attached to, and made dependent on, the Grand Lodge of Louisiana, and the M.W. Grand Master of that body was ex officio and by "inherent right" Grand High-Priest of the new Grand Chapter.

The question as to the legality of these proceedings had been foreclosed in 1829, by the admission of a representative from the Grand

---

[65] Reprint of Proceedings of the General Grand Chapter from 1798 to 1856, p. 194.

Chapter of Louisiana, in the person of Companion McConnell, on whose return to New Orleans the Grand High-Priest, Companion John Holland, convened the officers and members of the

Grand Chapter, who, by an official act, in regular assembly, enrolled themselves under the jurisdiction of the General Grand Chapter, in the manner prescribed by the 13th Section of the 4th Article of the General Grand Constitution; of which act it notified all the subordinate chapters under its jurisdiction, and directed similar action on their part, and enjoined a strict observance of the provisions of the General Constitution.

From 1829 to 1831 the Grand Chapter of Louisiana conducted all of her proceedings in good faith and true allegiance to the General Grand Chapter.

From 1831 to April, 1839, there was no meeting.

The subordinate chapters had ceased to exist, except Holland, No. 9, which kept up its work until the revocation of its Charter in 1841. In that year, the Grand Secretary of the Grand Lodge of Louisiana, by direction of the Grand Master, issued notices to certain Royal Arch Masons in New Orleans, to assemble and elect Grand Officers, with the intention of a reorganization of the State Grand Chapter.

This meeting did not occur; but another was soon thereafter called, and the High-Priest and three other officers of Holland Chapter were notified.

The usual Grand Officers were elected at this meeting, and the so-styled Grand Chapter of Louisiana was organized.

From the testimony submitted to the committee, it appeared that the High-Priest of Holland Chapter, Compn. Henry, was not present at this election; nor could the committee ascertain that there was any Companion present who was entitled to vote in an election of Grand Officers.

Shortly after this, Compn. Henry was officially notified by the Grand Secretary of the Grand Chapter of Louisiana of the organization of the Grand Chapter, and requiring of Holland Chapter her dues and returns from 1832 to 1838 inclusive.

Holland Chapter protested against this demand and asked for evidence of the legality of the organization of the Grand Body, which was refused, and Holland Chapter declined to recognize its authority.

The body, assuming to be the Grand Chapter, proceeded to revoke the Charter, and to expel the High-Priest and Secretary of Holland Chapter.

The Secretary, Compn. C.D. Lehman, made his appeal to the General Grand Chapter.

On July 24, 1843, he served the reputed Grand Chapter with a notice of his intention, and it was shown when this notice was served, the Grand High-Priest of the Grand Chapter, in his place, and in open chapter declared "that he did not acknowledge any other body, and was independent of the General Grand Royal Arch Chapter of the United States."

From the above statement it would appear that the Grand Royal Arch Chapter, organized in 1813, voluntarily surrendered its independent jurisdiction and enrolled itself under the General Grand Chapter, which body continued until 1831, and having ceased her operations by not meeting and electing officers, as required by the General Grand Constitution, it ceased to exist.

All the existing subordinate chapters came immediately under the jurisdiction of the General Grand Chapter, which alone had legal authority over the jurisdiction thus vacated, as by Article 2, Section 2, of the General Grand Constitution.

The deceased Grand Chapter could only be revived by Article 2, Section 9.

The committee recommended and which was unanimously adopted: That Holland Chapter, No. 9, be directed to resume its labors under the direction of its former officers and members, with power to fill existing vacancies, and that it be required to make its annual returns, and settle its dues with the General Grand Secretary.[66]

In the proceedings of the General Grand Chapter for 1847 we find in a report on Holland Chapter, No. 9, "that the Charter of said Chapter has been either lost or stolen; and that the dispensation under which it has been working for the past year expires by the terms of its own limitation with the present session of this General Grand Chapter.

They therefore respectfully recommend that the General Grand Secretary be authorized to execute a new Charter, to take the place of that which has been lost, etc., which was accepted."[67]

The General Grand Chapter at this session "Resolved, That there is not at this time any constitutional and legally authorized Grand Royal Arch Chapter in the State of Louisiana.

"Resolved, That the Association holding its meetings in the City of New Orleans, and assuming to exercise the functions and authority of a Grand Chapter of Royal Arch Masons is an irregular and

---

[66] Proceedings of the General Grand Chapter from 1798 to 1856, pp. 193-195.
[67] Ibid., pp. 218, 219.

unauthorized Masonic body; and it is hereby disowned and repudiated as spurious, clandestine, and illegal."

Masonic intercourse, public and private, was interdicted, and due notice of these resolutions was to be forwarded to the acting Secretary of said body by the General Grand Secretary.[68]

The Deputy General Grand High-Priest reported at this session, September 14, 1847, that since the session of 1844 he had issued dispensations to the following bodies in Louisiana: New Era, No. 2; Red River, No. 3; East Feliciana,[69] No. 4. No dates given.

He had also issued a dispensation to Holland Chapter, No. 1, at New Orleans, to continue work until the present session,[70] April 7, 1845, and a new Charter recommended, which was done as above stated.

When the Charter to East Feliciana, No. 4, was granted, by request of the chapter the name and place were changed to Clinton, to be located at Clinton.

At the same time charters were granted to New Era, No. 2, at New Orleans; Red River, No. 3, at Shreveport; viz.: September 15, 1847.[71]

At the fourteenth meeting of the General Grand Chapter, September 10, 1850, a committee reported that " on the personal knowledge of one of their own members who represents that State (Louisiana) in this Body, that those difficulties are now adjusted, and that the different Grand Bodies of that State, in all degrees of Masonry, are now united as one in that harmony without which our Order can not exist."[72]

At this session (1850) the General Grand King reported "that he had litfore Holland Chapter, No 1; New Era Chapter, No. 2; Red River Chapter, No. 3, and Clinton Chapter, No. 4, in the State of Louisiana, to organize and establish a Grand Chapter for that State; which they did in the City of New Orleans, on 1st day of May, 1848."[73]

Maine.

As the territory, occupied by Maine was a part of Massachusetts until it was made a State in 1820, the Grand Chapter of Massachusetts

---

[68] Proceedings of the General Grand Chapter from 1798 to 1856, p. 128
[69] Ibid., p. 209.
[70] Ibid., 209.
[71] Ibid., 225
[72] Ibid., p. 248.
[73] Ibid., p. 253.

granted a Warrant of Constitution to organize a chapter in Portland, Me., February 13, 1805.

The same Grand Chapter issued dispensations, December 17, 1819, to Montgomery, at Bath, and to New Jerusalem, at Wiscasset; on December 29, 1819, to Jerusalem Chapter, in Hollowell.

Henry Fowle, Deputy Grand High-Priest, constituted these three chapters, respectively, July 18, 19, and 21, 1820, which was reported by him to James Prescott, Grand High-Priest.

These three chapters, with Mt. Vernon Chapter, of Portland, met in convention in Portland, 1820, and adopted the constitution of the Grand Chapter of Massachusetts provisionally, and the Grand Chapter Officers were chosen and organized and constituted the Grand Chapter of Maine.[74]

The first reference to Royal Masonry in Maine by the General Grand Chapter is found in the proceedings for the triennial meeting, September 15, 1826,[75] when the committee reported the legal constitution of the Grand Chapter, and by resolution adopted, that Grand Chapter was recognized and received under the authority and sanction of the General Grand Chapter.

This Grand Chapter had the honor of having two of her Members selected as General Grand Officers in the General Grand Chapter of the United States, viz. : Robert P. Dunlap, General Grand High-Priest for three terms, in 1847, 1850, and 1853; and Josiah H. Drummond, General Grand High-Priest in 1871.

Maryland.

A circular letter from Concordia Chapter in Baltimore was issued to all the chapters in Baltimore and the "Encampment of Excellent, Superexcellent, Royal Arch" (In the District of Columbia), inviting them to send representatives to a convention to be held in the city of Washington, January 21, 1807, to take into consideration the propriety of forming a Grand Chapter for the State of Maryland and the District of Columbia.

Those chapters in Baltimore which met in this convention were Washington, Concordia, and St. John's.

We find from Compn. Edward T. Schultz's History of Capitular Masonry in Maryland that "Undoubtedly [Washington Chapter] was the Royal Arch Chapter of Jerusalem, instituted in 1787 by

---

[74] "History of Masonry and Concordant Orders," p. 616.
[75] Proceedings of General Grand Chapter, 1826, p. 82.

virtue of the dispensation or warrant of Lodge No. 7, Royal Arch Chapter of Jerusalem, at Chestertown, and was attached to Lodge No. 15, now Washington Lodge, No. 3." This chapter finally was merged with Concordia in 1822.

Companion Schultz informs us:[76] "It is probable that Royal Arch Chapters were attached to most of the active Lodges in the State.

Hiram Lodge, No. 27, at Port Tobacco, as we have seen, resolved to open a 'Royal Arch Chapter.' There is evidence to show that more than one dispensation was granted in the year 1797.

Brother David Kerr was at the time Grand Master, and by virtue of the power and control of the Royal Arch Degree, believed to be inherent in Grand Masters, issued his dispensations for the formation of these several Chapters which then, in connection with the Chapter attached to Washington Lodge, formed, June 24, 1897, the first Independent Grand Chapter in the United States.

The Grand Chapter claimed to have been organized in 1796 in Pennsylvania, was an appendage to the Grand Lodge of that State, and did not become independent until the year 1824."

In the above statement of Companion Schultz we heartily concur.

The Grand Chapter of 1797 in Maryland became dormant in 1803, and was revived in 1807, according to documents shown in Companion Schultz's history.[77]

A Grand Royal Arch Convention was held by the H. Royal Arch Chapters in the State of Maryland and District of Columbia in the city of Washington on January 21, 1807. Washington, Concordia, and St John's chapters of Baltimore, Federal and Washington Naval of Washington City and Potomac Chapter of Georgetown of the District of Columbia were present by their representatives.

This Convention resolved unanimously to organize a Grand Chapter for the State of Maryland and the District of Columbia.

They elected the Grand Officers, and opened the Grand Chapter in ample form. A committee was appointed to frame a constitution, which reported, and their report was unanimously adopted.

The degrees recognized by this Grand Chapter were Mark Master, Past Master, Most Excellent Master, and Royal Arch.

We make the following extract from Companion Schultz's Freemasonry in Maryland:[78]

---

[76] History of Capitular Masonry in Maryland," pp. 321, 322, 323.
[77] Ibid.
[78] Vol. i., pp. 317, 318.

"Since the finding of these books (old Records), documents have been brought to light, which in connection with them throw much light upon the early history of the Grand R.A. Chapter of Maryland, and the District of Columbia, which as it will be seen

Was the title of the body subsequently formed by the representatives of the chapters in Baltimore and Washington."

The great care, diligence, and indefatigable zeal of Companion Schultz manifested in his history, deserve especial mention by all succeeding historians of Masonry, for his valuable additions to the ancient history of Masonry in Maryland in all the branches – and we continue our extracts:

"Some months since we learned that the Masonic papers of Philip P. Eckel, which were supposed to have been lost or entirely destroyed, were in the possession of his granddaughter, Mrs.

David J. Bishop, living in this city (Baltimore), and who has since most kindly placed them at our disposal. These papers were found to be of great interest as they disclosed the existence of Masonic bodies held in Baltimore prior to the year 1800, that were not previously known or mentioned by any Masonic writer."

Brother Eckel was perhaps the most active and zealous Mason that ever lived in this jurisdiction; there is scarcely a record or document existing in this State, from about 1792 to 1828, that does not mention his name in some capacity.

Mackey says: "He was one of the most distinguished and enlightened Masons of his day;" and we add to this that he was evidently an "Inspector General" of the A.'. A.'. S.'. Rite.

Companion Schultz furnishes facsimile copies of several of the documents referred to, and to prove that a Grand Chapter existed in Baltimore is such a copy of a "dispensation" from David Kerr, Grand High-Priest, to Philip P. Eckel as High-Priest, to assemble a sufficient number of Companions to open and hold a chapter of Royal Arch Masons, etc., in Baltimore, which was to continue in force until June 20, 1797.

This dispensation is dated May 8, 1797.

No further records or documents of any description have been discovered in reference to the Grand Chapter organized in 1807, and the reorganization which occurred in the year 1814.

On May 9th of that year delegates from Chapters Nos. 1, 2, and 3 met in the city of Baltimore, when a constitution for the Grand Royal

Arch Chapter of the State of Maryland and District of Columbia was adopted and Grand Officers elected.[79]

This Grand Chapter continued with above title until the withdrawal of the chapters located in the District of Columbia, except Potomac, No. 8, at Georgetown, which elected to remain under the jurisdiction of Maryland.

This severance was done by the authority of the General Grand Chapter, August 30, 1822.[80]

After this the Grand Chapter of the District of Columbia ceased to exist, the chapters in Washington City and Alexandria had no Grand Head until 1841, when steps were taken to place the chapters in the District of Columbia under the jurisdiction of the Grand Chapter of Maryland.[81] This condition continued until May 7, 1867, when the three chapters in the District of Columbia which were under the jurisdiction of Maryland and District of Columbia, viz.: Columbia, Washington, and Mount Vernon, were duly organized, and constituted the Grand Chapter of the District of Columbia.

That this was regularly and lawfully accomplished, we refer to the proceedings of the General Grand Chapter for 1865.

The following was referred to a committee:

"Resolved, That the Royal Arch Chapters in the District of Columbia or any three of them, are hereby authorized to establish a Grand Chapter for the District of Columbia; and whenever such Grand Chapter shall be organized, the jurisdiction now exercised over the chapters taking part in the same, by the Grand Chapter of Maryland, shall cease."[82] That committee reported in 1868, and the Grand Chapter of the District of Columbia was sustained.

Massachusetts.

The Royal Arch Chapter of St. Andrew's was one of the three original chapters which met in convention in Boston, October 24, 1797, and issued the "Circular," which invited the assembling of a convention in Hartford, Ct., January 24, 1798, "to form and open a Grand Chapter of Royal Arch Masons, and to establish a Constitution for the government and regulation of all the chapters that now are or may be hereafter erected within the said States."[83]

---

[79] Schultz's "History of Maryland," vol. i., p. 325.
[80] Proceedings General Grand Chapter, 1826, P. 77.
[81] Ibid., 1841, p. 161; 1842, p. 181.
[82] Ibid., i865, P. 31.
[83] "Compendium," p. 7.

The first notice of conferring the Royal Arch degree which we find was August 28, 1769, in St Andrew's Chapter, called "Royal Arch Lodge," under the sanction of St. Andrew's Lodge Charter, No. 82, under the Registry of Scotland.

From August 12, 1769, until 1788, the title "Royal Arch Master" was employed.

Michigan.

At the fifth regular meeting, of the General Grand Chapter, held September 9, 1819, the committee reported that the General Grand High-Priest had granted a dispensation to Monroe Chapter, No. 1, at Detroit, December 3, 1818.[84]

At the twelfth meeting of the General Grand Chapter a dispensation was reported as having been granted, by the Dep. General Grand High-Priest, May 16, 1844, to St Joseph's Valley Chapter, No. 2, at Niles.[85] Also the same officer reported, at the thirteenth meeting, held September 14, 1847, that a dispensation had been granted (without date) to Jackson Chapter, No. 3, in Jackson.[86]

A Charter was granted to Monroe Chapter, No. 1, September 11, 1819;[87] and at the litfo of September 14, 1847, a Charter was granted to St. Joseph's Valley, No. 2;[88] and September 16, 1847, to Jackson Chapter, No. 3,[89] by vote of the General Grand Chapter.

The General Grand Scribe, in January, 1848,[90] authorized the chapters in Michigan to meet and organize a Grand Chapter for the State.

Minnesota.

The first notice of Royal Arch Masonry, in the proceedings of the General Grand Chapter, we find at the fifteenth meeting, held September 17, 1853, when the committee reported that "a number of companions at St. Paul, Minn., have petitioned the General Grand King for a dispensation," and recommended a dispensation to be issued by the present Deputy General Grand High-Priest.[91]

---

[84] "Compendium," p. 60.
[85] Ibid., p. 182.
[86] Ibid., p. 209.
[87] Ibid., p. 60.
[88] Ibid., p. 209.
[89] Ibid., p. 225.
[90] Ibid., p. 254.
[91] Proceedings, 1853, p. 320. (90 Ibid., 1856, p. 373.)

At the triennial session, September 11, 1856, a Charter was granted. Dispensations were issued by the General Grand High- Priest to the following chapters: Vermillion, No. 2, in Hastings, June 20, 1857; St. Anthony Falls, No. 3, in St. Anthony, January 5, 1858.

On September 14, 1859, charters were granted to these.

A convention was held, by authority of Compn. Albert G. Mackey, General Grand High-Priest, dated December 1, 1859, in St. Paul, December 17, 1859, a constitution was adopted and the Grand Chapter of Minnesota was regularly organized.

Mississippi.

At the sixth meeting of the General Grand Chapter, held September 14, 1826, the General Grand High-Priest reported having issued a dispensation to a chapter at Port Gibson, Miss.

On the 15th at the same meeting, a Charter was granted.[92]

September 14, 1841, it was reported that a dispensation was issued to Vicksburg Chapter, June 17, 1840; and a Charter was granted September 17, 1841.

At the twelfth session, September 10, 1844,[93] the Deputy General Grand High-Priest reported having issued dispensations to chapters in Mississippi as follows, viz. : to Columbus Chapter, February 7, 1842; and to Jackson, August 28, 1843.

The General Grand High-Priest reported having issued a dispensation to a chapter at Holly Springs, October 30, 1841.[94] At the thirteenth session, September 14, 1847, the General Deputy Grand High-Priest reported that he had authorized the consecration of three chapters in Mississippi since the session of 1844, for which charters had been ordered at that time, viz.: Columbus Chapter, at Columbus; Jackson Chapter, at Jackson; and Wilson Chapter, at Holly Springs.[95] He also reported having issued two dispensations to organize chapters: Carrollton Chapter, No. 7, at Carrollton; and Yazoo Chapter, No. 8, in Yazoo County.[96]

In compliance with a petition from the chapters in Mississippi, the General Deputy Grand High-Priest reported that, March 12, 1846, he had granted permission for those chapters to form a Grand Chapter

---

[92] Proceedings General Grand Chapter, 1798-1856, p. 89.
[93] Ibid., p. 163.
[94] Ibid., P. 78.
[95] Ibid., p. 209.
[96] Ibid., p. 209.

for that State; and he had been officially notified that the Grand Chapter had been duly organized, May 18, 1846.[97]

Missouri.

At the regular meeting of the General Grand Chapter (September 11, 1819) it was reported that the Grand High-Priest had granted a dispensation to form a chapter in Missouri Territory, at St.

Louis, on April 3, 1819,[98] and a Warrant was granted, September 16, 1826,[99] at the sixth meeting.

At the tenth meeting, September 14, 1838, the General Grand Scribe reported that a dispensation had been issued for a Charter to Palmyra Chapter, No. 2[100] (no date given).

The committee recommended a Charter to be issued whenever the provisions of the constitution should have been complied with.

A Charter, however, was not given by the General Grand Chapter, but after the formation of the Grand Chapter of Missouri, it was given October 16, 1847.

At the twelfth meeting of the General Grand Chapter, held September 10, 1844,[101] the Deputy General Grand High-Priest reported having issued dispensations to Liberty Chapter, No. 3, at Liberty, February 7, 1842; one to Weston Chapter, No. 4, at Weston, January 17, 1843; and one to Booneville Chapter, No. 6, at Booneville, March 3, 1843; one to La Fayette Chapter, No. 5, September 11, 1844. Charters were ordered to all chapters reported by the committee, viz.: Nos. 3, 4, 5, and 6.[102]

At the thirteenth meeting, held September 14, 1847, it was reported by the Deputy General Grand High-Priest that since the session of 1844 he had issued a dispensation to consecrate Booneville Chapter, No. 6, and he had issued dispensations to organize St. Louis Chapter, No. 8, at St. Louis, and Hannibal Chapter, No. 7, at Hannibal, No. On September 17, 1847, charters were ordered to be issued to Hannibal, No. 7, and St. Louis, No. 8.[103]

The convention to organize a Grand Chapter for the State of Missouri met in St. Louis, October 16, 1846, and the delegates of

---

[97] Ibid., p. 210.
[98] Ibid., p. 56.
[99] Ibid., p. 83
[100] Proceedings General Grand Chapter, 1798-1856, p. 153.
[101] Ibid., p. 181.
[102] Ibid., p. 185.
[103] Ibid., p. 232.

Chapters Nos. 1. 2, 5, and 6 were present, and did organize the Grand Chapter.

In the report of the General Grand Secretary of the General Grand Chapter, at the thirteenth meeting, held September 14, 1847, he states:

"In the month of November, 1846, I received notice of the formation of a Grand Chapter for the State of Missouri, purporting to be by authority from the General Grand Officers.

This, however, was an error; and on being informed by me that there had been no such authority given, it is believed no further proceedings have been had in the matter."[104]

We find the following minute in the proceedings of that day "To the General Grand Chapter:

"The Committee to whom was referred the action of the Grand Chapter of Missouri, have had the same under consideration, and respectfully report

"That the Grand Chapter of Missouri was formed, as we think, by the Chapters thereof in good faith, believing that they were fully authorized to do so, from conversations and correspondence with the Comp. General Grand Secretary.

Your Committee, however, believe that this organization was not strictly in conformity with the Constitution of this General Grand Chapter; therefore,

"Resolved, That all irregularities be removed, and that said Grand Chapter of Missouri be fully recognized, and that its representatives be invited to seats in this General Grand Chapter."[105]

Compn. J.W.S. Mitchell, of the Grand Chapter of Missouri, offered the following:

"Resolved, That the Chapters working by dispensation under this jurisdiction in Missouri be, and they are, required to pay dues to this General Grand Chapter up to the period when a Grand Chapter was organized in the said State of Missouri, viz.: October, 1846,"[106] which was adopted.

Montana.

The organization of the Grand Chapter of Montana, at Helena, June 25, 1891, was consummated in accordance with a call of the

---

[104] Ibid., p. 206.
[105] Proceedings General Grand Chapter, 1865, P. 25.
[106] Ibid., p. 31.

chapters and a Warrant which had been issued by the General Grand High-Priest, Companion David F. Day.

The chapters constituting the Grand Chapter were:
Dispensation
Charter Virginia City, No. 1, at Virginia City,
July 14, 1866 December 18, 1868

Helena, No. 2, at Helena,
December, 1867 December 18, 1868

Deer Lodge, No. 3, at Butte City,
October 10, 1874 November 25,

1874 Valley, No. 4, at Deer City,
July 22, 1880, August 27, 1880

Yellow Stone, No. 5, at Miles City,
January 2, 1886, October 1, 1886

Billings, No. 6, at Billings,
May 6, 1886, October 1, 1886

Livingston, No. 7, at Livingston,
July 15, 1886, October 1, 1886

Dillon, No. 8, at Dillon,
January 15, 1887, November 22,

1889 Great Falls, No. 9, at Great Falls,
March 13, 1889 November 22, 1889[107]
Proceedings General Grand Chapter, 1798 - 1856, p. 219[108]

Nebraska.

At the triennial communication of the General Grand Chapter, held September 8, 1865, the General Grand King reported:

"On the 21st day of November, 1859, I granted to sundry Companions at the City of Omaha, in Nebraska Territory, a dispensation to form and open a Chapter of Royal Arch Masons at that place, to be called Omaha Chapter, No. 1." He also reported having

---

[107] Ibid., p. 23.
[108] Ibid., p. 231

issued a dispensation, January 25, 1860, to Keystone Chapter, No. 2, at Nebraska City.

Also that on July 13, 1864, a dispensation had been granted to Nebraska Chapter, No. 3, at Plattsmouth. On the same day (September 8, 1865) charters were granted to all three of the above chapters.

By permission of the Deputy General Grand High-Priest a convention was held, March 19, 1867, and the Grand Chapter of Nebraska was regularly organized.

Nevada.

At the triennial of the General Grand Chapter, held September 8, 1865, the General Grand High-Priest reported having issued a dispensation, in May, 1863, to "Lewis Chapter," at Carson City, Nevada, which name was a compliment to himself (John L. Lewis).

This chapter received the Charter, dated September 8, 1865.[109] A dispensation was issued to Virginia Chapter, at Virginia City.[110] From the report, in the proceedings, it is very uncertain when the dispensation was issued.

The Charter was ordered September 18, 1868.

A dispensation was granted to Austin Chapter, at Austin, October, 1866, and a Charter, September 18, 1868.

A dispensation was issued to White Pine Chapter, at Hamilton, January 10, 1871; and a Charter, September 20, 1871.[111]

A convenion of these four chapters was held by authority of the General Grand High-Priest, November 18, 1873.

From the proceedings of the General Grand Chapter for November 21, 1874, we see in the report of the General Grand Secretary that a dispensation had been issued to St. John's Chapter, at Eureka, April 26, 1873; and also to Keystone Chapter, at Pioche, June 12, 1873.[112] The General Grand Secretary says: "The Chapters organized U.'. D.'.in Nevada, made returns and paid dues to date of the organization of the Grand Chapter of Nevada, of which they became components, in accordance with a custom hitherto approved by the General Grand Chapter."[113]

New Hampshire.

---

[109] Ibid., p. 31.
[110] Ibid., p. 23.
[111] Ibid., 1871, p. 33.
[112] Proceedings of General Grand Chapter, 1874, p. 41
[113] Ibid., P. 41.

In the session of the General Grand Chapter of the United States, held June 6, 1816, we find that the General Grand King reported that he had granted warrants or charters for St. Andrew's Chapter at Hanover, January 27, 1817; Trinity Chapel, at Hopkinton, February 16, 1807; Washington Chapter, in Portsmouth, November, 1815; Cheshire Chapter, at Keene, May 4, 1816;[114] and at this session the warrants were confirmed June 7, 1816.[115]

The Grand Chapter of New Hampshire was organized on June 10, 1819, and the General Grand Chapter was duly notified by John Harris, of New Hampshire, August 21, 1819, and the Grand Chapter was recognized by the General Grand Chapter at the session held September 9, 1819.[116] The General Grand High-Priest issued a Warrant to Union Mark Lodge, No. 1, in Claremont, July 3, 1818[117] which subsequently passed under the jurisdiction of the Grand Chapter of New Hampshire.

New Jersey.

The first official notice we find of the introduction of capitular Masonry in New Jersey, is in the proceedings of the General Grand Chapter for June 6, 1816.

The General Grand Scribe had granted a Warrant or Charter to Washington Chapter, Newark, May 26, 1813; to Cincinnati Mark Lodge, No. 1, Hanover, April, 1811; and to Union Mark Lodge, No. 2, Orange.[118]

At the triennial meeting, held September 16, 1826, the report of the General Grand High-Priest stated that a dispensation had been granted by him to Franklin Chapter, No. 3, and a Charter was granted.[119]

A special committee reported September 10th that a Charter had been granted to the State of New jersey, enabling the respective chapters therein to form and hold a Grand Chapter in the said State, by the Most Excellent General Grand High-Priest.[120]

---

[114] There were no meetings of General Grand Chapter between 1806 and 1816.
[115] "Compendium," fifth meeting of General Grand Chapter of United States, p. 56.
[116] Ibid., p. 55.
[117] Ibid., p. 60.
[118] Proceedings of General Grand Chapter for 1797 to 1856, p. 45.
[119] Ibid., p. 78.
[120] Proceedings of General Grand Chapter, 1797-1856, pp. 77, 82.

At the triennial session, September 10, 1819, a communication from a Companion from the State of New jersey on the subject of forming a Grand Chapter being referred to a committee, they repored, that it appears that there are two chapters in the State of New Jersey under the jurisdiction of the General Grand Chapter, and one under the authority of the State of Pennsylvania, which does not acknowledge the jurisdiction of the General Grand Chapter.

The committee were of the opinion that a Grand Chapter could not be formed until there were three chapters acknowledging the jurisdiction of the General Grand Chapter, which was accepted by that body.[121]

A dispensation was granted, September 23, 1854, to Enterprise Chapter, No. 2, at Jersey City,[122] and which was reported at the triennial meeting, September 9, 1856, and February 23, 1856, a dispensation was issued by the General Grand High-Priest to Boudinot Chapter, No. 5, at Burlington.

It was reported by the committee:

"Union Chapter, No. 1, Newark,[123] is the only regularly Chartered Chapter now immediately subordinate to this General Grand Chapter.

The following chapters have been working under dispensations from the General Grand Officers from the dates of their dispensations to this time, viz.: Enterprise, No. 2, jersey City; and Boudinot, No. 5, Burlington.[124] Hiram Chapter, No. 4, Eatontown, having been recognized by the General Grand High-Priest as heretofore stated, now stands a regular subordinate on the register of this General Grand Chapter."[125]

We find nothing said subsequently of the Grand Chapter of New Jersey.

A resolution was adopted in the General Grand Chapter at its session, September 17, 1841, that Hiram Chapter at Trenton be advised to place itself under the jurisdiction of the Grand Chapter of the State of New York, and that said Grand Chapter be advised to legalize the proceedings of Hiram Chapter subsequent to the dissolution of the Grand Chapter of New Jersey.[126]

---

[121] Ibid., p. 54.
[122] Ibid., p. 364.
[123] Ibid., p. 365.
[124] Ibid., p. 365.
[125] Ibid., p. 365.
[126] Ibid., p. 168.

The Deputy General Grand High-Priest issued a dispensation to Union Chapter, No. 1, for Newark,[127] March 13, 1848, and reported the same at the triennial held September 10, 1850, and also to Newark Chapter, No. 2, March 20, 1848 both of these had charters granted September 12, 1850.[128]

The General Grand Secretary reported at the session held September 13, 1853, viz.: "On the 23d of litfor I received from the Deputy General Grand High-Priest a letter from the High- Priest of Newark Chapter, stating the loss of the Charter of said Chapter; which letter was endorsed by Comp. Stapleton, advising the issuing of a dispensation enabling the Chapter to continue its work; which dispensation was issued by the General Grand High-Priest."[129]

It appears, however, that subsequently, September 17, 1853, Newark, No. 2 was merged into Union Chapter.

The peculiar condition of Royal Arch Masonry in New Jersey continued for some considerable length of time, and was not satisfactorily settled until the organization of the Grand Chapter, February 13, 1857.

Hiram Chapter, which, as above shown, was transferred to the jurisdiction of New York Grand Chapter, by the resolution of the General Grand Chapter, September 17, 1841, again desired to be under the jurisdiction of the General Grand Chapter; and in July, 1853, requested of the Grand Chapter of New York to be transferred thereto.

At the triennial of the General Grand Chapter, the report of the General Grand Secretary shows: "Upon examining the papers which came into my possession at our last triennial meeting, after the adjournment, I found among them a petition from the officers and members of Hiram Chapter, No. 4, Eatontown, New Jersey, directed to the General Grand Chapter, dated February 3, 1852, setting forth that, that Chapter was, many years before, chartered by the Grand Chapter of New Jersey, and continued to work under said Charter, so long as that Grand Chapter was in existence.

That it was then 'taken under the fostering care of the Grand Chapter of New York, to which it had ever since been subservient,' and praying to be acknowledged and registered as one of the subordinates of this General Grand Chapter.

---

[127] Proceedings of General Grand Chapter, 1797-1856, p. 250.
[128] Ibid., p. 257.
[129] Ibid., p. 293.

To the petition was appended full power from the Grand Chapter of New York to the petitioner to transfer their allegiance from the Grand Chapter of New York to this General Grand Chapter.

That petition seems, from the endorsement upon it, in the hand writing of Compn. Swigert, who acted as my assistant, to have been referred to the Committee on Chapters and Dispensations. It is not mentioned in the proceedings."[130] A correspondence ensued between the High-Priest of Hiram Chapter and the General Grand High-Priest Hon. R.P. Dunlap, who finally directed the General Grand Secretary to register Hiram Chapter on the roll of chapters subordinate to the General Grand Chapter, which was done November 14, 1854, and the High-Priest George Finch was duly notified thereof, and thereafter the returns were regularly made as a subordinate chapter to the General Grand Body.[131] A Charter was ordered for Hiram Chapter, September 11, 1856.[132]

The following chapters applied to the General Grand High-Priest for his consent to organize a Grand Chapter, viz.: Newark Chapter, No. 2; Hiram Chapter, No. 4, and Boudinot Chapter, No.5. This approval was dated January 24, 1857, and the Grand Chapter was regularly organized February 13, 1857.

New York.

It is very well settled that the Royal Arch degree was conferred in that jurisdiction under lodge charters, as it was elsewhere in the colonies, and prior to the formation of the Grand Chapter for the New England States and New York in 1798.

A Warrant was issued by the Duke of Athol, September 5, 1781, making Rev. William Walter the Provincial Grand Master, authorizing him to form a Provincial Grand Lodge in the city of New York.

The first meeting of this provincial body was held December 5, 1782.

At that date nine lodges existed in the city, and there were six military lodges of the British Army.

It is supposed by some writers, and probably it was correct, that Washington Chapter, of New York, styled the "Mother Chapter," originated in the above-mentioned Provincial Grand Lodge.

---

[130] Proceedings of General Grand Chapter for 1797 to 1856, p. 361.
[131] Ibid., 1856, p. 361.
[132] Ibid., 1856, p. 373.

The early records of Washington Chapter were destroyed by fire in New York, consequently its origin is unknown.

It, however, granted warrants for other chapters through a number of years, Hiram Chapter in Newtown, Ct., dated April 29, 1791, being the first one now known.

The following chapters assembled in convention in Albany, March 14, 1798, and organized and established a Deputy Grand Chapter subordinate to the Grand Chapter of the Northern States for the State of New York, viz. : Hudson, of Hudson, instituted in 1796; Temple, of Albany, instituted February 14, 1799; Horeb, of Whitestown; Hibernian, of New York City; and Montgomery, of Stillwater; dates of these three not known. Comp. Thomas Frothingham was elected Chairman and Comp. Sebastian Vischer, Secretary.

The constitution was read by Compn. Thomas Smith Webb, and Compn. De Witt Clinton was elected Deputy Grand High-Priest; John Hammer, Dep. Grand Secretary.

From the first, warrants were issued to organize Mark lodges and chapters, and prosperity attended the Royal Craft.

Thirty-three chapters and three Mark lodges were represented in the Grand Chapter in 1820.

The chapters increased to fifty-three in 1829, and sixty-one were represented in 1853; while in 1839 and 1840, following the Morgan affair, about thirteen only were reported.

As New York is the most populous State in the Union, so also does Masonry take the lead as to numbers in all the branches in Masonry.

The General Grand Chapter met in the city of New York in 1816, 1819, 1826, 1829, and 1841. DeWitt Clinton served as General Grand High-Priest from 1816 to 1826; Edward Livingston, 1829 to 1835; John L. Lewis in 1865, and James M. Austin in 1868.

At the meeting of the Grand Chapter of the Northern States, held January 10, 1799, Section 1 of Article 1. of the Constitution was changed, and that body assumed the title of General Grand Chapter of Royal Arch Masons for the six Northern States of America enumerated in the preamble.[133] The State organizations were, by Article II, Section I, required to drop the prefix Deputy," and were designated as "Grand Chapters."

---

[133] Proceedings of General Grand Chapter, 1797 to 1856, p. 19, and at p. 10 at session, January 26, 1798.

The six are enumerated in the preamble and New York is also added.

North Carolina.

At the thirteenth meeting of the General Grand Chapter of the United States, held September 14, 1847, in the city of Columbus, O., we find the following report of the General Grand Secretary, viz.:

"In the State of North Carolina there is no Grand Chapter.

The time was when such an institution existed there as a constituent of the General Grand Chapter; but it is believed that it ceased to exist about twenty years ago.

There are said to be Chapters at Halifax, Tarborough, Fayetteville, and Wilmington; but they are not in correspondence with the General Grand Chapter, although some of them, if not all, were instituted under its immediate jurisdiction."

"Note. – Since the foregoing was written I have received a printed copy of the Minutes of a Convention of delegates from the several chapters, by which it appears a Grand Chapter has been reorganized for the State of North Carolina.

Whether this organization be in strict compliance with the Constitution or not, there can be no doubt it was the intention of the chapters so to do, as the whole proceeding seems to be with a view of regaining their former position in the Confederation."

We have carefully referred to the proceedings of the General Grand Chapter, from the thirteenth meeting in 1847 back to the commencement of 1797, and find that the first notice of a chapter in North Carolina was at the fourth meeting, June 6, 1816, being a special in consequence of a lapse in 1813, reported when a Charter was to have been issued to Concord Chapter, at Wilmington, May 4, 1815, by the General Grand King.

He had also issued a Charter to Phoenix Chapter, at Fayetteville, September 1, 1815.[134]

We found also that at the sixth meeting, held September 14, 1826,[135] the Deputy General Grand High-Priest, Compn. Fowle, had granted a Warrant to Wadesborough Chapter, at Wadesborough, in 1822 (no date given).

At this meeting there was no delegate present from North Carolina.

---

[134] "Compendium," p. 46.
[135] Ibid., p. 72.

When the "Memorial" of the Grand Chapter of Kentucky was presented to the General Grand Chapter at its sixth meeting, September 14, 1826, asking for a dissolution of the latter body, it was referred to a committee, and at the same meeting the committee reported the answers of all the Grand Chapters, and North Carolina is stated as concurring with the Kentucky Grand Chapter's resolution.[136] At the meeting of the General Grand Chapter (September 14, 1847) above referred to, the matter concerning a Grand Chapter in North Carolina being referred to a committee, the following report was made:

"That they have had the same under consideration and find their proceedings to be regular.

They assembled as appears by their printed proceedings, on the 28th of June, 1847; three chapters were represented; they proceeded to elect Officers and adopt a Constitution; in which, however, your committee would remark there appear to be several unconstitutional articles or sections, and we would respectfully recommend that the Grand Chapter of North Carolina be recognized as a legal Grand Chapter on their altering and amending their constitution to conform to that of this General Grand Chapter in the following particulars noted by your committee[137] (omitted).

Which recommendation was adopted." So that the Grand Chapter of North Carolina was legally authorized September 16, 1847.

At the fourteenth triennial session, September 15, 1850, Companion L.L. Stephenson was present as proxy, for the Grand High-Priest.[138]

North Dakota.

After the chapters located in South Dakota, by consent of the Grand Chapter of Dakota, on January 6, 1890, had organized their Grand Chapter, on January 9th following, the representatives of Missouri, No. 6, at Bismarck; Casselton, No. 7, at Casselton; Cheyenne, No. 9, at Valley City; Keystone, No. 11, at Fargo; Jamestown, No. 13, at Jamestown; Lisbon, No. 29, at Lisbon, met in convention, and were constituted, by Companion Theodore S. Parvin, by authority of a dispensation from the General Grand High-Priest, Noble D. Larner, and the Grand Chapter of North Dakota was organized in ample form with the following constituent chapters: Missouri, No. 1, at Bismarck;

---

[136] "Compendium," p. 70.

[137] Ibid., p. 155.
[138] Ibid., p. 175.

Casselton, No. 2, at Casselton; Corinthian, No. 3, at Grand Forks; Cheyenne, No. 4, at Valley City; Keystone, No. 5, at Fargo; Jamestown, No. 6, at Jamestown; Lisbon, No. 7, at Lisbon.

The first annual convocation was held on Grand Forks, June 18, 1890.

The membership reported of the seven chapters was three hundred and fifty-five.

Ohio.

The very first notice of Royal Arch Masonry in Ohio is found in the proceedings of the fourth meeting of the General Grand Chapter, held June 6, 1816, where it is reported that the General Grand Scribe had granted a Warrant or dispensation to Washington Chapter at Chillicothe, O., September 20, 1815,[139] which was confirmed on June 7, 1816.[140] The Committee on Examination of Credentials reported:

"On examination it appears that American Union Chapter, of Marietta, originated in the year 1792; that Cincinnati Chapter existed prior to the 27th of January, 1798; that Horeb Chapter had authority from the Deputy Grand High-Priest of the State of Maryland and District of Columbia dated 8th March, 1815, which Grand Chapter is in connection with the General Grand Chapter of the United States."[141]

Cincinnati Chapter started the effort to form a Grand Chapter by sending an invitation to the other chapters to meet at Worthington, October 21, 1816; and on the 24th of that month the Grand Chapter was regularly organized.

The chapters constituting the Grand Chapter were: American Union, No. 1; Cincinnati, No. 2; Horeb, No. 3; Washington, No. 4.

At the fifth meeting of the General Grand Chapter, held September 9, 1819, it was "Voted, That the Grand Chapter of Ohio be now received into the Union of the State Grand Chapters, under the jurisdiction of this General Grand Chapter."[142] The above quotation is taken from the history of the "Capitular degrees," by Comp. Alfred F. Chapman, who stated: "On the second day of the Meeting a Committee was appointed to examine the Credentials and reported as follows: "viz., the above quotation.

Pennsylvania.

---

[139] Proceedings of General Grand Chapter, 1797-1856, p. 45.
[140] Ibid., P. 45.
[141] "History of Masonry and Concordant Orders," p. 626.
[142] Proceedings of General Grand Chapter, 1797-1856, p. 52.

Grand H.R.A. Chapter. – The first chapter of R.A. Masons formed in Pennsylvania was that working under the Warrant of Lodge No.3, and its date was anterior to 1758.

From that period until the fall of the year 1795 all Royal Arch chapters were attached to subordinate lodges under the jurisdiction of the Grand Lodge.

At an Extra Grand Lodge of the Commonwealth of Pennsylvania, held November 17, 1795, "A letter was received and read, signed by Brother Matthias Sadler, as Grand High-Priest of a Grand Royal Arch Chapter, by him said to be established under the several warrants of Lodges No. 19, 52, and 67, held in the city of Philadelphia, and, on motion, the Grand Lodge considering such action irregular, suspended the warrants of the three lodges named until the next Grand Communication.

At an adjourned meeting of the Grand Lodge, held November 23, 1795, the committee appointed on the 17th of same month to take into consideration the action of Lodge 52, etc., reported fully on the matter and offered the following resolutions, which were adopted:

"'Whereas, The supreme Masonic jurisdiction over all Lodges of Ancient York Masons, held in Pennsylvania, has uniformly been and is duly and legally vested in the Grand Lodge of Pennsylvania;

"'And whereas, The number of Royal Arch Masons is greatly increased, insomuch that other Chapters are established in this city and in other parts of Pennsylvania;

"'And whereas.

It was always contemplated that such Chapters, regularly held, should be under the protection of this Grand Lodge;

"'And whereas.

It is the prevailing wish of the Royal Arch Masons within this jurisdiction that a Royal Arch Grand Chapter should be opened under the authority of this Grand Lodge.

Be it therefore, and it is hereby resolved, that a Grand Royal Arch Chapter be opened under the immediate sanction of the Grand Lodge of Pennsylvania.'"

At a meeting of the Grand Lodge, held March 5, 1798, "Rules and Regulations for the government of the Grand Holy Royal Arch Chapter, held under the protection of, and supported by the Grand Lodge of Pennsylvania, unanimously agreed to and established a Grand Chapter, held in Philadelphia, February 24, 1798," were confirmed.

In the declaration, preceding these rules and regulations, was the following:

"Ancient Masonry consists of four degrees, the three first of which are that of the Apprentice, the Fellow Craft, and the sublime degree of Master; and a brother being well versed in these degrees, and having discharged the offices of his lodge, particularly that of Master, and fulfilled the duties thereof with the approbation of the brethren of his lodge, is eligible, on due trial and examination by the Chiefs of the Chapter to whom he shall have applied, and by them found worthy of being admitted to the fourth degree, The Holy Royal Arch."

The first of the rules declared:

"That no Chapter of Holy Royal Arch shall be held or convened within the commonwealth of Pennsylvania or Masonic jurisdiction thereunto belonging, but under the authority and sanction of a regular subsisting warrant granted by the Grand Lodge according to the old institutions, and by the consent of said lodge first signified to the Grand Chapter."

Subsequently the degrees of Mark Master and Most Excellent Master were permitted to be conferred (so as to enable Companions of Pennsylvania to enter chapters in other States), but the conferring of them was not to be considered as a recognition of them as degrees of Ancient York Masonry.

This state of affairs continued until May 17, 1824, when the dependent Grand Chapter to the Grand Lodge was closed sine die.

And on the same day, "At a meeting of the Companions of the Holy Royal Arch, convened at the Masonic Hall," it was "Resolved, That the Companions now present do organize themselves into a Grand Holy Royal Arch Chapter," and on the 24th of the same month officers were elected, Companion Michael Nisbet being the first Grand High-Priest of the Independent Grand Chapter, and which now controls all the degrees of its sister Grand Chapters with the exception of that of Past Master, which the Grand Lodge still controls.

The Grand Chapter of Pennsylvania is not a constituent of the General Grand Chapter of the United States.

Rhode Island.

Washington Chapter, "Mother," of New York, gave a Charter to Providence Royal Arch Chapter, September 3, 1793, and was with the other chapters in the organization of the Grand Chapter of Rhode Island, March 12, 1798.

This Grand Chapter took part in the organization of the General Grand Chapter[143] and continued therewith until the war period (1861-65), and as the General Grand Chapter's sessions were thereby interrupted, this Grand Chapter, as well as some others, held that in consequence of the non-attendance at the regular sessions, the General Grand Chapter had been dissolved, and the Grand Body remained out of the Union until the session held October 12, 1897, when she again sent her representatives and rejoined the Union.

This action was resolved upon at the ninety-ninth annual convocation of the Grand Chapter of Rhode Island, held March 9, 1897.[144]

South Carolina.

A Warrant was granted by the Grand Chapter of New York, February 1, 1803, to Carolina Chapter, in Charleston.[145] At the third regular meeting of the General Grand Chapter, January 9, 1806, the General Grand Officers reported having granted a Warrant for a chapter at Beaufort, S.C., by the name of Unity Chapter, which was then confirmed.[146] The dispensation for this chapter had been issued March 1, 1805.

In consequence of the war with Great Britain there was no meeting of the General Grand Chapter until 1816, which was the fourth, being a special.

At the meeting of 1806 a petition for a chapter in Charleston, by Bryan Sweeny and others, was presented and refused, because it was not recommended by any adjacent chapter.[147]

The Grand Chapter for the State of South Carolina was instituted May 29, 1812.

We can not find any reference to the organization of the Grand Chapter of South Carolina in the proceedings of the General Grand Chapter; but at the fourth meeting, held June 6, 1816, Thos. Smith Webb is reported as proxy for Wm. Voung, the Grand High-Priest, and Foster Burnet as proxy for Benj. Phillips, Grand Scribe; therefore, that

---

[143] "Compendium of Proceedings General Grand Chapter of United States," p. 8.
[144] Proceedings General Grand Chapter, 1897, P. 29.
[145] Proceedings Grand Chapter of New York in "History of Masonry and Concordant Orders," p. 629.
[146] Proceedings General Grand Chapter, 1806, p. 30.
[147] Ibid., p. 31.

Grand Chapter was duly recognized as a constituent of the General Grand Chapter.

We must presume that during the war period, as was reported to the General Grand Chapter, "the situation of the country was such at that time as to render it highly inconvenient for the General Grand Chapter to convene."[148] This Grand Chapter was also represented at the meetings held in 1826 and 1829, and not again until 1844, and then not until 1859.

During the years 1861 to 1865 that Grand Chapter refused to withdraw its allegiance: "And, by a resolution adopted in 1861, the oaths of office and of initiation have included allegiance to the General Grand Chapter," was stated with pride, in the sessions of 1862-65 by Albert Mackey, General Grand High-Priest and Past Grand High-Priest of the Grand Chapter of South Carolina.[149]

South Dakota.

When it was decided by the chapters of Dakota Grand Chapter to organize two Grand Chapters, viz., for North and South Dakota, a convention was held by all the chapters located in South Dakota.

There were present the representatives of the following chapters, viz.: Yankton, No. 1, at Yankton; Aberdeen, No. 14, at Aberdeen; Mitchell, No. 16, at Mitchell; Brookings, No. 18, at Brookings; Orient, No. 19, at Flandreau; Rabboni, No. 23, at Webster.

Companion Theodore S. Parvin was present, and by authority of a dispensation issued to him, as Deputy, by General Grand High-Priest Noble D. Larner, which was confirmed by the then General Grand High-Priest David F. Day, he constituted the Grand Chapter of South Dakota in ample form.

Tennessee.

March 2, 1818, the General Grand High-Priest issued a dispensation to Cumberland Chapter, in Nashville, Tenn.,[150] which received a Charter at the session of the Gencral Grand Chapter, September 11, 1819.[151]

At the meeting held September 15, 1826, it was reported that dispensations had been issued to the following chapters, viz. : Franklin Chapter, at Franklin, March 25, 1824; Clarksville Chapter, at

---

[148] Proceedings General Grand Chapter, 1816, p. 41.
[149] Ibid., 1865, p. 11
[150] Ibid., 1819, p. 60.
[151] Ibid., p. 60.

Clarksville, December 11, 1824; LaFayette, at Columbia, January 5, 1825.

At the same session charters were ordered to be issued.[152] At the session September 16, 1826, the Grand Chapter of Tennessee was regularly recognized as having been duly organized and constituted,[153] and became a constituent of the General Grand Chapter.

Texas.

At the meeting of the General Grand Chapter, held December 1835, an application was made by Comps. Samuel M. Williams, James H. C. Miller, and others associated with them, for a Charter to constitute a chapter of Royal Arch Masons in Texas.[154] The committee, to whom this was referred, recommended, December 9th, that a Warrant or Charter be issued to them by the name of San Filipe de Austin, Royal Arch Chapter, No. 1.[155]

At the meeting held in 1850, Austin Chapter, No. 6, petitioned to have the name changed to Lone Star, No. 6.[156]

At the meeting of General Grand Chapter, September 14, 1850, the following chapters received charters, the General Grand King having reported that dispensations had been issued to them by him, viz.:

Name	Dispensation	Charter Granted
Washington Chapter	No. 2.	May 5, 1848... September 12, 1850
Jerusalem Chapter	No. 3	March 10, 1849 Dispensation contd
Trinity Chapter	No. 4	March 14, 1848... Dispensation contd
Brenham Chapter	No. 5	April 14, 1849... September 12, 1850
Austin changed to Chapter	No. 6.	April 14, 1849... September 12, 1850
Lone Star San Jacinto Chapter	No. 7.	January 22, 1850 Dispensation cont'd
Washington	No. 8	No date, 1850...

---

[152] Proceedings General Grand Chapter, 1826, p. 78.
[153] Ibid., p. 82.
[154] Ibid., 1835, p. 129.
[155] Ibid., p. 133
[156] Ibid., 1850, pp. 252, 257, 258, 268, 272.

changed to Chapter		September 13, 1850
Brazos Rising Star Chapter	No. 9	February, 1850... September 14, 1850

Those chapters in the above table having their dispensations continued were recommended and authorized to surrender them, and receive charters from the Grand Chapter of that State, if one be organized previous to the next meeting of the General Grand Chapter.

"The First Grand Chapter of the Republic of Texas was formed by a convention of Royal Arch Masons, delegates from San Filipe de Austin Chapter, of Galveston; Cyrus Chapter, of Matagorda; Lone Star Chapter, of Austin, and Rising Star Chapter, of San Augustine.

The Convention met in the city of Austin on the 14th of December, 1841."[157]

The Grand Chapter was organized and the constitution adopted.

San Filipe de Austin Chapter declined to sign the constitution and withdrew from the convention.

The constitution was adopted and ratified on December 21, 1841.

It was signed by B. Gillespie, Grand High-Priest, and attested by H.W. Raglin, Grand Secretary. Compn. George Lopas, the Grand Secretary of the Grand Chapter of Texas, in 1895, was instructed to prepare a reprint of the proceedings of the Grand Chapter, which be accomplished, and the valuable results of his labors appear in two beautiful volumes, from which we are enabled to gain all the information as to the condition of capitular Masonry in the State of Texas.

It is probable that no convocation was held in 1842.

The proceedings of 1844 to 1849 included, as also the original constitution, were printed and given verbatim in the reprint.

The Grand Chapter met in 1848, but the proceedings were not printed.

When, "for the sake of peace and harmony among the Craft," this Grand Chapter was dissolved, there were nine chapters, viz.: Cyrus, No. 1, at Matagorda; Lone Star, No. 3, at Austin; Rising Star, No. 4, at San Augustine: Washington, No. 5, at Washington; De Witt Clinton, No. 6, at Clarksville; Jerusalem, No. 7, at Alta Mira (Fanthorp's) ;

---

[157] "Historical Sketch," by George Lopas, Grand Secretary, 1897, p. 3.

Houston, No. 8, at Houston; Brenham, No. 12, at Brenham, and Trinity, No. 13, at Crockett.

The compiler, Compn. Lopas, was unable to account for the missing Nos. 2, 9, 10, 11 and was unable to learn of their names or locations.[158]

The chapter San Filipe de Austin, No. 1, to be located at San Filipe de Austin, in consequence of unforeseen events was never opened at that place, but was opened at Galveston, June 2, 1840, four years and a half later.

This was reported to the General Grand Chapter in 1844, and, on September 12th, by a resolution adopted, the removal was approved.[159]

A certain Scotchman, Dugald McFarlane, organized a chapter in Matagorda, in 1837, and named it Cyrus Chapter, having neither Warrant or Charter.

Doubts having arisen as to its legality, in 1841, they petitioned the Grand Lodge of the Republic of Texas for a dispensation to open a chapter.

A dispensation was issued to them December 10, 1841.

At the same time dispensations were also issued to Rising Star Chapter, at San Augustine, and Lone Star Chapter, at Austin.[160]

After the organization of the Grand Chapter they addressed a memorial to the Grand Lodge of Texas, and after setting forth certain reasons litfore, respectfully asked the Grand Lodge "to relinquish and surrender all jurisdiction and control over the Royal Arch Chapters and Royal Arch Masons in the Republic of Texas upon the surrender of the dispensations heretofore granted by your worshipful body."[161]

This was granted by the Grand Lodge of Texas.

All the irregularities of these chapters in Texas in the early years were respectively cured by the action of the General Grand Chapter in the one case of San Filipe de Austin Chapter, and the Grand Lodge of the Republic of Texas as to the other chapters.

The General Grand Chapter, however, did not recognize the Grand Chapter of Texas as having been regularly constituted, as they had not asked permission to organize from that body, and the General Grand Chapter decided to suppress it by mild means.

---

[158] Ibid., p. 3.
[159] Proceedings General Grand Chapter, p. 191.
[160] Ruthven's Reprint," p. 101.
[161] Ibid., vol. i., p. 112.

In 1847 they passed a resolution forbidding Royal Arch Masons under that jurisdiction from holding Masonic intercourse with the Grand Chapter of Texas, its subordinates, and those acknowledging its authority.

"At the formation of the Grand Chapter of Texas in the city of Galveston, December 30, 1850, the following chapters were represented: San Filipe de Austin, No. 1, chartered by the General Grand Chapter, December 9, 1835; Washington, No. 2, Brenham, No. 5, and Brazos, No. 8.

"Of the Chapters organized by authority of the General Grand Chapter, all but San Filipe de Austin, No. 1, surrendered their authority from the General Grand Chapter to the Grand Chapter of Texas, and received their charters, dated June 25, 1851, and signed by the Grand Officers elected at the second annual convocation in the town of Huntsville, June 24, 1851."

"San Filipe de Austin, No. 1, never received a charter from the Grand Chapter of Texas until June 22, 1860."

"Many of the Companions who belonged to Chapters under the First Grand Chapter of the Republic of Texas, believing the action of the General Grand Chapter in regard to Royal Arch Masonry in Texas unwarranted and unjust, refused to be 'healed' under the new organization, and were thereby debarred from enjoying the privileges for which they had worked so earnestly and long.

Others accepted the situation until such time as they should be able to sever an alliance that was unsought and always distasteful."

"The time came in 1861, when, on the 17th of June, the Grand Chapter adopted the following resolution:

"Resolved, That all connection between this Grand Chapter and the General Grand Chapter of the United States is dissolved and forever annihilated by the separation of our State from that government."[162]

The Grand Chapter of Texas has steadily refused all overtures from the General Grand Chapter to return to the fold from which she withdrew in 1861. Tempus lit omnia" (Time cures all things), and we feel assured that, with the passing away of the present generation, with its prejudices, so will pass away that feeling in the Grand Chapter of Texas which now keeps her out of the fold, especially as some of her best members never left the General Grand Body.

---

[162] "Historical Sketch," P. 7.

Utah.

December 13, 1872, Utah Chapter, No. 1, Salt Lake City, had a dispensation issued, and a Charter was granted November 25, 1874.[163]

A dispensation was issued for Ogden Chapter, No. 2, at Ogden, March 11, 1881; and Ontario, No. 3, at Park City, October 26, 1882; and charters to these two were granted August 15, 1883.[164] Utah has no Grand Chapter, and is under the control of the General Grand Chapter.

Vermont.

The first notice of Royal Arch Masonry we have is in the proceedings of the General Grand Chapter, at its third regular meeting, held January 9, 1806, where it is stated that a communication from Rutland in the State of Vermont, signed by Nicholas Goddard, Grand Secretary, was presented, informing the General Grand Chapter of the formation of the Grand Royal Arch Chapter in the State of Vermont, etc.[165] At this first day of the meeting the General Grand Chapter, by resolution, admitted the said Grand Chapter of Vermont into union with that body.[166]

From the records of the Grand Chapter of New York we learn that a Warrant for a Mark Master Mason's Lodge was granted at Bennington, January 30, 1799.

Also that the Deputy Grand High- Priest issued a dispensation to Jerusalem Chapter, in Vergennes, March 25, 1805; and the Grand Chapter granted it a Charter, February 5, 1806.[167]

A Grand Chapter was organized in Vermont, December 20, 1804, but there is no record to be found when, nor by whom, Royal Arch Masonry was introduced into the State.

From the proceedings of the Grand Chapter of New York we also learn that in February, 1805, the matter of the formation of a Grand Chapter in Vermont was under consideration, and it was the opinion that there ought to be at least three regular Royal Arch Chapters to form a Grand Chapter, and also they say that "your Committee have had authentic evidence from respectable sources, that there were but three members at the formation of the aforesaid Grand Chapter."[168]

---

[163] Proceedings General Grand Chapter, 1870 p. 56.
[164] Ibid., 1883, pp. 96, 97.
[165] Proceedings General Grand Chapter, 1806, p. 39.

[166] Ibid., P. 29.
[167] "History of Masonry and Concordant Orders," p. 633.
[168] Ibid., p. 633.

A protest was made against the effort to form the Grand Chapter; nevertheless we find that the General Grand Chapter did recognize the organization of that Grand Chapter, as above stated.

The last annual convocation was held in 1832, six years after the great anti-Masonic excitement commenced, Compn. Nathan B. Haswell (Blessed be his memory) being then Grand High-Priest, who also was present at the triennial convocation of the General Grand Chapter in 1832.

At the session of 1844 Compn. Haswell said:

"At the last triennial meeting of your body in New York I had the honor to present a communication giving an account of the state of Masonry in Vermont.

In accordance with a duty I owe the fraternity and in behalf of many good and true Masons in my State I have now further to report that nothing has occurred since that period to warrant the resuming of our Masonic labors.

"In no State of our Union has the anti-Masonic spirit gained so strong a foothold as in Vermont.

Although she has been divested of the political power that for years worked her curse, still her old leaders continue restless and troublesome; and under the abolition excitement which now pervades the State they still exert a secret influence hostile to our institution, which time, patience, and perseverance can alone conquer.

"Mortifying and unpleasant as it is to be compelled by the continued force of circumstances to suspend our Masonic labors, prudence dictates a course so important to the well-being and future welfare of the whole fraternity.

"We look forward, however, to a period when we can peacefully resume them and when public opinion shall do us justice, and sanction a course thus adopted; then shall our obscure but not lost Pleiad again break forth, diffusing new light and heat, in the Masonic Constitution [Constellation perhaps].[169]

"We now ask your fraternal advice in our difficult movements.

And in behalf of the Companions and brethren in Vermont, whose fidelity has never been shaken, I submit this report.

"NATHAN B. HASWELI, High-Priest and Grand Master."

In February, 1848, Jerusalem Chapter, No. 2, was reopened by a dispensation from the General Grand Scribe.

---

[169] Proceedings of General Grand Chapter, 1844, pp. 183, 184.

The Grand Lodge of Vermont was revived in 1847; and soon following this event the Companions of the Grand Chapter made a movement toward the revival of the Grand Chapter, and under the direction of Companion Haswell, who was the last Grand High-Priest, and sanctioned by the Deputy-General Grand High-Priest, the Grand Chapter was reorganized July 18, 1849.

There were three chapters which took part in the reorganization: Jerusalem, No. 2, at Vergennes; Burlington, No. 12, at Burlington and LaFayette, No. 15, at East Berkshire.

In October, 1849, the Grand High-Priest granted a renewal of the Charter to Champlain Chapter, at St. Albans.

June 11 1850, an attested copy of the original Charter of this chapter was shown in the Grand Chapter with proof of original Charter having been destroyed by fire.

Champlain Chapter paid $25, under the ruling, and was revived and represented at that grand convocation.[170]

Since that period the Grand Chapter has continued to be represented in the General Grand Chapter.

Virginia.

The introduction of Royal Arch Masonry into Virginia in 1753 was no doubt similar to its introduction into Pennsylvania and other States north of it, by means of Royal Arch lodges, so-called, because the Royal Arch degree was permitted to be conferred under the lodge Charter, and we have recently seen the discovery by Bro. S.J. Quinn, of Fredericksburg, of the fact that in that ancient town there was such a lodge, in which the Royal Arch degree was conferred, earlier than in any other place in the colonies; and very soon after that degree had been introduced into the work of the lodges in England.

It has been said, by others, that the introduction of the Royal Arch degree into Virginia was by Bro. Joseph Myers, who was the successor of Da Costa, who had opened, under the authority of Bro. Michael Moses Hayes, a Sublime Grand Lodge of Perfection in 1783, at Charleston, S.C. Bro. Myers subsequently settled in Richmond, Va., and then and there introduced the Holy Royal Arch of the Ancient Accepted Scottish Rite, which was taught in Virginia until 1820, when the ritual of the English degree was adopted, whose officers consisted of High-Priest, King, and Scribe, while the former were High-Priest, Captain of the Host, and Captain General.

---

[170] "History of Masonry and Concordant Orders," p. 633.

Bro. John Dove, in his history of the Grand Chapter of Virginia, uses the following language:

"Royal Arch Masonry was taught and practiced in this State during the latter part of the last century, under the authority of a Master's Warrant, until the want of some specific legislation seemed evidently indicated for the internal government of the Royal Arch Chapters, which were then growing in number and increasing in members."

This was in the early part of 1806, and from his acknowledged intellectual ability, in connection with the record of his constant attendance at every meeting of the Grand Chapter of Virginia from December 17, 1818, to December 17, 1868, he was well qualified to decide with authority.

In discussing the matter of substitutes he said: "We have been in the constant use of them since 1792, and have as yet seen no evil result therefrom."

From the date above mentioned by Comp. Dove, viz., 1792, when the Royal Arch was conferred, we may be safe in our statement that as early as 1792 Royal Arch Masonry was practiced in Virginia.

We also, from his statement, may be assured that in Virginia the degree of Past Master was in the chapter series and had been in Virginia since 1790, and whatever may have been the full ritual under lodge warrants, it was practiced until 1820.

At a convocation of the Grand Chapter of Virginia, held January 7, 1820, it was "Resolved, That our enlightened Companion, James Cushman, H.-P. of Franklin Chapter, No. 4, Connecticut, be requested to exemplify the mode of work at present adopted by the General Grand Chapter of the United States, it appearing from his credentials that he is fully competent."

On January 18, 1820, the degree of Mark Master, Past Master, Most Excellent Master, and Royal Arch Mason were exemplified by him and after "most solemn deliberation" were adopted, "that harmony and unity should prevail throughout the Masonic world, and more especially the United States."

From 1820 until December 17, 1841, the council degrees of Royal and Select Masters were controlled by a Grand Council.

At the latter date, by mutual agreement, these degrees were placed under the control of the Grand Chapter, and the following resolutions give the order of succession:

"Resolved, That hereafter the degrees in subordinate chapters be given in the following order, to wit: Mark Master, Past Master, Most

Excellent Master, Royal Master, Select Master, and Royal Arch." May 1, 1808, the Grand Chapter of Royal Arch Masons of Virginia was established, in compliance with a proposition from a convention held in "Norfolk Borough," when it appeared that the "Grand United Chapter of Excellent and Superexcellent Masons of Norfolk had proposed to the Royal Arch Chapters of Richmond, Staunton, and Dumfries to establish a Supreme Grand Royal Arch Chapter for the State of Virginia."

This movement was entirely independent of the General Grand Royal Arch Chapter of the United States, and that Grand Chapter has always held aloof from the General Grand Body.

The Supreme Grand Chapter established Magnolia Chapter, No. 16, at Appalachicola, and Florida Chapter, No. 32, at Tallahassee, Fla., which united with the other chapters in Florida in forming the Grand Chapter of that State.

Washington.

November 1, 1869, a dispensation was granted to Seattle Chapter, No. 1, in Seattle.[171] A dispensation was granted to Walla Walla Chapter, No. 2, in Walla Walla, February 13, 1871. Charters were granted at the meeting of General Grand Chapter, September 20, 1871.[172]

From difficulties encountered within the first chapter it did not succeed, and its Charter was suspended by the General Grand High-Priest, May 25, 1873, and reported by him at the meeting held November 2, 1874.[173] The report of the committee to whom this action had been referred, as also a memorial from members of that chapter, recommended that the action of the General Grand High-Priest be approved; and that the memorial be referred to that officer with power to restore or arrest the Charter of said chapter, as in his judgment he may deem best for the interest of Royal Arch Masonry.[174]

On August 27, 1880, the Charter was declared forfeited and that number of said chapter be assigned to Walla Walla Chapter.[175]

A dispensation was granted to Spokane Chapter, No. 2, at Spokane Falls, November 1, 1881; and one to Seattle, No. 3, at Seattle January 2, 1833.

---

[171] Proccedings Grand Chapter, 1871, p. 33.
[172] Ibid., p. 33.
[173] Ibid., 1874, p. 15
[174] Ibid., p. 55
[175] Ibid., 1880, p. 69.

At the meeting August 15, 1883, charters were granted to both of these chapters.[176]

A convention having been called to meet at Spokane Falls, June 6, 1884, the General Grand High-Priest decided that a letter of a should first have been obtained before holding a convention, and gave his authority to hold a convention at Walla Walla October 2, 1884.[177] (May 10, 1884, the General Grand High-Priest had granted a dispensation to Tacoma Chapter, No. 4, which by order passed to the jurisdiction of the Grand Chapter.)

This convention was held at that date by the three chapters above mentioned.

West Virginia.

After the State of West Virginia was erected and the Grand Lodge of the new State had been regularly organized, May 11, 1865, the Companions of the various chapters, numbering nine, who were under the Constitution of the Grand Chapter of Virginia, deemed it proper to follow the example of the lodges, and organize a Grand Chapter for the new territory.

This movement started in Wheeling Union Chapter, No. 19, Wheeling.

A memorial was issued by Wheeling Union Chapter, which sought permission to organize a Grand Chapter for the State.

The following chapters approved the memorial: Jerusalem Chapter, No. 55, in Parkersburg, November 17, 1870; Star of the West Chapter, No. 18, at Point Pleasant, November 21, 1870; and Nelson Chapter, No. 26, at Morgantown, November 30, 1870.

The Grand Chapter of Virginia took action upon the memorial, December, 1870, and gave consent, "upon the same terms and conditions, and with the same limitations, as the consent of the Grand Lodge of Virginia was given to the formation of a Grand Lodge for the State of West Virginia."

A convention was held November 16, 1871, in Wheeling, and the four chapters above mentioned were represented by their delegates; in addition to these were delegates from Lebanon Chapter, No. 9, at Martinsburg.

The Grand Chapter of West Viyginia was duly and constitutionally instituted, the Grand Officers were chosen and installed by Most Excellent John P. Little, Grand High-Priest of the Grand

---

[176] Ibid., 1883, p. 97.
[177] Proceedings Grand Chapter, 1886, P. 20.

Chapter of Virginia, who took occasion to warn the Companions against a union with the General Grand Chapter.[178] This warning, like that which oftentimes only excites the curiosity

Of the Warnee, has had the effect of bringing the Grand Chapter of West Virginia into the fold, which we trust will be followed by the Mother of the Old Dominion.

Wisconsin.

The Deputy-General Grand High-Priest, at the triennial meeting of the General Grand Chapter held September 10, 1844, reported having granted a dispensation to two chapters in Wisconsin Territory, viz.: February 16, 1844, to Milwaukee, No. 1; and Washington, No. 2, in Plattesville, July 2, 1844.[179] At the meeting September 14, 1847, the same officer reported having issued a dispensation to Southport Chapter, No. 3, in Southport (no date);[180] and also that his proxy had consecrated Washington Chapter, No. 2, at Plattesville, a Charter having been granted to said chapter, September 11, 1844.[181] A Charter was granted to Southport, No. 3, at the meeting held September 17, 1847.[182]

By authority of the Deputy-General Grand High-Priest under date of January 10, 1850, a convention was held in Madison of the delegates of the three chapters, and the Grand Chapter of Wisconsin was duly constituted, February 14, 1850.

The Deputy-General Grand High-Priest having received officially the printed proceedings and grand constitution under date of July 5, 1850, he authorized Argulus W. Stark to install the Grand Officers, which was done August 7, 1850.

Wyoming.

At the triennial meeting of the General Grand Chapter held September 19, 1871, the General Grand High-Priest reported that he had issued a dispensation to a constitutional number of Companions to form a chapter at Cheyenne, Wyoming Territory, under the name of

---

[178] "Masonic History of Concordant Orders," p. 636.

[179] Proceedings of General Grand Chapter, 1844, p. 182.
[180] Ibid., 1847, p. 209.
[181] Ibid., 1844, p. 185, note.
[182] Ibid., 1847, p. 228.

Wyoming Chapter, No. 1,[183] which was chartered, September 20, 1871.[184]

Evanston Chapter, No. 2, at Evanston, received a dispensation dated April 25, 1876;[185] and Lebanon, No. 8, at Laramie City, had a dispensation granted March 15, 1877; and these two had charters granted August 24, 1877.[186]

Garfield Chapter, No. 4, at Rawlins, had a dispensation issued March 25, 1884; and a Charter granted October 1, 1886.[187] These chapters are under the immediate jurisdiction of the General Grand Chapter, never having organized a Grand Chapter.

---

[183] Ibid., 1871, p. 15.
[184] Ibid., p. 33.
[185] Ibid., 1877, p. 92.
[186] Proceedings of General Grand Chapter, 1877, pp. 92, 93.
[187] Ibid., 1886, p. 125.

CHRONOLOGICAL MEMORANDA OF IMPORTANT TRANSACTIONS OF THE GENERAL GRAND CHAPTER![188]

October 24, 1797. – Preliminary meeting of three chapters in Boston, Mass.

January 24, 1798. – Organization of the "Grand Royal Arch Chapter of the Northern States of America." September, 1798. – First meeting after organization for the choice of Officers.

January 9, 1799. – Adjourned meeting; change of name to that of General Grand Royal Arch Chapter of the Northern States of America.

January 9, 1806. – Change of name to that of General Grand Chapter of Royal Arch Masons for the United States of America.

September, 1812, was, by resolution, fixed as the time, and New York City as the place, for the next Septennial Session.

June 6, 1816. – Held in New York City, by reason of failure to meet in 1812.

Constitution changed, so as to have a Depay General Grand High-Priest.

September, 1819. – Held agreeably to adjournment.

February, 1823. – Adjournment was to Washington, District of Columbia, at this time, but not held.

September, 1826. – Met according to previous notice. Meetings made triennial.

November, 1832. – Held in this month on account of cholera in Baltimore during September.

September, 1862. – Appointed to meet at Memphis, Tenn., but not held on account of Civil War then prevailing.

---

[188] Ibid., 1897.

September, 1871 – Constitution amended, admitting Past Grand High-Priests as permanent members.

November, 1874. – Constitution amended, making the first four Past General Grand Officers permanent members.

October 13, 1897. – Centennial Celebration at Baltimore, Md.

CHAPTER LVII

HISTORY OF THE INTRODUCTION OF FREEMASONRY INTO EACH STATE AND TERRITORY OF THE UNITED STATES

The Cryptic Degrees

In the Freemason's Library and General Ahiman Rezon, by Samuel Cole, P.M., published in Baltimore in 1826, we find a list of forty-three degrees which was taken from a "late publication, 1816," which the author states are conferred in the Sublime Grand Lodges in Charleston, S. C., in the city of New York, and in Newport, R.I., which we have heretofore quoted.

"Besides those degrees, which are in regular succession, most of the Inspectors are in possession of a number of detached degrees, given in different parts of the world, and which they generally communicate, free of expense, to those brethren who are high enough to understand them. Such as Select Masons, of 27, and the Royal Arch, as gnven under the Constitution of Dublin, etc., etc."

In a description of the degree of Select Master, the writer says: There is reason to believe that this degree was in use long before those of Most Excellent or Mark Master."[189]

It is well enough to quote from the charge to a Select Master, to indicate its proper place in the "curriculum" of the degrees: "Companion - Having attained to this degree, you have passed the circle of perfection in Ancient Masonry."[190]

This indicates that the Select degree closed all the degrees appertaining to the "Secret Vault," as it really did, up to 1826 at least.

---

[189] Freemason's Library," Cole, p. 220.
[190] Ibid., p. 223.

The edition of the above work of 1817 contains an article by Hezekiah Niles on the Select degree, in which he says: "Though this beautiful Degree is known to some persons in many parts of the United States, we are not informed that it is worked anywhere but in Baltmore. We have been told that a regular Chapter of Select was held at Charleston, S.C., many years ago, but believe it has declined.[191]

Bro. John Dove of Virginia, says: "This beautiful Degree is comparatively of Modern Origin, having been, with the Degree of Royal Master, in the possession of a distinguished Chief, in the State of Maryland, as a purely honorary Degree, elucidatory of, and appendent to Royal Arch Masonry, and by him conferred without fee; he delegated authority to others, to use them, in the same way, until the year 1824, when the Grand Chapter of Maryland, with his consent, took charge of the Degrees, and ordered them to be given before the Most Excellent Master; where all intelligent workers in the Royal Arch must at once perceive the propriety of their location."[192]

Brother A.G. Mackey says: "For many years there have been three distinct claims urged for jurisdiction over these degrees, in America - first, by the Supreme Council of the 33d Degree; next by some of the Grand Chapters; and lastly by the Grand Councils, composed of the subordinate Councils of each State."

"Connected with this question of jurisdiction is another in reference to the historical origin of the Degrees, and, as the person or persons, by whom they were first introduced into America.

The Masons of Maryland and Virginia contend, that the Royal and Select Degrees were introduced by Philip P. Eckel, of Baltimore, one of the most distinguished and enlightened Masons of his day, who, in 1817, communicated them to Jeremy L. Cross, and gave him authority to confer them in every Royal Arch Chapter which he might visit in his official character." This clearly shows that they were to be subsequent to the Royal Arch.

Dr. Robert Folger says: "The Masons of that day (1816) were divided in opinion concerning the proper place to which these degrees (Royal and Select) belonged.

One party preferred that they should be kept separate, and left where they were - a separate system."

At the fourth meeting of the General Grand Chapter, June 6, 1816, a discussion took place upon the proposition for the admission of the Grand Chapter of Maryland and the District of Columbia, William

---

[191] Schultz's "History of Masonry in Maryland," vol. i., p. 335.
[192] Ibid., p. 336.

James Hughan, Philip P. Eckel and Benj. Edes being the representatives of that Grand Chapter.

We learn from the published minutes of that meeting, that a committee made the following report:

"The undersigned having been appointed a Committee for the purpose of conferring with M.'. E.'. Comps. Philip P. Eckel and Benjamin Edes, delegates of the Grand Royal Arch Chapter of the State of Maryland, beg leave to report that they have had an interview with the above named Companions, from whom they received the following proposition, to wit: The Grand Chapter of the State of Maryland and District of Columbia is willing to support the Constitution of this General Grand Chapter.

It will not grant any warrants out of its District and will discountenance all chapters formed contrary to the General Grand Constitution; but requests that it shall not be forced to alter its mode of working, if any difference should exist, at present, and to be received on an equality with the other Grand Chapters.

"Under a consideration of all the above circumstances, your Committee recommend that the said Grand Chapter of the State of Maryland be admitted to an union with this General Grand Chapter.

"(Signed by the Committee).

The Undersigned, delegates from the Grand Chapter of Maryland and District of Columbia, agree to the above report.

"Signed P.P. ECKEL, G.'. H.'. P.'.
"BENJ. EDES."

This report being read and accepted, it was thereupon voted to receive the said Grand Chapter of the State of Maryland and District of Columbia under the jurisdiction of the General Grand Chapter.[193] Folger, referring to this meeting of the General Grand Chapter, says: "The whole matter then came up for discussion, Mr. Eckel, of Maryland, taking a very prominent part in advocating the Union of these two degrees with the services of the Royal Arch Chapter.

The discussion became warm and lasted the better part of two days, when the motion to unite them was rejected.

Whereupon, immediately after adjournment, the State Grand Council of Royal Masters was formed, and the different Councils came under that governing power, and continued so up to 1828.

---

[193] Proceedings General Grand Chapter, 1816, p. 44.

It was this move on the part of the General Grand Chapter, in refusing a recognition of those degrees, that determined Mr. Cross in his future course.

"Mr. Eckel, the Baltimore delegate, then went home; and when Cross, who at that session of the General Grand Chapter had been appointed and confirmed as General Grand Lecturer, started on his lecturing tour, he stopped at Baltimore and purchased and received the privilege from Eckel and Niles to erect and establish councils of Royal and Select Masters throughout the Southern and Western States. This privilege he carried out pretty effectually, beginning with New Jersey; and all the councils in existence in those States, mentioned in his narrative, were established by himself, also the Eastern States, except Rhode Island." Bro. Edw. T. Schultz, in commenting upon what Folger had published as above, said:

"From the above quotations it will be perceived that it was the general belief that the control of the Royal and Select Degrees were vested in Eckel and Niles.

"But we think Bros, Dove, Mackey, and Folger, and others, make a great mistake in coupling the Royal Master's Degree with the Select, in connection with the names of Eckel and Niles; for there is no evidence whatever to show that these Brethren ever exercised or claimed control of the Royal Master's degree, or that they were even in possession of that degree, at the periods named by them."[194]

From Bro. Josiah H. Drummond we learn that, on apparently good authority, Eckel did not get the Royal Master's degree until 1819; when he and Benj. Edes, of Baltimore, received it from Ebenezer Wadsworth, of New York. Bro. Schultz thinks "this is probably true, for there is no mention of that degree being worked in this jurisdiction (Maryland) in any document, or upon the records of the Grand Chapter or its subordinates earlier than 1850. Bro. Cole, in 1817, speaks of it incidentally, but not as among the degrees conferred."[195]

Cole's edition of 1826 (p. 319), says Royal Master and Ark Master or Noachite."

These are considered as merely preparatory, and are usually conferred immediately before the solemn ceremony of exaltation.[196] It will be remembered it at on page 220 of Cole we quoted him as saying that among those degrees communicated "to those brethren who are

---

[194] Schultz, "History," vol. i-, p. 339.
[195] Ibid., p. 338.
[196] Cole, p. 319.

high enough to understand them, such as Select Masons of 27" and the Royal Arch, as given under the Constitution of Dublin, etc.

This evidently shows that even as late as 1826 these two degrees of Royal and Select were not united; and also, that the Royal Master preceded the Royal Arch; and it was most likely that the Select degree followed the Royal Arch.

We show herewith a facsimile copy of the original commission to Jeremy L. Cross, from Eckel and Niles.

To all whom it may concern

Imprest with a perfect conviction that a knowledge of the misteries of the degree of Royal Arch are eminently promoted by a knowledge of those revealed in the Council of Select Masons; and Whereas, the said degree of Select is not so extensively known as its wants and the good of the Craft require - Therefore Know Ye, That reposing especial confidence in my beloved and trusty Companion, Jeremy L. Cross. I do hereby, by the high powers in me vested, authorise and empower him to confer the said degree as follows (viz.): In any place where a regular chapter of Royal Arch Masons is established, the Oficers or Members approving, he may confer said degree according to its rules & regulations, but only on Royal Arch Masons, who have taken all the preceding degrees, as is required by the General Grand Chapter. When a competent number of Select Maosns are thus made, he may grant them a warrant to open a Council of Select and confer the degree and do all other business appertaining thereto.

Given under my hand and Seal at Baltimore, the 27th day of May, A.D. 1817, and in the year of the Dis. 2817, Sigm Philip L. Eckel Thrice Illustrious & Grand Puissant in the Grand Council of Select at Baltimore & Approved as G.G. Scribe.

Approved and attested as Ill. in the Grand Council.

H. Niles

The Select degree was recognized by the constitution of the Grand Chapter of Maryland adopted in 1824, but the Royal Master's degree is not mentioned.[197]

Bro. Schultz continues: "Furthermore, the Warrant granted to Cross, by Eckel and Niles, a copy of which, taken from a photograph

---

[197] Schultz, p. 338.

copy of the Original, in the possession of Bro. Wm. R. Singleton, of Washington, is here inserted, and from which it will be seen that the Select Degree alone is mentioned."

In the first warrants issued by Cross under this commission, the Companions were empowered "to form themselves into a regular Council of Select Masters," but in the warrants issued by him in 1819 and thereafter, the High Powers in him vested, by the Grand Council at Baltimore, were enlarged to include the Royal Master's degree.[198]

It is well to state that from the action subsequently taken by Grand Chapter of Maryland in 1827, from documents submitted, "upon the subject of the institution of the Select Degree independent of the Grand Royal Arch Chapter," which were referred to a committee, who recommended that a circular be sent to the several Grand Chapters, regarding the matter, and which was adopted.

Cross was charged with having abused the "authority delegated or meant to be delegated" to him, and it had been asserted that he had been expelled by the Grand Chapter but Bro. Schultz assures us that there is nothing in the records to warrant such an assertion." Moreover, Cross did not belong to any chapter under the jurisdiction of the Grand Chapter of Maryland.[199]

Cross, it is said, established about thirty-three councils in various parts of the United States.

He also delegated others, with power in like manner to issue warrants for councils of Royal and Select Masters.

"From all that has been stated, it is evident, not only that Eckel and Niles claimed to have had the supreme control and authority over the Select degree, but that this claim was generally regarded valid; and it is equally as evident, we think, that these Brethren never claimed the control of the Royal Master's degree." "It has always been a question of much interest with Masonic writers to know the source whence these Brethren received their authority, and the control of the Select degree.

An old document, that most unexpectedly came to the knowledge of the writer about a year ago, settles that question beyond a doubt.

It is as follows:

"Whereas, In the year of the Temple, 2792, our thrice illustrious Brother Henry Wilmans, Grand Elect, Select, Perfect Sublime Mason, Grand Inspector General, and Grand Master of Chapters of the Royal Arch, Grand Elect and Perfect Master's Lodges and Councils,

---

[198] Ibid.
[199] Ibid.

Knight of the East, Prince of Jerusalem, Patriarch Noachite, Knight of the Sun, and Prince of the Royal Secret, did by and in Virtue of the powas in him legally vested, establish, ordain, erect and support a Grand Council of Select Masons in the City of Baltimore, and wrought therein, to the great benefit of the Craft, and to the profitable extension and elucidation of the Mysteries of Masonry:- and Whereas, we the subscribers to these presents are by regular succession possessors of all the rights, privileges and immunities and powers vested in any way whatsoever in the said Grand Council of Select Masons, considering the great advantages that would accrue to the Craft, in an extension of the knowledge of the Royal Secret, as introductory to, and necessary for, the better understanding of the Superior Degrees.

"Know all, whom it may concern, that we do hereby authorize and empower our trusty and beloved Companions K.S....K. T.... H.A.... of the same, to open and to hold a Chapter of Select Masons in the City of Baltimore and under such By-Laws and regulations as may be enacted and established for the government of the same subject to the following general rules and regulations.'" (Which we omit.)

From some cause the dispensation was not used, but the fact is fully and emphatically stated by Eckel and Niles, under their hand and seal, that they were, "by regular succession, possessors of all the rights, privileges, and immunities and powers vested in any way whatsoever in the said Grand Council of Select Masons," which has been instituted in the city of Baltimore, in the year 1792, by Henry Wilmans, "Grand Inspector General."

"This document, in connection with the Rules and Regulations of the Lodge of Perfection (referred to above), leave no room for doubt that Wilmans was an Inspector of the Rite of Perfection, and that he exercised, in the City of Baltimore, in 1792, the powers claimed by such Inspectors.

But from whom did Wilmans acquire his powers of 'Grand Inspector General,' and the authority 'to establish, ordain, erect and support a Chapter of Select Masons?'"

"We regret that we can not answer the question, nor could the learned Brethren in vaious parts of the country, to whom we applied.

The name of Wilmans does not appear upon any register or document in the archives of the Supreme Council of the Southern Jurisdiction, or upon any other known document or record containing the names of the early Inspectors.

From the fact that in both the documents he is styled 'Grand Inspector General,' while those deriving their powers from Morin are styled 'Deputy Inspectors,' led to the supposition that he might have derived his powers from Europe; acting upon which supposition, letters were addressed to the Grand Lodges at Berlin and Bremen.

While the result of the correspondence, which ensued, was of an interesting nature, nothing in regard to his Masonic character could be learned.

"It has been ascertained that Wilmans was a native of Bremen, and that he emigrated to this country as early at least as the year 1790, and settled in Baltimore.

The first mention of his name, on the records of the Grand Lodge, is in connection with Concordia Lodge, in 1793, of which he was appointed the first or Charter Master.

In the same year he was elected Deputy Grand Master and in the following year, Grand Master of Masons in Maryland.

The register of the Old Zion Lutheran Church, of this city, shows that he died in 1795."

"In a MSS. book of Moses Holbrook, of South Carolina, written in 1829, it is stated that Joseph Myers, a Deputy Inspector General, deposited in the year 1788, in the archives of the Grand Council of Princes of Jerusalem at Charleston, 'a certified copy of the Royal and Select Master's degrees received from Berlin.'"

"This is evidently an error, so far as it relates to the Royal Master's degree.

As intimated, the degree was first known in the Eastern States, and the earliest reliable mention of it there, is in the year 1809." "Bro. Holbrook wrote his book in 1829, at which time both degrees were conferred at Charleston, and naturally he connected the two in his statement, making a similar error that others do, when stating that Eckel and Niles claimed the control of the Royal Master's degree. The book referred to contains also the statement, that somewhere about the year 1788, Joseph Myers was for a time located at Baltimore."

"Did Wilmans receive the Select degree from Myers, or did Myers receive it from Wilmans?"

"If the degree came from Berlin, it is quite probable that Wilmans brought it with him, as he came from Germany, about the time mentioned for the deposit, in the MSS. of Holbrook."

"There is a tradition existing in the Eastern States, that Eckel received the degree from a Prusian, temporarily sojourning in Baltimore.

The period of Wilmans' residence in Baltimore was perhaps not over eight years, and with some propriety, he might have been regarded as a sojourner - and a Prussian."

"It is stated, but upon what authority we know not, that the Royal and Select degrees were conferred by Andrew Franken at Albany in 1769, and that he conferred them upon Samuel Stringer, who afterwards removed to Maryland; but we have not been able to find this name upon any of the records of this jurisdiction."

"These statements or traditions, it will be seen, all point to Maryland as the source from whence the select degree, and (as the writers will have it) Royal Master's degree also, were subsequently introduced into other parts."[200]

Folger says Eckcl, at the session of the General Grand Chapter, advocated "the Union of the degrees with the services of the Royal Arch Chapter."

"From 1824 to 1852, the Select degree only was worked in the chapters in Maryland and District of Columbia.

After 1852, both degrees were worked in Councils specially convened for the purpose, after the Most Excellent and prior to the Royal Arch."[201]

The true history of the origin and progress of the Cryptic Rite in the several States, if it were possible to produce it, would prove of great interest to the Masonic student.

From the preceding pages, taken mostly from the labors of Companion Edw. T. Schultz in his valuable History of Masonry in Maryland, we learn that, while the degrees of Royal Master and Select of Twenty-seven may have been conferred in various places prior to 1792, yet we must concede that the organization of the Council of Select Masons in Baltimore by Philip P. Eckel and Hezekiah Niles, under the sanction of Henry Wilmans, was the very first organized effort to propagate the rite in this country.

Companion Schultz has shown, very clearly, that we can not go beyond the date of that organization, so far as any ancient records have been discovered.

After Companion Jeremy L. Cross had been appointed the Grand Lecturer of the General Grand Chapter, at the session of 1816 - we learn, from several sources, that Cross went to Baltimore in 1827 - and there, no doubt, was initiated into the degree of Select Master and recoved the Warrant from Eckel and Niles which is referred to on the preceding page of this chapter.

A photograph copy of the original is in the possession of the present writer.

---

[200] Schultz, "History of Maryland," vol. i., pp. 335 to 344.
[201] Ibid., p. 344.

This photo copy was submitted to the daughter of Bro. Eckel, who was the wife of Brother, Hon. Elijah Stansbury, Ex-Mayor of Baltimore, and they both certified that they recognized his signature; and, moreover, sent the writer an original letter written by Bro. Eckel in 1819.

These evidences were submitted to experts in handwriting, and the certificate to Cross was pronounced a forgery because the real later signature was of so much better caligraphy than the signature in the suspected paper, as, according to the expert's idea, it should not have been better, being two years older!!! The writer has in his possession several other papers signed by Eckel, and in no two of them do his signatures correspond.

Our duty as a historian requires this statement to be made. Our own opinion is yet, that the document shown by Cross was a veritable commission from Eckel and Niles to propagate the degree, and the Masonic World should be glad thereof; as by his means, the rite spread rapidly in the South and West.

The writer was made a Royal and Select Master, in one of Cross's councils, in St. Louis, Mo., in 1841, about the time the Grand Council of the State was organized, as he then copied their records into the record-book.

The Grand Chapter of Maryland, having incorporated the Select degree into the chapter work in 1824, in 1828 that Grand Chapter sent communications to other Grand Chapters suggesting the propriety of the several Grand Chapters in the United States assuming jurisdiction over the degrees of Royal and Select Masters.

In the Grand Chapter of South Carolina, this matter was referred to a committee, who reported February 26, 1829, which report was unanimously adopted by the Grand Chapter :

"That Committee, after extensive and careful investigation, reported, that in February, 1783, Dr. Dalcho and many others received those degrees in Charleston in the sublime Grand Lodge of Perfection, then established in that city.

That when the Grand Council of Princes of Jerusalem was established in Charleston, February 20, 1788, Joseph Myes, one of the Deputy-Inspectors who established it, deposited in the Archives certified Copies of the degrees of Royal and Select Masters from Berlin in Prusia, to serve for the future guidance and government of that new body.

That from 1788, the Grand Officers and Supreme Council of Inspectors-General, at Charleston, had been steadily in the habit of conferring these degrees; and in 1828, numbers of councils of Select

Masters were acting under their authority in the Southern and Western States.

"The Committee had seen and perused the first copy of those degrees that ever came to America, and old copies of Charters that had been returned by Councils, in States where Grand Councils had been formed, and Charters obtained from such Grand Councils.

And the Committee reported, that these degrees had been under regular and independent Masonic protection and authority for more than forty-six years, and were so circumstanced in the United States, at a period long prior to the establishment of Grand or General Grand Royal Arch Chapters, or even of Chapters of Royal Arch Masons, in any part of the world; and that the Grand Chapter of South Carolina ought to avoid all collision with contemporary Masonic jurisdictions, regularly established, and much longer in existence than their own; and so reported a formal resolution (which the Grand Chapter unanimously adopted) that it was 'improper and inexpedient to assume a jurisdiction over the said degrees, and thus to interfere with the rights and privileges of our brethren in another and higher order of Freemasonry.'

"Of the Illustrious brothers Myers, Spitzer and Forst, that Committee said, 'the above named three respectable Brethren and Companions are, and steadily have been, Members and Officers of the said Council of Princes of Jerusalem.

Their evidence therefore, must be conclusive upon these points.'

"The same Committee (Royal Arch Masons, be it observed, and a Committee of a Royal Arch Chapter, enquiring into its own jurisdiction) said of the Brothers and Companions, Dr. F. Dalcho, Dr. Isaac Auld, Dr. James Moultrie, Senior, and Moses C. Levy, Esq., who received these degrees in Charleston in 1783, from the sublime Grand Lodge of Perfection: 'Three of the above named Brothers are still living, venerable for their years and warm attachment to the glorious cause of Freemasonry, and highly respected and esteemed for their standing in the community where they have so long honorably sojourned, and they are still members of the same Sublime Body.' There is still further testimony to be adduced. The report to the Grand Chapter, which we have quoted, was made by Compn. Moses Holbrook, its Chairman, and unanimously adopted; the Grand Chapter thus affirming, the veracity of the Masonic Witnesses, whose testimony was adduced.

In 1830 the same Compn., Holbrook, was M.'. P.'. Grand Commander of the Supreme Council of Sovereign Grand Inspectors

General of the 33 degree for the Southern jurisdiction of the United States at Charleston.

"In February, A.I. 2383, the M.'. E.'. G.'. High-Priest of the Grand Chapter of South Carolina, John H. Honour, who was then and still is (1853) M.'. P.'. W.'. Commander of the Sup.'. Council, S.'. G.'. I.'. G.'. of 33 degree, for the Southern Jurisdiction of the United States at Charleston, stated in his address to the Grand Chapter, that he had in his possession a manuscript copy of the degrees of the Royal and Select Masters, in which there was a note in the handwriting of Brother Holbrook dated March 15, 1830, in these words:

In Brother Snell's book is written the following:

"'Supreme Council Chamber, Charleston, S. C., 10th Feb., 1827.

"'I hereby certify that the detached degrees, called Royal and Select Master, or Select Masters of 27, were regularly given by the Sublime Grand Lodge of Perfection (No. 2 in the U.S.A.), established by Brother Isaac Da Costa, in Charleston, in Feb., 1783, one of the original Members of which Most Illustrious Brother Moses C. Levy, is still alive and a Member of it to this day, without ceasing to be so for a day; and further, that at the first establishment of a Grand Council of Princes of Jerusalem, in Charleston, February, 1788, by the Ill.'. Dep.'. Inspectors General, Joseph Myers, B. M. Spitzer, and A. Forst, Brother Myers (who succeeded Brother Da Costa after his decease) deposited a certified copy of the Degrees from Berlin, in Prussia, to be under the guidance and fostering protection of the government of the above Grand Council of Princes of Jerusalem.'

"Brother Myers shortly after this (Feb. 20, 1788,) resided some time in Norfolk, Richmond, and Baltimore, previous to his removal to Europe, and he communicated a knowledge of these degrees to a number of brethren in those cities.

The original copy is still in my keeping, and agreeably to the obligations of the same, and the Grand Constitutions governing those degrees, viz.: Royal and Select Mason Of 27, it is correct and lawful to give them either to Sublime Masons, who have arrived to the Knights of the Ninth Arch (13th) or to the Companions of the 3d Arch (Royal Arch Masons)."

From this statement, of those who held the control originally, it will be observed that it was the design, always, to confer, at least the Select degree, only on those who had a knowledge of the Royal Arch degree; hence to impart the mysteries of the Ninth Arch to anyone "beneath the dignity of the Royal Arch," was to invert the true order of succession, so essential in all Masonic degrees.

It has been asserted by some that the Cryptic degrees had been worked in this country earlier than 1783; as early perhaps as 1766 in the city of Albany, and that they were brought from France, and not from Prussia.

Brother Pike said in his report:[202]

"We can soon learn how it was that the Council degrees came about 1766 from France and not from Prussia.

In 1761, the lodges and Councils of the superior degrees being extended throughout Europe, Frederic II. (or the Great), King of Prussia, as Grand Commander of the Order of Princes of the Royal Secret, or 32d degree, was by general consent acknowledged and recognized as Sovereign and Supreme Head of the Scotch Rite."

"On the 25th October, 1762, the Grand Masonic Constitutions were finally ratified in Berlin, and proclaimed for the government of all Masonic bodies working in the Scotch Rite over the two hemispheres; and in the same year they were transmitted to Stephen Morin, who had been appointed, in August, 1761, Inspector General for the New World by the Grand Consistory of Princes of the Royal Secret, convened at Paris, under the presidency of Chaillon de Joinville, representative of Frederic, and Substitute-General of the Order.

It will be remembered that the 33 degree was not then created; and, under Frederic the Great, there was no rank higher than the 32 degree, nor any body superior to a Consistory.

When Morin arrived in the West Indies, he, agreeably to his patent, appointed M. Hayes a Deputy Inspector General, with the power of appointing others when necessary.

It was under this authority, coming, it is true, from the Consistory of Paris held by that consistory as the delegate and representative of Frederic the Great, that the Lodges of Perfection in Albany and Charleston were established, with authority to confer these detached degrees."

"Many rites flourished in Europe awhile and died.

The French and Scotch Rites reduced the degrees practiced by their votaries, the former to seven, the Seventh being the Rose Croix, the latter to thirty-three and some auxiliary degrees.

---

[202] "History of Masonry and Concordant Orders," p. 649.

By common consent it became Masonic law that the first three degrees were the joint property of all, but the others, the peculiar property of the inventors.

Royal Arch Masonry separated itself from 'Blue' Masonry, organized itself, invented three new degrees, and commenced an independent existence.

The Royal and Select Masters formed themselves into councils, and after a time they, too, organized themselves into Grand Councils, and claimed an independent existence.

The Supreme Council did not deny the right, but simply retained their original right to confer the degrees, and Charter councils in States where no Grand Councils have been organized."

The following is a copy of a decree issued by the Supreme Council A.'. A.'. A.'. S.'. Rite of the Northern jurisdiction, the true copy of which was sent to the Southern jurisdiction and was presented to the writer many years since by General Albert Pike.

"The Supreme Grand Council of Sov. Grand Inspectors General for the Northern Masonic District and jurisdiction of the U. States of America duly, lawfully, and constitutionally assembled on the 10th day of June, 1850, at its Grand East, the City of New York, in its Supreme Grand Council of Princes of Jerusalem do declare and make known as follows:

"That in addition to the regular series of degrees and order of the ancient and accepted rite, the said rite had, from time immemorial, been in possession of, and claims as its exclusive property, a number of detached degrees which are illustrative of, connected with, and necessarily appendant to certain degrees in said right or departments thereof: and that the Supreme Grand Council, as the sole conservators of said rite, in said Northern Jurisdiction, is sacredly bound to preserve intact and free from any amalgamation with foreign rites or Masonic Bodies, not acknowledged by us or our said rite, all and every one of the detached degrees referred to.

"That two of such detached degrees, called 'Royal Master' and 'Select Master,' or 'Select Masons of 27,' having in various ways and at different times fallen into the hands of persons in no way connected with the sublime system of free Masonry, or the said 'ancient and accepted rite,' have been and are now cultivated in a garbled form, by bodies styling themselves Masonic, and working under self-assumed powers and authority in this regard, claiming the right to grant charters to confer them; and, moreover, that these degrees, in some places of this jurisdiction, have become amalgamated with a Modern American rite, and are also claimed as the property of the American Royal Arch Chapters.

"This Supreme Grand Council therefore, as in duty bound, protests against this invasion of its rights and privileges, and further declares and makes known that the said degrees of Royal and Select Master, from their nature or character, and the history they develop, and circumstances upon which founded, can not, except in an anachronistic and improper manner be conferred disconnected from the ineffable degrees, and lodges of perfection (14th degree ancient and accepted rite) and that said degrees belong not only characteristically and historically, but legitimately, to 'Ineffable Masonry' and 'Lodges of Perfection,' and do not appertain and can not consistently and lawfully be made an appendage to any Masonic system except said 'Sublime System,' nor to any rite except said 'ancient and accepted rite.'

"And whereas, such assumed authority over the detached degrees aforesaid, may, as we have reason to believe in some instances, have been exercised in good faith, but without a due appreciation of our rights and prerogative in regard to them, this Supreme Grand Council for the sake of harmony is willing to confer and advise with our illustrious Brethren, the Southern Supreme Grand Council at Charleston, S. Carolina, and act in concert with them in adopting such measures in reference to those degrees, as may be mutually adjudged most feasible and proper, without infringing in any way whatever upon our Supremacy over the said degrees.

"'Deus meumque jus,' "J.J.J. GOURGAS, Sovereign Grand Commander of 33d" for the Northern D. and J., U.S.A.
JILES F. VATES, Insp. Lieut Grand Commander.

"N.B. - Signed on the original by Arch d Bull, Sov. Gr. Insp. General 33d; K.H. Van Rensselaer, Sov. Gr. Insp. Gen 33 d, and Francis Turner, Prince of Jerusalem Rose + H.R.D.M.; K.H.; S.P.R.S, and now a member of this Supreme Grand Council.

"To the Supreme Grand Council of the 33 degree, ancient and accepted rite,' at their Grand East, the City of Charleston, S. Carolina.

"Through their Illus. Brother, Albert G. Mackey, M. D., Grand Secretary General of their H. E."

A true copy, W.R. SINGLETON, 33d.

The Supreme Council of the Southern Jurisdiction held to the same contention until at a meeting of the Supreme Council at Baltimore, May, 1870, they surrendered all claim to these degrees.

Dr. Olivar, in his Historical Landmarks,[203] gives an account of the legend of the Secret Vault as discovered in the construction of theSecond Temple, as follows:

"The foundations of the Temple were opened, and cleared from the accumulation of the rubbish, that a level might be procured for the commencement of the building.

While engaged in excavations for this purpose three fortunate sojourners are said to have discovered our ancient stone of foundation, which had been deposited in the secret crypt by Wisdom, Suength, and Beauty, to prevent the communication of ineffable secrets to profane or unworthy persons.

"The discovery having been communicated to the prince,[204] prophet and priest of the Jews, the stone was adopted as the Chief Corner-Stone of the re-edified building, and thus became, in a new and more expressive sense, the type of a more excellent dispensation.

An avenue was also accidentally discovered, supported by seven pairs of pillars, perfect and entire, which, from their situation, had escaped the fury of the flames that had consumed the Temple, and the desolation of war that had destroyed the city.

"The Secret Vault, which had been built by Solomon as a secure depository for certain secrets that would have inevitably been lost without some such expedient for their preservation, communicated by a subterranean avenue with the King's palace; but at the destruction of Jerusalem, the entrance having been closed by the rubbish of falling buildings, it had been discovered by the appearance of a keystone among the foundations of the Sanctum Sanctorum.

A careful inspection was then made, and the invaluable secrets were placed in safe custody."

Brother Mackey says:[205]

"To support this legend there is no historic evidence and no authority except that of the Talmudic writers.

It is clearly a mythical symbol, and as such we must accept it.

We can not altogether reject it, it is so intimately and so extensively connected with the symbolism of the Lost and recovered Word, that if we reject the, theory of the Secret Vault we must abandon all of that symbolism, and with it the whole of the science of Masonic symbolism.

---

[203] Vol. ii., p. 434.

[204] Zerubbabel was Tirshatha (Governor).

[205] "Encyclopoedia of Freemasonry," p. 852.

Fortunately there is ample evidence in the present appearance of Jerusalem and its subterranean topography to remove from any tacit, and as it were, conventional assent to the theory, features of absurdity and impossibility.

"Considered simply as a historic question, there can be no doubt of the existence of immense vaults beneath the superstructure of the original Temple of Solomon.

Prime, Robinson, and other writers, who in recent times have described the topography of Jerusalem, speak of the existence of these structures, which they visited, and, in some instances, carefully examined." Dr. Barclay (City of the Great King) describes in many places of his interesting topography of Jerusalem, the vaults and subterranean chambers which are to be found beneath the site of the Old Temple.

"In the earliest ages the cave or vault was deemed sacred.

The first worship was in cave-temples, which were either natural or formed by art to resemble the excavations of nature.

"The vault was, in the ancient mysteries, symbolic of the grave; for initiation was symbolic of death, where alone Divine Truth is to be found.

The Masons have adopted the same idea.

They teach that death is but the beginning of life; that if the first or evanescent temples of our transitory life be on the surface, we must descend into the Secret Vault of death before we can find that sacred deposit of truth which is to adorn our second temple of eternal life.

It is in this sense an entrance through the grave into eternal life, that we are to view the symbolism of the Secret Vault.

Like every other myth and allegory of Masonry, the historical relation may be true, or it may be false; it may be founded on fact, or be the invention of imagination, the lesson is still there, and the symbolism teaches it, exclusive of the history."

The above quotations; have been made because the present writer had devoted many years to the study of the topography of Jerusalem and its immediate vicinity in connection with his studies in the various Masonic rites which locate their mysteries in that city and in and about the Temple area now called Harem-esh Sheriff. His conclusions are that not a single degree in Masonry can properly be located near the city of Jerusalem nor on or in the "Sacred Area" of the Temple.

So far as the caves or cisterns which are to be found under the surface of the "Area" at the present day did give a key to those who formulated the Cryptic degrees, he feels assured that the originators of those degrees did have some knowledge of their existence - but with accurate maps of that "Area" and the location of every vault or cistern before us, furnished by the accurate survey of Captain Chas. Warren in 1867, we could not for one moment entertain the belief that such a system of vaults or arches ever existed there, as described in our lectures of any of the Rituals - but we do believe that these rituals, being symbolic and allegorical, were founded upon the fact of vaults found in that locality.

We can refer to the legend of Enoch and his vaults, erected to conceal the sacred delta, constructed by him and his son Methuselah, after the ineffable NAME of Deity had been revealed to him, and which name he had engraved upon the delta, which by the command of God, he was to conceal and secure, for future generations to discover.

These vaults, nine of them, were securely constructed, and two pillars were erected, and placed near, with inscriptions to indicate the locality of the vaults.

It is possible that the pillars were destroyed and carried away by the flood.

The fable further states that when King Solomon commenced the preparation of the ground on Mount Moriah for the temple, his workmen broke into these vaults and found certain mysterious things there; and upon reporting to King Solomon what they had found, he directed them to cease their labors, as he supposed the vault had been a secret place for the worship of the gods of the original inhabitants of Canaan.

God, however, notified him in a dream that he should proceed; as he had designed that spot for the erection of the Temple for his worship, as it had been thrice dedicated, first by Enoch when he constructed the vaults and made the deposits of these mysterious emblems - second, on this spot Abraham erected the altar to sacrifice his son Isaac[206] - and third, by his father David, where he erected the altar on the threshing floor of Arauna and sacrificed to stay the hand of the destroying Angel.[207]

There is no doubt whatever in the mind of the writer but that the inventors of the degrees above the three original degrees - such as the Royal Arch and Select, designed to demonstrate to the postulant the value of the great and now ineffable and mysterious name of Deity.

---

[206] Gen., ch. xxii.
[207] 1. Chron., ch. xxi., verses 25 to 27.

It is well known to all students of the ancient mysteries of the Orient that after the initiation of a candidate in the lower mysteries, and a certain period having elapsed, by many severe tests, lustrations by the four elements and trials, he was invested with the great WORD in a very solemn and mysterious manner, by the Archi-Magus, who alone could communicate this word to the postulant.

In receiving this word, was conveyed to him by its interpretation, the meaning of all the preceding ceremonies.

Those who arranged the series of degrees as above mentioned, from the Entered Apprentice to the Select Master, designed that in the last degree there should be a full explanation of all that which was concealed in the various forms and ceremonies, and in our present lectures in that degree it is very evident that such was the design sign of closing the Ancient Craft Masonry with the Select of Twenty-seven, "to pass the Circle of Ancient Craft Masonry."

GENERAL GRAND COUNCIL.

In 1871 the Grand Council of Massachuseas undertook the task of bringing mder out of the disordered condition of the Cryptic Rite in the United States, and having enlisted the valuable services of our most distinguished Companion, Hon. Josiah H. Drummond, of Maine,[208] who, in compliance with their request, called a convention, and fourteen Grand Councils were represented at the meeting in New York City, June 12, 1872, at which the following was adopted:

"Whereas, In some jurisdictions the question has been mooted of surrendering the Cryptic Degrees to the Chapters; and

"Whereas, There are many Companions who have received the degrees in Chapters or from Sovereign Inspectors of A.'.A.'.S.'. Rite, therefore

"Resolved, That it is the sense of this Convention that the Cryptic degrees should be under the exclusive jurisdiction of Grand Councils, and that no one should be recognized as a regular Companion of the Rite who had not received the degrees in a lawfully constituted Council or by authority of the Supreme Council of the A.'.A.'.S.'. Rite previous to the date, or has been lawfully healed."

The convention adopted a uniform system of nomenclature, which has since been generally adopted.

---

[208] Drummond, "History of Grard Council in United States," p. 89, in the Cryptic Rite

In June, 1873, another meeting of the Convention was held in New York and nineteen Grand Councils were represented.

The following was adopted:

"That the order of the succession of the degrees be: First, Royal Master's; second, Select Master's; and that it be left optional with each Grand Council to confer the super-excellent Master's degree as an honorary degree."

The convention announced as its opinion that a General Grand Council of the United States should be formed. Subsequently meetings were held, December, 1874, in New Orleans; August, 1877, in Buffalo, N.Y.; at which latter meeting twenty-two Grand Councils were represented, and also Ontario, Canada.

The convention met at Detroit, August 23, 1880, when a constitution was adopted which it was required should be adopted by not less than nine regular Grand Councils, and then should become operative.

The General Grand Recorder, George W. Cooley, gave notice, February 23, 1881, that the Grand Councils of New York, Minnesota, Ohio, Indiana, Maryland, Tennessee, Massachusetts, Alabama, and Louisiana had ratified the constitution.

On March 1, 1881, Hon. Josiah H. Drummond, General Grand Master, issued his circular to the officers, and also announced that the Grand Council of South Carolina had adopted the constitution.[209] The first sesion was held pursuant to this circular, at Denver, Col., August 14, 1883, and the following Grand Councils were represented: California, Florida, Indiana, Kansas, Louisiana, Maryland, Maine, Massachusetts, Minnesota, Missouri, New Hampshire, Ohio, New York, South Carolina, Tennessee, and Vermont. (Forever blessed be their memory.) Of those seventeen who originally acceded to the first formation of the provisional General Grand Council, in 1880, these were absent: Georgia and Alabama; and South Carolina had since given her adhesion.

Alabama, having been with the seventeen Grand Councils to join in the formation of the provisional General Grand Council in 1880, was never represented at any subsequent assembly.

We will now, in a more regular manner, give the history of the formation of the General Grand Council.

---

[209] Proceedings, 1883, p. 20.

The General Grand Council of the United States was organized at a convention of delegates of seventeen Grand Councils which met at Detroit, Mich., August 23, 1880.

The action of this convention was at once approved by the following Grand Councils: New York, Minnesota, Ohio, Indiana, Maryland, Tennessee, Massachusetts, Alabama, and Louisiana.

South Carolina Grand Council soon thereafter organized, and ratified the constitution of the General Grand Council and resumed work.

In the address of the General Grand Master, Josiah H. Drummond, at the first Triennial Assembly, held at Denver, Col., August 14, 1883, he states: "At the time of the formation of the provisional General Grand Council there were twenty-three Grand Councils, which had not adopted the 'Mississippi Plan.'

"Of these, seventeen, viz., Alabama, California, Florida, Georgia, Indiana, Kansas, Louisiana, Maine, Maryland, Massachusetts, Minnesota, Missouri, New Hampshire, New York, Ohio, Tennessee, and Vermont, have become constituents of the General Grand Council.[210]

Of the other six, five continue to exist, but have not become constituents of this body, viz., Connecticut, Michigan, New Jersey, Pennsylvania, and Rhode Island.

Some of these, however, have the matter under consideration.

It is understood why Connecticut has not given her adhesion is, the law of this body, that persons receiving the degrees in Chapters, or in Councils appurtenant to Chapters, can not be recognized.

"The remaining one of twenty-three, North Carolina, at its session held in June last undertook to dissolve and turn the degrees over to the Chapter.

While this occasions regret, it is no matter of surprise, because Royal Arch Masonry is at an exceedingly low ebb in that State, and it sometimes seems a matter of doubt whether the Grand Chapter itself will be able to maintain its existence.

"Grand Councils at the advent of the 'Mississippi Plan' existed in other States, as follows: Arkansas, Illinois, Iowa, Kentucky, Mississippi, Nebraska, South Carolina, and Wisconsin.

All of which accepted in some form the general features of the 'Mississippi Plan.'

---

[210] Proceedings General Grand Council, 1883, p. 7.

"The Grand Councils of Arkansas, Illinois, and Kentucky have reorganized, but have not as yet ratified and adopted the General Grand Constitution.

The Grand Council of Illinois never formally dissolved, but maintained its existence and undertook to surrender the degrees to the Grand Chapter; this action had been rescinded by both grand bodies, and the Grand Council now exists with all its powers, and I trust with its pristine vigor."[211]

We have followed thus far the history of the Cryptic Rite as given by Companion Josiah H. Drummond in his address to the General Grand Council at the first Triennial Assembly, three years after the inauguration of that body.

He further stated the following Grand Councils had taken no definite action, viz., Iowa and Nebraska.

Mississippi had taken action in reference to the over-whelming sentiment of the Craft, which looks toward reorganizing the Grand Council System.

The situation in Wisconsin is anomalous; the Grand Council surrendered the degrees to the Grand Chapter, which authorized the conferring of them in a council appurtenant to a chapter,[212] so that in theory, if not in practice, each chapter had a council appurtenant to it, the chapter officers being the officers of the council.

But in 1881, in consequence, as I understand, of objections to the recognition of persons receiving the degrees in such councils, a convention of the delegates of these councils was called, and a Grand Council of Royal and Select Masters was organized.[213]

We have given the above very interesting information as to the several States wherein the Cryptic Rite was worked in this place rather than in the separate individual jurisdictions, as it greatly saves space and time, reserving both of these for the details property belonging to each subordinate jurisdiction as to the organization of the constituent councils in each, as it will appear under the alphabetical arrangement.

Note. - Companion Drummond in the above sketch begins with Alabama, but that Grand Council never appears in any subsequent proceedings as a constituent of the General Council.

Alabama.

---

[211] Ibid., General Grand Master's Address.

[212] Charters issued to chapters in 1848-49 provided for this usage.-EDITOR.
[213] Ibid.

The information which we have been enabled to obtain concerning Cryptic Masonry in Alabama is somewhat vague.

It is supposed that John Barker, of the A.'.A.'.S.'. R.'. Southern Jurisdiction, started the first councils of Royal and Select Masters, under his authority as Deputy Inspector-General.

It is conceded that a Grand Council was organized in 1838 (December 13th).[214] This Grand Council repudiated, very properly, the course of the Grand Chapter of Virginia, in capturing the degrees of the council, and incorporating them with the chapter work, in 1843.

The council also, in 1849, protested against the Grand Consistory of Charleston granting (of) these degrees in its jurisdiction.[215]

This Grand Council met, with some omissions, as in 1840, 1861, 1862 or 1863, until in 1886 it was dissolved, when all branches of Masonry in that State were much depressed. Since then, however, matters have greatly improved.

This Grand Council was never connected with the General Grand Council after 1881, although one of the first to join in the organization in 1880.

Arizona.

The proceedings of the Triennial assembly of the General Grand council of 1897 show that the following councils secured their warrants

Dispensation Granted.
Chartered

Olive Council, No.1. At Prescott, July 1, 1893. August 22, Phoenix, U.D. At Phoenix, April 4, 1895. Surrendered February 17, 1897 Tucson, U.D. At Tucson, April 5, 1895. Surrendered September 2, 1897

Arkansas.

Four subordinate councils were, at an early date, chartered by the Supreme Council A.'. A.'. S.'. R.'. of the Southern Jurisdiction.

These four councils were formed by the State Grand Council, November 6, 1860.

In 1878 the Companions adopted the system of incorporation with the chapters; but in 1881 resumed the independent form; and in 1886 united with the General Grand Council, and is yet within that organization.

---

[214] "History of Masonry and Concordant Orders," p. 661.
[215] Ibid.

On the 25th of April, 1899, they had the sad misfortune to lose their Grand Recorder Companion James A. Henry.

California.

The Grand Council of Alabama granted charters to organize two councils in California.

One council was chartered by the Grand Council of Tennessee, and one by the Grand Council of Texas. These four councils organized a Grand Council, June 26, 1860. In 1880 this Grand Council united with the General Grand Council in its organization.

Colorado.

The following councils were organized in Colorado under the General Grand Council:

Dispensation Granted.	Chartered.
Denver, No. 1, Denver	January 16, 1892. August 21, 1894.
Rocky Mountain, No. 2 Trinidad	March 24, 1893 August 21, 1894.
Durango, No. 3, Durango	May 16, 1893. August 21, 1894.
Akron, No. 4, Akron	May 23, 1893. August 21, 1894.
Canon City, No. 5, Canon City	June 5, 1893 August 21, 1894.
Gunnison, U.D, Gunnison.	
Pueblo, No. 7, Pueblo,	April 10, 1894. August 21, 1894.

All of these councils are reported as being in existence at the Triennial held in 1897. At that session the General Grand Master reported that he had issued dispensations as follows:

To Hiram Council, at Greely, with sixteen members, December 8, 1894; but no interest being taken, the dispensation was surrendered, December 9, 1896.

To Zabud Council, at Colorado Springs, with thirty-two members, May 27, 1895.

This council made reports for 1895, 1896, and 1897; paid dues for 1895 only, and asked for a Charter; but does not appear in the list of councils whose dispensations were continued; nor was it chartered.

To Leadville Council, at Leadville, June 10, 1895, and dispensation was surrendered, November 10, 1896.

Hiram, U. D., Greely, December 8, 1894, and surrendered.

Zabud, U. D., Colorado Springs, May 27, 1895, and continued.

Leadville, U. D., Leadville, June 10, 1895, surrendered.

Connecticut.

In 1818 Companion Jeremy L. Cross was very industrious in propagating the Cryptic Rite, and succeeded in forming ten councils in Connecticut.

The first Grand Council of Select Masters for the State was organized by that name as claimed.

There are no records of this body up to 1830. In 1825 the two degrees of Royal and Select Masons were recognized.

From 1826 to 1846, in consequence of the Morgan episode, very little if anything was done in this as well as other branches of Masonry.

Since the revival, in all the States where the anti-Masonic spirit had prevailed, Masonry has taken a "new and prolonged lease," and flourishes to a much greater degree than ever before in its history.

The sons and grandsons of the bitterest anti-Masons of 1830 are now the most zealous in their efforts to spread abroad the glad tidings of peace on earth and good-will toward men."

Connecticut Grand Council does not belong to the General Grand Council, which is much to be regretted.

The benefits of her union with that body would be mutual.

Delaware.

It is said that Jeremy L. Cross, when on his lecturing tour in the early days, visited Delaware and conferred the degrees in Wilmington and Newcastle. We have no further information from that State.

District of Columbia.

The Cryptic degrees are first mentioned, in the history of Masonic degrees in the District of Columbia, in the records of the Grand Chapter which was organized in 1822.

At the Semi-Annual Convocation held June 9, 1829, the report of the Committee on Correspondence refers to a circular letter which had been sent by the Grand Chapter of Maryland to each Grand Chapter in the United States; which is as follows:[216]

"M.E. Sir and Companion:

"I am instructed by the Grand Chapter over which I have the honor to preside, to address you, and through you your Grand Chapter, upon the unsettled state of the degree of Select Mason, a subject deemed by us of sufficient importance to claim the particular attention of your Grand Chapter.

"This degree existed under the authority of a distinguished Chief in the State of Maryland, but without the recognizance of our Grand Chapter for many years; until, in the year 1824, upon the revision of our Constitution, it appearing, evident that the Select Degree not only has an intimate connection with, but is in a measure necessary, as preparatory to and elucidatory of that of the Royal Arch; it was formally recognized by our Grand Chapter, and required to be given by our subordinate Chapters in its proper order immediately preceding that of the Royal Arch.

Under this arrangement we have since progressed, much to our satisfaction; but it is with regret that we have learned that Councils or Chapters of Select Masons have been established in some of our sister States, independent of Royal Arch Masonry, avowedly in pursuance of, but, as we are satisfied, through a great mistake or actual abuse of any authority delegated, or meant to be delegated, in relation to the Select Degree.

We would, therefore, beg leave respectfully to recommend to your Grand Chapter the consideration of this degree, and the circumstances under which it exists, within your jurisdiction; with the hope that you will see it to be for the general interest of the Craft to take the degree under your recognizance and control, to whom of right it belongs, and thereby do away with what is felt to be a grievance, by those distinguished Chiefs, whose authority, delegated to a limited extent, and for special reasons, has been perveaed for sordid purposes, by the creation of an independent order, never contemplated by them; and which we believe to be inconsistent with the spirit and best interests of our institution.

"Respectfully and fraternally, &c."

This was never officially communicated to the Grand Chapter of the District of Columbia by the Grand Chapter of Maryland, but was taken from the printed proceedings of that body, pp. 15, 16, and 17.[217]

---

[216] Proceedings of Grand Chapter of District of Columbia, 1822-1833, p. 108.

[217] Proceedings of Grand Chapter of District of Columbia, p. 109.

That committee also reported: "The Grand Chapter of North Carolina had determined that the degree should come under the jurisdiction of State Grand Chapters, and recommended it to the favorable consideration of the General Grand Chapter.

The Grand Chapter of Maine had referred the subject to a Committee.

It remains for the Grand Chapter to take such orders in the premises as it shall seem proper."

The Grand Chapter of Ohio has passed a resolution of which the following is a copy, and which has officially been communicated to this Grand Chapter for its consideration. "At a regular communication of the Grand Chapter [of Ohio] in January, 1829, the following resolution was adopted:

"Resolved, That it is the opinion of this Grand Chapter that the General Grand Chapter of the United States ought to be dissolved.

"BELA LATHAM, "Grand Secretary."

A committee to whom the subject was referred reported:[218]

"That they are decidedly of the opinion that the Royal and Select Master's Degrees should be recognized by and conferred under the direction of the several Grand Chapters of the respective States and Territories of the Union.

With regard to the proper time when these degrees should be conferred, whether before or after the Royal Arch Degree, they decline expressing an opinion, preferring that this point should be left to the determination of the General Grand Chapter; and they recommend that the representatives from this Grand Chapter to that body, at its Triennial meeting, in September, be instructed to conform in their proceedings on this subject, to the tenor of the foregoing." This was laid on the table for the present.

When taken up again, it was "Resolved, That the further consideration thereof be postponed till the first Tuesday in August next; and that in the meantime the Grand Secretary be directed to forward a copy of the report this day made on that subject to the several Councils of Royal and Select Masters in the District of Columbia."[219]

At the special convocation, held August 31, 1829, the following appears: Companion Baldwin, from a committee appointed by the Council of Royal and Select Masters of the City of Washington (which body had been addressed on the subject by the Grand Secretary,

---

[218] Ibid., 113.
[219] Proceedings of the Grand Chapter of the District of Columbia, p. 115.

pursuant to order) presented to the Grand Chapter the following letter and report, viz.:[220]

"WASHINGTON, August 31, 1829.

At a special meeting of the Council of Royal and Select Masters, held at the Central Masonic Hall, on Saturday, the 29th of August, instant, the written report having been presented and read, was, on motion, ordered to be transmitted to the Grand Chapter of the District of Columbia at their next meeting.

"JOHN CAROTHERS, T.I.G.M. W.W. BILLINGS, Recorder."

Report.

"The Committee appointed by the Council of Royal and Select Masters of the City of Washington, to whom was referred the propriety of extending the jurisdiction of the General, Grand, and Subordinate Royal Arch Chapters so as to embrace the Degrees of Royal and Select Masters, have the honor to report:

"That they have had the subject under consideration, and are duly impressed with its vast importance.

After the most mature deliberation they have corne to the following conclusions: That Masonic light in its principles, and the order of its development, is fixed and unchangeable! That whatever power the Fraternity may have over forms and ceremonies, yet no body of Masons, however exalted, neither have nor can assume the power of changing the original landmarks, or altering its clements.

Your committee are confident, from an intimate acquaintance with all the degrees, that those of 'Royal and Select Master' are not only posterior in order to the 'Royal Arch,' but that in our opinion it would not be consistent with ancient Masonry to make them previous.

"Whether the interests of the Craft would be promoted by this extended jurisdiction, your Committee are unable to say; but should that course be thought advisable, by the General Grand Chapter, in its solemn deliberation, your Committee are decidedly of the opinion that it can only be done under the following restrictions:

"1st. That the Degrees of Royal and Select Masters can only be conferred on Royal Arch Masons.

"2d. No one can be an officer of any Chapter who is not both a Royal and Select Master.

"Without these restrictions your Committee can never consent to a change in the present established mode of proceeding.[221]

---

[220] Ibid., 119.
[221] Proceedings of the Grand Chapter of District of Columbia, p. 120.

"All of which is most respectfully submitted.
"E. BALDWIN, "W.W. BILLINGS,
Committee." "J.A. KENNEDY,

The report of a committee made in June last on the subject of the degree was taken up and read, and was passed by a majority of one vote only, and on motion it was "Resolved, That the Grand Secretary transmit to the General Grand Secretary copies of the two reports above stated, together with the proper credentials of the proxies appointed to represent this Grand Chapter in the General Grand Chapter of the United States, at its ensuing meeting in New York; and that the Grand Secretary do prepare the proper instructions."

At the meeting of the General Grand Chapter, September 11, 1829, the question came up for action on a communication from Comp. J.K. Stapleton, upon which a suitable committee made the following report, and it and the resolutions were adopted:

"Whereas, It is satisfactorily proved to this General Grand Chapter, that the Constitution of the Councils of Royal and Select Master Mason, in different parts of the United States, by sundry persons, has been without any legitimate authority,

"And Whereas, Those degrees are conferred in some chapters, under the authority of the General Grand Chapter; and whereas it was proved that it was the only and sole intention of the Most Excellent Companions from whom these degrees emanated that they should be conferred under the authority of Royal Arch Chapters; therefore,

"Resolved, That this General Grand Chapter cordially recommend to the different Councils in the United States to adopt measures to place those degrees under the authority of the State Grand Chapters.

"Resolved, That authority be, and is hereby, granted to the several Grand Chapters, under the jurisdiction of the General Grand Chapter, to make such arrangements as shall be found necessary for conferring the degrees of Royal and Select Masters in Royal Arch Chapters; provided always that no Grand Chapter, within the limits of which is a Grand Council, shall authorize the Royal Arch Chapters under the jurisdiction to confer such degrees without the consent of such Grand Council."

We have no records or accounts whatever in the District of Columbia as to what became of the "Council," or Councils, if more than one, which is referred to above.

The chapters in the District continued to confer the Royal and Select degrees prior to the Royal Arch, until in 1833, when the Grand Chapter was dissolved. Several of the chapters again joined the Grand Chapter of Maryland, which body, thereafter, in 1844, added to its nomenclature "the District of Columbia," and the Council degrees were worked within the chapters prior to the Royal Arch, until May 23, 1867, when the Grand Chapter of the District of Columbia was again organized; and on that day, the new Grand Chapter, by resolution, unanimously dropped those degrees from the curriculum of the chapter work, being well satisfied that they did not properly belong to the chapters. Soon after the organization of the Grand Chapter in 1867, Companion Benjamin B. French, the Inspector-General of the Southern Jurisdiction for the A.'.A.'.S.'.R.'., for the District of Columbia, issued three dispensations to form three new councils of Royal and Select Masters, for the District of Columbia.

Those who had recoved those degrees in regular organized councils refused to join in this movement.

Soon after this, the question was agitated as to the legality and propriety of thus inaugurating a new method of propagating the Cryptic degrees, and the result was, these three councils went into "innocuous desuetude." When the time was deemed judicious, the present writer, with eight others, who had been regular Council Masons, prepared a petition to the Grand Council of Massachusetts for a dispensation to open LaFayette Council.

This was granted August, 1870, with the writer as Most Illustrious Master.

The Grand Officers of the Grand Council of that State came to Washington and opened LaFayette Council.

Inasmuch as the great body of Royal and Select Masons in the District had received the degrees of Royal and Select Masters in their several chapters prior to the Royal Arch, it was decided that all such Royal Arch Masons, as well as those who had never received the Council degrees, should be received at a nominal price (five dollars) for those degrees.

Accordingly, in two nights sessions the Grand Officers conferred the Royal, Select, and Super-excellent degrees upon 158 R.A. Masons.

A Charter was granted December 14, 1870, and the council started with flying colors and great success.

This council continued with some measure of prosperity for several years, when from internal dissensions the members lost their interest and in a few years ceased to attend, and the council died out.

When the General Grand Council of the United States was organized in 1881, the present writer, after correspondence with Companion Josiah H. Drummond, the General Grand Master, and a few members of the defunct body, petitioned for another council to be called "Washington," with the principal officers of the deceased LaFayette Council at the head. A dispensation was granted, and started with good prospects.

At the next meeting of the General Grand Council a Charter was granted.

Since that time Washington Council, No. 1, has continued to grow, but not as rapidly as she should.

Indeed, the District of Columbia should have several councils in prosperous operation, and that, too, under the constitution of a Grand Council for the District.

Florida.

The Southern Supreme Council, exercising its undoubted right of control at that time over the degrees of Royal and Select Masons, through some one of her inspectors, perhaps in South Carolina, had, previous to 1858, issued at different times warrants to form three councils in Florida.

The present writer is personally aware of the one existing at Warrington, adjoining the navy-yard at that locality, as he reported for duty as Chief Constructing Engineer at that naval station February, 1857, and found a thriving lodge, chapter, and council in full operation, and it was his great pleasure to assist in the work in all of these bodies at that time.

January 13, 1858, these three councils organized a Grand Council, at the time of the agitation of who should control these degrees.

After much discussion the Grand Chapter of Florida declined to act.

The Grand Council became a member of the General Grand Body.

There have been no proceedings of the body issued since 1882, and there have been no meetings since 1884. In the proceedings of the General Grand Council for 1897 there is a broad black mark across the page opposite to Florida, where the Grand Recorder's name should have been, but in the tables of annual assemblies from 1894 to 1896 Florida appears with names of the Grand Officers.

Georgia.

We learn that one of the deputies of the Southern Supreme Council, Abram Jacobs, conferred the degree of Select of Twenty-seven in the State of Georgia.

On May 2, 1826, a Grand Council was organized by the authority of the Inspector-General of the Supreme Council, which is noticed in the publications of that day.

June 25, 1841, three councils met, and a Grand Council was established by the authority of the Supreme Grand Council of the 33 degree, in Charleston, S.C. They adopted the constitution of the former Grand Council of 1826. That body, having ceased to work, became dormant and the records were lost.

In the revised constitution of 1842 they claimed to be the highest source of legitimate Masonic authority in the State of Georgia, and of right ought to have the government and superintendence of all councils of Royal and Select Masters within its jurisdiction.[222] This Grand Council belongs to the General Grand Council and is reported in the proceedings of 1897.

Idaho.

A council was organized in Idaho by a dispensation from the Officers of the General Grand Council, viz., Idaho Council, No. 1, at Pocatillo, December 15, 1896 - which was annulled afterward; also a dispensation for Adoniram Council, at Boise, January 30, 1896. Dispensation continued until next assembly.

Illinois.

The Grand Council of Kentucky having issued charters to several councils in the State of Illinois, a Grand Council was organized March 10, 1854. In 1877 the degrees were surrendered to the control of the Grand Chapter of Royal Arch Masons, notwithstanding that in 1854 it refused to heal Royal and Select Masters who had been made in the chapters.

The Grand Council, however, continued its annual sessions, its constituents being composed of the mixture of regularly made Council Masters and those made in the chapters.

---

[222] "History of Masonry and Concordant Orders," p. 662.

This did not prove satisfactory, and in 1882 the Grand Council and Grand Chapter agreed to resume their old condition. Illinois Grand Council is an independent Grand Body.

Indiana.

In the State of Indiana the Council degrees were given in the chapter work.

After the General Grand Chapter's decision, councils were chartered by the Grand Councils of Kentucky and Ohio.

Chapter Royal and Select Masons were "healed" and the Grand Council of Indiana was organized December 20, 1855.

Iowa.

When Royal Arch Masonry was first planted in Iowa, the Council degrees were part of the chapter work.

After the decision of the General Grand Chapter, in regard to these degrees, Companions were "healed" by the authority of the Grand Master of the Grand Council of Illinois.

Charters were issued by that Grand Council to councils in Iowa, which subsequently organized the Grand Council of Iowa, January 2, 1857. In 1878 the Grand Council merged itself into the Grand Chapter of Iowa, nineteen councils having been duly organized prior to that time.

To the present day those degrees are merged into the chapter of Royal Arch.

Kansas.

Three councils of Royal and Select Masters were chartered by the Grand Council of Missouri, in the State of Kansas, and December 2, 1867, these three councils organized a Grand Council of Royal Select and Super-excellent Masons.

Kentucky.

The Select degree was carried into the State of Kentucky by J.L. Cross, when in 1817 he made his official tour through the Western States as General Grand Lecturer of the General Grand Chapter.

December 10, 1827, six councils met by their delegates and organized a Grand Council of the State, which is said to be the result of John Barker's efforts in behalf of the Supreme Council of the Southern Jurisdiction, A.'. A.'. S.'. R.'. This jurisdiction felt the effects of the

Morgan anti-Masonic period from 1830 to 1840, when the Grand Council met only once.

The degrees were merged into the chapter from 1878 to 1881.

After the organization of the General Grand Council the Grand Council of Kentucky was re-organized.

Companion H.B. Grant, M.'. Ill.'. Gr.'. Master, in his annals mentions the case of a Thrice Illustrious Master of a council who communicated the degrees outside of a council, and who construed his obligation to mean that he could not confer the degrees except in a council, but could communicate the degrees, and so directed the record to be made as if conferred in a council.

This was declared by the Grand Master to be irregular, and required recognition to be refused until they were "healed" in open council.

The Grand Council of Kentucky is an independent body.

Louisiana.

It is stated that John Barker in 1827 organized Holland Council, No. 1, in New Orleans, and in the "tableau" of the Grand Chapter of Louisiana in 1828 it is referred to.

When in or about 1850 Capitular Masonry was re-organized, Cryptic Masonry was also revived.

Four councils formed a Grand Council February 10, 1856.

One of these was Holland, No. 1. The others had been chartered by the Grand Councils of Kentucky and Alabama.

Maine

At an early period a council had been organized in Maine, working under the General Grand Chapter.

The Grand Council of Massachusetts organized three councils, and these, by their delegates, formed the Grand Council, May 3, 1855.

Maryland

In the introduction of this history of the Cryptic Rite, the connection of Eckel and Niles, as leaders at an early date, was noticed.[223] The Select degree was then only recognized as an appendant to the regular curriculum of degrees of the A.'. A.'. S.'. R.'. which was controlled by the Deputy Inspectors of that rite.

---

[223] See pp. 1549, 1550.

This was prior to 1800, and perhaps extended into the present century, as late as the date of the certificate, or dispensation, given to Cross.

We have seen, under District of Columbia, the steps which were taken, as eady as 1824 to incorporate these degrees with the chapter work and to precede the Most Excellent Master's degree.

This union of the Cryptic with the Capitular system continued until 1872, when, by law, the Grand Chapter separated them.

Six council after this (May 12, 1874) organized the present Grand Council of the State, which became a member of the General Grand Council and so continues.

Massachusetts.

In 1817 a voluntary council of Royal Masters was organized by Benjamin Gleason and others, and subsequently obtained the sanction of Columbian Council of New York.

A Select council was formed at Springfield, May 28, 1818, by J.L. Cross.

Six councils, at different times, having been organized, their delegates met February 8, 1826, and on June 15, 1826, completed the formation of a Grand Council.

The records of this body having been lost during the anti-Masonic period, nothing is known concerning these degrees until the re-organization in 1847.

From the year 1853 the Grand Council has met regularly and great prosperity has followed.

It is asserted that Hiram Council, at Worcester, with 1,070 members in 1897, is the largest council of Royal and Select Masters in the world.

Michigan

The Grand Council of Connecticut had chartered three councils in the State of Michigan, and these, by their delegates, met in convention on January 13, 1858, and organized a Grand Council for the State.

In 1856 that Grand Council granted a Charter for a council at Detroit.

This Grand Council is independent, and chapter - made Royal and Select Masons are not in favor.

Minnesota

The Grand Council of Iowa having chartered three councils in Minnesota, December 12, 1870, these three by their delegates organized a Grand Council.

The council which had been chartered by the Grand Council of New York in 1855 soon became dormant.

This Grand Council is a member of the General Grand Council.

Mississippi.

From our careful examination into the early history of Cryptic Masonry in the State of Mississippi, we find that John Barker, before mentioned as agent for the Southern Supreme Council, established at Natchez, Miss., a Grand Council of Princes of Jerusalem in 1829, which assumed the control of the Royal and Select Master's degrees, and under the auspices of the Council of Princes of Jerusalem seven councils were organized, and these by their delegates organized a Grand Council January 19, 1856.

After the close of the war, in 1865, a number of the councils having surrendered their charters, and others having become dormant, the Grand Council, which had assemtacd annually, in 1877 adopted a plan which became widely known as the "Mississippi Plan," which provided:

"Each Royal Arch Chapter shall hereafter open within its bosom, under its charter, as a Chapter of Royal Arch Masons, a Council of Royal and Select Masters; the officers of the Chapter corresponding in rank to those of the Council.

"All the Royal Arch Masons who have not received the degrees of Royal Master and Select Master shall be entitled to have the same conferred or communicated on their request and without charge; but candidates who shall hereafter receive the Royal Arch degree shall immediately thereafter, and in connection with the Royal Arch degree, receive the degrees of Royal and Select Master without additional charge."

The Grand Council was dissolved, and this plan was adopted in many jurisdictions, the General Grand Chapter having placed on record at Lexington, Ky., at the meeting September 16, 1853, the following resolution:

"Resolved, That this General Grand Chapter and the governing bodies of Royal Arch Masonry affiliated with, and holding jurisdiction under it, have no rightful jurisdiction or control over the degrees of Royal and Select Master."

"Resolved, That this General Grand Chapter will hereafter entertain no question or matter growing out of the government or working of these degrees while in their present position."[224]

All of the independent jurisdiction except Iowa, which adopted the Mississippi Plan," have rescinded the same and returned to the council organization.

In 1888 the Grand Council of Mississippi at its session that year adopted the following:

"Resolved, That the Grand Royal Arch Chapter hereby releases control of the Cryptic Degrees and recommends that the Grand Council of Royal and Select Masters resume its former jurisdiction of the degrees.

"That Chapters are hereby prohibited from communicating and conferring the Cryptic Degrees, recognizing the authority of the Grand Council in all matters pertaining to said degrees." In February, 1888, the Grand Council of Mississippi met, six of the officers being of those elected in 1877. Six councils were represented.

At the sixth triennial assembly of the General Grand Chapter, which met in Baltimore, Md., October 11, 1897, the following paper was unanimously adopted:

"Whereas, The report of Companion Josiah H. Drummond as chairman of the Committee on Correspondence of the Grand Council of Maine for the year 1894, and the Address of Companion Frederic Speed, Grand Master of the Grand Council of Mississippi for the year 1895, present facts that conclusively show that a misunderstanding has existed in the minds of our Companions in Mississippi for some years past, as to the attitude of General Grand Council towards the Grand Council of Mississippi; therefore be it "Resolved, That the General Grand Council, through its Grand Master, extend to the Companions of the Grand Council of Mississippi its fraternal greetings and its best wishes for the prosperity of the Cryptic Rite in Mississippi."[225]

Also this minute appeared: "Most Illustrious Frederic Speed, Grand Master of the Grand Council of Mississippi, was announced and received with the Grand Honors, escorted to the East, and greeted by the Most Puissant Grand Master in a happy and felicitous manner.

"Companion Speed thereupon addressed the General Grand Council in very eloquent language; thanking the Puissant Grand Master for the cordiality of his reception, etc.

---

[224] Proceedings of the General Grand Chapter, 1856, p. 317.

[225] Proceedings General Grand Council, 1897, p. 79.

The above preamble and resolution was then read and Companion Speed spoke feelingly as follows:

"'Most Illustrious Sir and Companions:

"'When I say that the reading of the resolution, which I have just heard, affords me the most sincere satisfaction and pleasure, I but feebly voice the emotions of my heart.

If I know myself or the great-hearted men who comprise the Cryptic Masons of Mississippi, I can honestly say that we have taken no pleasure in the long estrangement which has unfortunately divided us, and I am sure they will receive with no less happiness than I now do, the message of peace and good will which come to us, through the action of this most illustrious Body.

Receive then, Sir, this right hand as a pledge, in their name, of reconciliation and peace, given with a determination to forget the past, and to strive in the bonds of friendship and brotherly love, with you, for the upbuilding of the temple of the Lord, letting the past bury its dead, and acting in the living present, heart within and God overhead.

Whom God hath joined together, let no man put asunder."[226]

Missouri,

It is said by very good authority that Cross, in his tour through the West, conferred the Select degree in Missouri; in what year is uncertain.

Also it is said that the Royal degree was introduced as early as 1828.

In 1841 there were three councils in the State: one in St. Louis, one at Palmyra, and where the other was located the present writer can not recollect. At that time, 1841-42, he was in St. Louis and received the Royal and Select degrees in Missouri Council, No. 1, at St. Louis, about the time the Grand Council met.

Immediately after the Grand Council closed he wrote up and recorded the transactions of the Grand Council.

These bodies became extinct, as well as some councils which had been chartered by the Grand Council of Kentucky.

May 21, 1864, the Grand Council was organized.

In 1848 the writer having gone to Independence to construct a local railroad, found the Council degrees incorporated in the chapter by the Charter, to be worked subsequent to the Royal Arch.

---

[226] Ibid., p. 82.

Montana.

The following councils in Montana received dispensations from the General Grand Council, viz.:

Glendive, at Glendive April 22, 1896. Dispensation. October 12, 1897. Chartered.

Custer, at Miles City, October 24, 1897. Dispensation, Annulled.

Adoniram, at Livingston, May 13, 1897. Continued.

Mystic at Bozeman, May 20, 1897. Continued.

Zabud, No. 2, at Butte, May 22, 1897. October 12, 1897.

Montana, at Dillon, October 24, 1897. Annulled.

Deer Lodge, at Deer Lodge, June 10, 1897. Annulled.

Anaconda, at Anaconda, June 11, 1897. Annulled.

Hellgate, at Missoula, September 1, 1897 Continued.

Hiram, at Kalispell, September 2, 1897, Annulled.

These councils were all reported at the triennial of the Supreme Council in 1897.

Nevada.

The following councils were organized by dispensations issued by the Grand Officers of the General Grand Council for Nevada.

Dispensation.

Carson, at Carson, September 3, 1896.
Continued.

Mountain, at Virginia City, September 4, 1896.
Continued.

Reno, at Reno, September, 1896.
Continued.

Eureka, at Eureka, September 21, 1896.
Continued.

These were reported to the triennial of the General Grand Council in 1897.

New Mexico
The following, councils were granted dispensations, by the Officers of the General Grand Council, for New Mexico, viz.
Deming, No. 1, at Deming, April 8, 1887.
November 19, 1889.

Las Vegas, at Las Vegas, March 16, 1895.
Annulled.

Santa Fe, at Santa Fe, May 1, 1895.
Continued.

Hiram, at Albuquerque, May 7, 1895.
Annulled.

Alpha, at Raton, May 11, 1895.
Annulled.

Nebraska.
Omaha Council was organized July 8, 1867, by a Charter from the Supreme Council of the Southern Jurisdiction.
Two other councils were chartered by the Grand Council of Kansas.

The Grand Council was formed by the delegates of the above-mentioned three councils, November 20, 1872.

In 1878 the councils adopted the "Mississippi Plan." In 1886 the Grand Council was revived, and then afterward joined the General Grand Council, where she is now.

New Hampshire.

August 5, 1815, four Companions organized a council of Royal Masters at Hopkinton, N.H. J.L. Cross, in 1819, instituted another council of Select Masons, at Hopkinton; these two were united in 1822.

On July 9, 1823, a Grand Council was formed.

During the period from 1835 to 1855 the councils were dormant.

The above two councils, Orphan and Columbian, after 1855 were revived, and Adoniram Council, which had been chartered by the Grand Council of Connecticut united and formed a Grand Council, June 11, 1862.

New Jersey.

Kane Council, No. 11, was chartered by the Grand Council of New York; and two other councils, viz., Scott, No. 13, at New Brunswick, and Gebal, No. 14, at Tretiton, were chartered by the Grand Council of Pennsylvania.

These three councils organized the Grand Council, November 26, 1860.

It has always been an independent Grand Council.

New York.

The earliest time when we find any organization in the State of New York of the Council degrees is September 10, 1810; at which time a meeting of Royal Masters was held in St. John's Hall, in New York City, and a council of Royal Masters was opened, with Companion Thomas Lowndes presiding; and it was determined to organize a Grand Council to be called Columbian Council of Royal Master Masons for the City of New York.

Thomas Lowndes was elected and installed Thrice Illustrious Grand Royal Master.

Nineteen members, Royal Master Masons, were present.

It is thought, and no doubt correctly so, that this was the very first council formed, and was regarded as authority, as on the evening of

December 6, 1817, a petition was received from a council organized in Boston, asking the sanction of Columbian Council for its formation.

This was granted, and Benjamin Gleason was recognized as T.I.G.M. of the said new council.

From the records of Columbian Council it appears that a council of Knights of the Round Table was convened, as also a Chapter of Illustrious Knights of the Holy Order of the Garter, wherein Companions were installed Knights of the Illustrious and Invincible Order of St. George of Cappadoci, by which latter title the Order was sometimes known.

Thomas Lowndes was annually elected T.I.G.R.M. from the organization, September 2, 1810, to July 9, 1820, and presided at every meeting.

Five Companions received the degree of Superexcellent Master December 22, 1817.

There is no record of the Select Master's degree earlier than November 25, 1821.

In January, 1823, it was "Resolved, That it is expedient to form a Grand Council of Royal Master Masons and Select Masons for the State of New York, and that T.I.G.R.M. Thomas Lowndes be requested to call a convention of all the present and past Grand Royal Masters and Deputy Grand Royal Masters and Grand Wardens in this city, in order to carry into effect the formation of said Grand Council." A convention was held January 25, 1823, and a Grand Council of Royal and Select Masters was formed Thomas Lowndes being elected M.I.R.G.M., which council continued until June 4, 1860, when it united with a Grand Council which had been organized in the city of New York, May 27, 1854, by delegates from councils of Royal and Select Masons working under the authority of the Grand Council of Connecticut.

In the formation of the General Grand Council the New York Companions took a very active part.

North Carolina.

At a very early date Masonry was introduced into North Carolina. A Warrant for a lodge, called "Royal White Hart Lodge," at Halifax, was granted August 21, 1767, and the first Grand Council was formed at Fayetteville, June 21, 1822.

At the convention for the organization of this body five councils were represented, they having all been chartered by the Supreme Council of the Southern Jurisdiction.

The effort to incorporate the degrees with the chapter did not succeed.

The Grand Chapter had endeavored to control the degrees, but in 1859 "Resolved, That this Grand Chapter, after due consideration, hereby disclaims for itself and subordinates any and all control over the Royal and Select Master's degrees." The Supreme Council of Southern jurisdiction chartered, by Dr. A, G. Mackey, as agent, three councils, and a Grand Council was organized June 6, 1860.

In consequence of the War no meeting was held until 1868. This body was dissolved in 1883, and the degrees were turned over to the Grand Chapter.

In 1887 the Grand Council was re-organized.

It is now an independent body.

Ohio.

John Barker, the agent of the Supreme Council Southern Jurisdiction, at a very early day organized five councils in Ohio.

J.L. Cross had been in Ohio perhaps as early as 1817; some authors say 1816; we think not, as he had not received his commission as General Grand Lecturer until the session of the General Grand Chapter, June 8, 1816.

Moreover, as the General Grand Chapter refused the proposition, at that session, to incorporate the degrees in the chapter work, and as it is asserted by Folger that Cross went to Baltimore, and the paper issued by Eckel and Niles is dated in 1817 (May 27th), the very fair presumption is that Cross did not attempt to confer the Select prior to the date of his authority, whether that "paper" was genuine or a forgery, as Companion Josiah H. Drummond has pronounced it to be. Companion Drummond has traced the "itinerary" of Cross through Western Pennsylvania, Ohio, Kentucky, Mississippi, and Louisiana, and thence to Baltimore, May, 1817.

In 1827 a council was established at Cleveland by Charter from the Grand Council of New York.

A Grand Council for the State was organized January 6, 1830, by the five councils organized by John Barker.

North Dakota.

The following councils received their dispensations from the Officers of the General Grand Council, viz.:

Dispensation.	Charter.

Casselton, No. 1, at Casselton,	December 7, 1888 November 10, 1889.
Hilkiah, No. 2, at Jamestown,	September 1, 1893 August 21, 1894. Dispensation.
Hiram Council, at Valley City	December 31, 1895. Continued.
Rae Council, at Grand Forks	January 2, 1896. Annulled.
Zabud Council, at Devil's Lake	January 3, 1896 Annulled.
Towner Council, at Towner	January 6, 1896
Continued Adoniram Council, at Fargo.....	February 15, 1896
Continued Damascus Council, at Wahpeton	February 18, 1896 Annulled.
Mizpah Council, at Park River	March 15, 1896 Annulled.
Tyrian Council, at Lisbon	April 6, 1896 Continued
Bismarck Council, at Bismarck	April 20, 1896 Continued

Oregon.

By authority of the General Grand Master of the General Grand Council, Companion A.H. Hodson was authorized to convene not less than five Royal and Select Masters, and to confer the degrees upon not exceeding nine Royal Arch Masons.

A dispensation was issued to Pioneer Council, U. D., at McMinnville.

Three councils convened February 3, 1885, and formed a Grand Council for Oregon under the jurisdiction of the General Grand Council.

Pennsylvania.

October 26, 1847, two councils in Pennsylvania, and one in Texas, formed the Grand Council.

This Grand Council disbanded and was re-organized in 1854.

Papers of the meetings from 1847 to 1851 have been found, but it seems no regular records were ever kept.

It was proposed in the Grand Council, in 1854, to turn the degrees over to the control of the Council of Princes of Jerusalem, which, however, was not accepted; and December 30, 1854, the Grand Council was re-organized.

It is an independent jurisdiction, but does not recognize those who have received the degree in chapters.

Rhode Island.

A meeting of Royal Masters was convened in Providence, R.I., March 28, 1818, and May 19th "Resolved, That the degree of Select Master be attached to this Council." J.L. Cross gave that council a Charter in 1819.

For many years this council was dormant, and no meeting was held until 1841.

The Grand Councils of Massachusetts and Connecticut issued charters to other councils, and the Supreme Council of Northern Jurisdiction A.'.A.'.S.'.R.'. gave authority to confer the degrees of Royal and Select Master upon a Charter for a Lodge of Perfection at Newport, which in 1870 was revoked, a Grand Council having been organized on October 30, 1860, from which a Charter was obtained.

This Grand Council is independent.

South Carolina.

In the preface to this chapter much of the early history of the Cryptic degrees has already been given in detail.

The Supreme Council of the Southern Jurisdiction had great influence in the direction of the government of the Cryptic Rite in South Carolina.

Nine councils of Royal and Select Masons were chartered in the years of 1858 and 1859.

The Supreme Council in 1860 waived its rights, and a Grand Council was regularly formed, February 15, 1850.

In 1880 the "Missisippi Plan" was adopted.

However, in 1881, the Grand Council was re-organized and became a member of the General Grand Council.

South Dakota.
The following councils received dispensations from the Officers of the General Grand Council in South Dakota:
Alpha Council, No. 1, at Sioux Falls...D. April 11, 1891.
C. July 21, 1891.
Lakota Council, No. 1, at Deadwood........September 7, 1895.
Annulled.
Black Hills Council, No. 1, at Hot Springs.....September 9, 1895.
Annulled.
Zabud, Council No. 1, at Yankton.........September 25, 1895.
Annulled.
Scotland, Council No. 1, at Scotland........October 1, 1895.
Surrendered.
Omega, Council No. 1, at Salem...........October 10, 1895.
Continued.
Hiram, Council No. 1, at Canton..........October 30, 1895.
Annulled.
Koda, Council No. 1, at Flandreau.......October 31, 1895.
Surrendered.
Brookings Council, No. 1 at Brookings... November 1, 1895.
Annulled.
Aberdeen Council, No. 1 at Aberdeen........November 4, 1895.
Annulled.
Adoniram Council, No. 1 at Webster.........November 6, 1895.
Annulled.
Emanuel Council, No. 1 at Millbank........November 14, 1865.
Annulled.
Mitchell Council, No. 1 at Mitchell........November 28, 1895.
Annulled.
Oriental Council, No. 1 at Pierre..........December 12, 1895.
Annulled.
Mystic Council, No. 1 at Huron...........December 30, 1895.
Surrendered.
Faulk Council, No. 1 at Faulkland.......December 31, 1885.
Annulled.

Tennessee.

Two councils derived their authority to organize councils in the State of Tennessee from the Supreme Council of the Southern Jurisdiction. Two other councils had obtained charters from the Grand Council of Kentucky, and one other had received a dispensation from the Grand Council of Alabama.

These five councils by their delegates organized a Grand Council, October 13, 1847.

This Grand Council united with the General Grand Council.

Texas.

From the history of the Cryptic Rite in Pennsylvania we learn that a council of Texas united with two councils in Pennsylvania in the organization of a Grand Council in 1847; hence these degrees must have been worked in a council in Texas at that time.

June 24, 1856, a Grand Council for Texas was organized, which was disbanded in 1864, and the degrees remanded to the chapters, which can be conferred upon Royal Arch Masons only.

Utah.

The following dispensaions were issued by the Grand Officers of the General Grand Council to form councils in Utah, viz.:

Summit Council, at Park City, September 2, 1895, which was very soon surrendered.

Utah, No. 1, at Salt Lake City, dispensation granted February 13, 1892, and chartered August 21, 1894.

Vermont.

After J.L. Cross had made his tour in the South and West he was in Vermont in July, 1817.

In a letter from Haverhill, N.H., he says: "I made no further tarry until I arrived at Windsor, Vermont, where I established a council of Select Masons.

They, finding that the degree was full of information, and that it could not be given antecedent to that of the Royal Arch, wished for a warrant to empower them to confer it, upon which I granted them one in the words following." (Omitted.)

Cross was made a Royal Arch Mason in Champlain Chapter, No. 1, at St. Albans, Vt., July 11, 1815, while engaged as a lecturer to the lodges.

Companion Drummond claims that the first permanent body of Select Masters was the council formed by Cross at Windsor, Vermont, July 5, 1817. He founded a council at Bradford, also, in 1817.

By himself or by his deputy, John H. Cotton, Cross organized nine councils.

The Warrant of the counch at Bennington having been preserved, we give it, as follows:

"To all whom these presents may come, GREETING:

"Know ye, that by the high powers in me vested by the Thrice Illustrious and Grand Puissant in the Grand Council of Select Masters, held at the City of Baltimore, in the State of Maryland, North America, I do hereby constitute and empower the within named Companions to form themselves into a regular Council of Select Masters, and I do hereby appoint my worthy Companion Samuel S. Young to be first Thrice Illustrious Grand Master, Zacheus Hovey, to be first Illustrious Deputy Grand Master, and Oliver Abell to be the Principal Conductor, and I do grant them full power, with their constitutional number, to assemble, open, and confer the Degree of Select master, and do all other business appertaining to said degree, for which this shall be their warrant, until revoked by the Grand Puissant.

And I do further direct said Council to hold its meetings at Bennington, Bennington County, and State of Vermont.

Given under my hand at Bennington this twenty-third day of May, A.D. 1818, and of the Discovery 2818.

"Signed JOHN H. COTTON, "Acting Deputy Puissant in Grand Council."

These councils continued until 1826-1828.

During the Morgan anti-Masonic period, like all other branches of Masonry, nothing was done.

A re-organization took place in 1849, under their original warrants, until 1854.

Four of these councils organized a Grand Council August 10, 1854.

Vermont united with the General Grand Council.

Virginia.

In the previous history of the rite we have shown that Myers remained for some time in Virginia and was in Norfolk and in Richmond, where he communicated the degrees of Royal Master and Select of Twenty-seven, under his authority as Inspector of the A.'.A.'.S.'. Rite.

Jeremy L. Cross, it is said, established a council of Select Masters in December, 1817, in Richmond, and soon thereafter in Portsmouth and other towns.

A Grand Council was formed in 1820 and often failed to meet, as in 1829 to 1839, and in 1847 was dissolved, and the degrees were remanded or rather turned over to the chapters, where they have remained to the present time.

These degrees are conferred in the chapter preceding the Royal Arch under the mistaken idea that the incidents therein related occurred at the building of the Temple, and those of the Royal Arch were laid at the rebuilding thereof, forgetting that, as allegorical representations, they should of necessity for proper instruction be, as they were originally designed, subsequent to the "Mason of the Royal Arch," or thirteenth of the A.'.A.'.A.'.R.'.

Washington.

The General Grand Council by its Officers issued dispensations to Washington to organize councils as follows:

	Dispensation.	Chartered.
To Tacoma, No. 1, at Tacoma	February 9, 1891.	July 21, 1891.
To Colfax, No. 2, at Colfax	June 9, 1893.	August 21, 1894.
To Mt. Baker, No. 3, at New Whatcom	June 14, 1893	August 22, 1894.
To Spokane, No. 4, at Spokane	July 8, 1893	August 21, 1894.
To Pomeroy, No. 5, at Pomeroy	July 16, 1893	August 22, 1894.
To Seattle, No. 6, at Seattle	May 9, 1894	August 21, 1894.

These councils, by order of the General Grand Master, issued May 31, 1895, were assembled by their representatives, June 5, 1895, and the adoption of a constitution and the election of their Officers were duly and regularly constituted, and the Officers were installed by the Special Deputy, Elijah M. Beatty, and so reported to the General Grand Recorder.

Zabud Council, No. 7, at Walla Walla, had a dispensation granted December 8, 1874, and was reported for 1895.

This council became a constituent, under a Charter, of the Grand Council of the State, chartered June 8, 1896.

Wisconsin.

The Grand Council of Ohio chartered three councils in Wisconsin, and a Grand Council was organized by the delegates of these three October 28, 1857.

By arrangement and consent the degrees were turned over to the Grand Chapter in 1878.

In 1881 a Grand Council was again organized by delegates from forty-nine councils.

Wisconsin is an independent Grand Council.

Wyoming.

The following dispensations were issued by the Grand Officers of the General Grand Chapter for Wyoming, viz.:

Cheyenne Council, at Cheyenne June 24, 1895.
Surrendered June 5, 1896.

Laramie Council, at Laramie July 4, 1896.
Annulled.

Zabud Council, at Evanston September 2, 1895.
Annulled.

Tyrus Council, at Green River September 3, 1896.
Surrendered.

Sheridan Council, at Sheridan May 12, 1896.
Annulled.

ABSTRACT OF RETURNS OF SUBORDINATE COUNCILS FOR THE YEAR 1896

Name of Grand Lodge	Held at	Membership.
Washington, No. 1	Washington, D.C.	125
Olive, No.1	Prescott, Ariz	10

Phoenix, U.D.	Phoenix, Ariz.	
Tucson, U.D.	Tucson, Ariz.	
Canon City, No. 5	Canon City, Col.	32
Hiram, U.D.	Greeley, Col.	16
Zabud, U.D.	Colorado Springs, Col.	35
Leadville, U.D.	Leadville, Col.	30
Glendive, U.D.	Glendive, Mont.	12
Custer, U.D.	Miles City, Mont.	9
Adoniram, U.D	Livingston, Mont	8
Mystic, U.D	Bozeman, Mont	15
Zabud, U.D	Butte, Mont	22
Montana, U.D	Dillon, Mont	12
Deer Lodge, U.D	Deer Lodge, Mont	11
Anaconda, U.D	Anaconda, Mont	12
Deming, No. 1	Deming, N.M	37
Las Vegas, U.D	Las Vegas, N.M	
Santa Fe, U.D	Santa Fe, N.M	16
Hiram, U.D	Albuquerque, N.M	
Alpha, U.D	Raton, N.M	15
Casselton, No. 1	Casselton, N. Dak	23
Hilkiah, No. 2	Jamestown, N. Dak	20
Hiram, U.D	Valley City, N. Dak	22
Rae, U.D	Grand Forks, N. Dak	19
Zabud, U.D	Devil's Lake, N. Dak	13
Towner, U.D	Towner, N. Dak	11
Adoniram, U.D	Fargo, N. Dak	17
Damascus, U.D	Wahpeton, N. Dak	10
Mizpah, U.D	River Park, N. Dak	9
Tyrian, U.D	Lisbon, N. Dak	11
Bismarck, U.D	Bismarck, N. Dak	18
Alpha, No. 1	Sioux Falls, S. Dak	23
Lakota, U.D	Deadwood, S. Dak	21
Black Hills, U.D	Hot Springs, S. Dak	16
Zabud, U.D	Yankton, S. Dak	16
Scotland, U.D	Scotland, S. Dak	11
Omega, U.D	Salem, S. Dak	10
Hiram, U.D	Canton, S. Dak	14
Koda, U.D	Flandreau, S. Dak	17
Brookings, U.D	Brookings, S. Dak	16
Aberdeen, U.D	Aberdeen, S. Dak	14

Adoniram, U.D	Webster, S. Dak	14
Emanuel, U.D	Milbank, S. Dak	10
Mitchell, U.D	Mitchell, S. Dak	19
Oriental, U.D	Pierre, S. Dak	15
Mystic, U.D	Huron, S. Dak	14
Faulk, U.D	Faulkton, S. Dak	13
Utah, No. 1	Salt Lake City, Utah	38
Summit, U.D	Park City, Utah	22
Cheyenne, U.D	Cheyenne, Wyo	
Laramie, U.D	Laramie, Wyo	18
Zabud, U.D	Evanston, Wyo	13
Tyrus, U.D	Green River, Wyo	17
Sheridan, U.D	Sheridan, Wyo	12

SUBORDINATE COUNCILS UNDER THE IMMEDIATE JURISDICTION OF THE GENERAL GRAND COUNCIL, 1896.

Council	Location.	Date of Dispensation.	Date of Charter.
DISTRICT OF COLUMBIA.			
Washington, No. 1	Washington	No dispensation	August 14, 1883.
ARIZONA.			
Oliver, No.1	Prescott	July 1, 1893	August 22, 1894.
Phoenix, U.D.	Phoenix	April 4, 1895	Surrendered.
Tucson, U.D.	Tucson	April 5, 1895	Surrendered.
COLORADO.			
Denver, No. 1	Denver	Jan. 16, 1892	August 21, 1894.
Rocky Mountains	No.1 Trinidad	March 24, 1895	August 21, 1894.

Durango, No. 3	Durango	May 16, 1893	August 21, 1894.
Akron, No. 4	Akron	May 23, 1893	August 21, 1894.
Canon City,	No. 5 Canon City	June 5, 1893	August 21, 1894.
Pueblo, No. 7	Pueblo	April 10, 1894	August 21, 1894.
Hiram, U.D.	Greeley	Dec. 8, 1894	Surrendered.
Zabud, U.D.	Colorado Springs	May 27, 1895	Dispensation
Leadville, U.D.	Leadville	June 10, 1895	Surrendered.
IDAHO.			
Idaho, U.D.	Pocatillo	Dec. 15, 1896	Annulled.
Adoniram, U.D.	Boise	Jan. 30, 1897	Dispensation continues.
MONTANA.			
Zabud, No. 2	Butte	May 22, 1896	October 12, 1897.
Glendive, U.D.	Glendive	April 22, 1896	Dispensation continued.
Custer, U.D.	Miles City	April 24, 1896	Annulled.
Adoniram, U.D.	Livingston	May 13, 1896	Dispensation continued.

Mystic, U.D.	Bozeman	May 20, 1896	Dispensation continued.
Montana, U.D.	Dillon	May 24, 1896	Annulled.
Deer Lodge, U.D.	Deer Lodge	June 10, 1896	Annulled.
Anaconda, U.D.	Anaconda	June 11, 1896	Annulled.
Hellgate, U.D.	Missoula	Sept. 2, 1896	Dispensation continued.
Hiram, U.D.	Kalispell	Sept. 2, 1896	Annulled.
NEVADA.			
Carson, U.D.	Carson	Sept. 3, 1896	Dispensation continued.
Mountain, U.D.	Virginia City	Sept. 4, 1896	Dispensation continued.
Reno, U.D.	Reno	Sept. 19, 1896	Dispensation continued.
Eureka, U.D.	Eureka	Sept. 21, 1896	Dispensation continued.
NEW MEXICO.			
Deming, No. 1	Deming	April 25, 1887	November 19, 1889.
Las Vegas, U.D.	Las Vegas	March 16, 1895	Annulled.
Santa Fe, U.D.	Santa Fe	May 1, 1895	Dispensation continued.
Hiram, U.D.	Albuquerque	May 7, 1895	Annulled.
Alpha, U.D.	Raton	May 11,	Annulled.

		1895	
NORTH DAKOTA.			
Casselton, No. 1	Casselton	Dec. 17, 1888	November 19, 1889.
Hilkiah, No. 2	Jamestown	Sept. 1, 1893	August 21, 1894.
Hiram, U.D.	Valley City	Dec, 31, 1895	Dispensation continued.
Rae, U.D.	Grand Forks	Jan. 2, 1896	Annulled.
Zabud, U.D.	Devil's Lake	Jan. 3, 1896	Annulled.
Towner, U.D.	Towner	Jan. 6, 1896	Dispensation continued.
Adoniram, U.D.	Fargo	Feb. 15, 1896	Dispensation continued.
Damascus, U.D.	Wahpeton	Feb. 18, 1896	Annulled.
Mizpah, U.D.	Park River	March 15, 1896	Annulled.
Tyrian, U.D.	Lisbon	April 6, 1896	Dispensation continued.
Bismarck, U.D.	Bismarck	April 20, 1896	Dispensation continued.
SOUTH DAKOTA.			
Alpha, No. 1	Sioux Falls	April 11, 1891	July 21, 1891.
Lakota, U.D.	Deadwood	Sept. 7,	Annulled.

		1895	
Black Hills, U.D.	Hot Springs	Sept. 9, 1895	Annulled.
Zabud, U.D.	Yankton	Sept. 25, 1895	Annulled.
Scotland, U.D.	Scotland	Oct. 1, 1895	Surrendered.
Omega, U.D.	Salem	Oct. 10, 1895	Dispensation continued.
Hiram, U.D.	Canton	Oct. 30, 1895	Annulled.
Koda, U.D.	Flandreau	Oct. 31, 1895	Surrendered.
Brookings, U.D.	Brooking	Nov. 1, 1895	Annulled.
Aberdeen, U.D.	Aberdeen	Nov. 4, 1895	Annulled.
Adoniram, U.D.	Webster	Nov. 6, 1895	Annulled.
Emanuel, U.D.	Milbank	Nov. 14, 1895	Annulled.
Mitchell, U.D.	Mitchell	Nov. 28, 1895	Annulled.
Oriental, U.D.	Pierre	Dec. 12, 1895	Annulled.
Mystic, U.D.	Huron	Dec. 30, 1895	Surrendered.
Faulk, U.D.	Faulkton	Dec. 31, 1895	Annulled.
UTAH.			
Utah, No. 1	Salt Lake City	Feb. 13, 1892	August 21, 1894.
Summit, U.D	Park City	Sept. 2, 1895	Surrendered.
WASHINGTON			
Zabud, U.D.	Walla Walla	Dec. 8, 1894.	Became Constituent

			Grand Council of Washington.
WYOMING.			
Cheyenne, U. D	Cheyenne	June 24, 1895	Surrendered.
Laramie, U. D	Laramie	July 4, 1895	Annulled.
Zabud, U. D	Evanston	Sept. 2, 1895	Annulled.
Tyrus, U. D	Green River	Sept 3, 1895	Surrendered.
Sheridan, U. D.	Sheridan	May 12, 1896	Annulled.

SUMMARY OF GRAND COUNCIL RETURNS FOR THE YEAR 1896.

From the Proceedings of the General Grand Council, 1897.

Grand Council.	Held at	Membership.
Arkansas	Little Rock	321
California	San Francisco	901
Florida	Milton	72
Georgia	Macon	518
Indiana	Indianapolis	2,525
Indian Territory	Muskogee	97
Kansas	Wichita	797
Louisiana	New Orleans	207
Maine	Portland	2,189
Maryland	Baltimore	555
Massachusetts	Boston	5,294
Minnesota	St. Paul	734
Missouri	Springfield	704
Nebraska	Omaha	371
New Hampshire	Concord	1,416
New York	New York City	3,932
Ohio	Sandusky	4,222

Oregon	East Portland	189
South Carolina	Charleston	133
Tennessee	.Nashville	507
Vermont	Burlington	1,056
Washington	Seattle	215
Subordinates of General G Council		962

INDEPENDENT GRAND COUNCILS.

Grand Council.

Alabama
Montgomery
Connecticut
Hartford
Illinois
Chicago
Kentucky
Covington
Michigan
Coldwater
Mississippi
Jackson
New Jersey
Trenton
North Carolina
Wilmington
Pennsylvania
Lancaster
Rhode Island
Providence
Wisconsin
Milwaukee

FOREIGN GRAND COUNCILS.

Canada, Ontario
Barrie, Ontario
England and Wales, London

New Brunswick, St. John

CHAPTER LVIII

HISTORY OF THE GRAND AND SUBORDINATE COMMANDERIES IN THE SEVERAL STATES AND TERRITORIES OF THE UNITED STATES

Templar.

THE records of the early conclaves of the General Grand Encampment are the only sources of any definite information in regard to the introduction of the Templar Order into the several Masonic jurisdictions.

Whoever, therefore, has gone over the pages of those early records for any extended information will say, that for want of order and exactness they will compare with any other defective records now extant.

Discrepancies in dates continually occur, even within a few pages of each other, so that the compiler, after a diligent search and memoranda taken, will very soon have to alter the same.

We can refer any reader, for example, to the statistical tables of the dates of organization of the several Grand Commanderies in the Proceedings of 1880 and of 1895 for comparison.

In many cases in the reports of the General Grand Officers, as to the formation of the subordinate commanderies, it is said frequently: "Since the last conclave I have issued dispensations to the following subordinate Commanderies," without giving any dates whatever, leaving the compiler the difficult task of searching in the future pages for the definite years, months, and dates to find when these commanderies had their dispensations issued to them.

This was a constant source of error in dates, and, frequently, was a great annoyance in the preparation of this sketch.

We trust that should errors in dates be found hereafter the finder will consider the quandaries of the compiler, and especially if he should undertake to rectify our errors.

We have endeavored sedulously and faithhfully, as historian, to gather all the facts upon record, to give a truthful narrative of the formation of the subordinate bodies, as well as the constitutions of them also; and the organization of the Grand Commanderies in the several jurisdictions.

While all this has been an arduous task, there has been mingled with the task quite a pleasurable sensation in traveling over the "sacred ground" of "Templarism"; and our "pilgrimage" has yielded much satisfaction in making the acquaintance of so many distinguished knights who wrought so hard in building up an institution, which from the small beginnings of the eighteenth century, at its end, has resulted, in the close of the nineteenth century, in one of the most magnificent "Orders" the world has ever witnessed.

The Knight Templar order, as it is now constituted in the United States, has no rival in the world, and to emphasize its influences for good the Grand Encampment of the United States should, at its very next conclave, carry out the design of our most distinguished and lamented Knight, J.Q.A.

Fellows, to make the city of Washington the permanent headquarters, and erect such a Temple as would be commensurate with the dignity and importance of the Magnanimous Order of Knights Templars of the United States of America.

Note.-Dates of all the blanks marked with an asterisk could not be ascertained.

Alabama.

The Grand Commandery of Knights Templars for the State of Alabama was organized December 1, 1860, by the representatives of five commanderies, viz.:

Washington (Marion), at Marion; chartered in 1844. (No history.)

Mobile, No. 2, at Mobile; formed April 7, 1848, and chartered May 8, 1851.

Tuscumbia, No. 3, at Tuscumbia; formed August 1, 1848; chaptered October 12, 1850.

Montgomery, No. 4, at Montgomery; formed October 17, 1853; chartered September 19, 1853.

Selma, No. 5, at Selma; formed May 15, 1838; chartered September 16, 1859.

Arizona.

The Grand Commandery of Arizona was formed by Warrant from the Grand Encampment of the United States November 16, 1893.

The first commandery was Arizona, No. 1, at Tucson, February 22, 1883;[227] by dispensation, which was surrendered September 2, 1897.

Then followed:

Ivanhoe, No. 2, at Prescott, by dispensation September 30, 1892, and chaqered December 2, 1892.

Phoenix, No. 3, Phoenix, by dispensation October 7, 1892, and chartered November 14, 1892.

Arkansas.

The Grand Commandery of Arkansas was constituted May 25, 1872.

The first commandery organized was Hugh de Payens, No. 1, at Little Rock, December 20, 1853,[228] which received a Charter September 10, 1856.

Hugh de Payens, No. 3, at Fort Scott; dispensation granted April 13, 1867; chartered September 18, 1868; constituted October 11, 1868[229].

Jacques De Molay, No. 3; dispensation granted December 30, 1868,[230] and chartered September 21, 1871.[231]

Baldwin, No. 4, Fayetteville; dispensation April 28, 1871;[232] chartered September 21, 1871.[233]

Bertrand de Guesclin, Camden;[234] dispensation issued April 13, 1867 chartered September 10, 1868.[235]

California.

---

[227] Proceedings General Grand Encampment, 1883, p. 19.
[228] Ibid., 1865, p. 114.
[229] Ibid., 1868, p. 65
[230] Ibid., p. 30.
[231] Ibid., 1871, p. 224.
[232] Ibid. p. 31.
[233] Ibid
[234] Ibid., 1868, p. 13.
[235] Ibid., p. 65.

The Grand Commandery of Knights Templars for California was organized August 10, 1858, under the Warrant of the then Grand Master of the General Grand Encampment of the United States, Sir William B. Hubbard.

The first commandery formed in California was San Francisco, No. 1, at San Francisco, November 10, 1852, and chartered November 1, 1853.

The second was Sacramento, No. 2, at Sacramento, May 23, 1852, and chartered February 6, 1854.

The third was Pacific, No. 3, at Columbia, February 20, 1856, and chartered September 10, 1856.

Colorado.

The Grand Commandery was constituted March 14, 1876.

The commanderies were:

Colorado, No. 1, at Denver; dispensation granted January 13, 1866, and chartered September 10, 1868 constituted January 26, 1869.[236]

Central City, No 2, at Central City; dispensation granted November 8, 1866,[237] and chartered September 18, 1863.[238]

Pueblo, No. 3, at Pueblo; dispensation granted September 10, 1874, and chartered December 3, 1874.

Connecticut.

The Grand Commandery was constituted between 1829 and 1832, according to the list in the Proceedings of 1856, p. 358; but in the Proceedings of 1898 the date is given September 13, 1827.

We assume the first date to be correct, as in the Proceedings of the Grand Encampment we find the Grand Encampment of Connecticut represented at the fifth meeting, held November 29, 1832, but not so represented at the fourth meeting, September 14, 1829, nor is any mention made of the formation of the Grand Body in the minutes of said meeting of 1829, which would have been if the Grand Commandery had been organized.

The first commandery formed was Colchester, at Colchester; Charter dated September, 1819.

---

[236] Proceedings General Grand Encampment, 1868, p. 65.
[237] Ibid., p. 12.
[238] Ibid., 1871, p. 29.

The second was New Haven, at New Haven; dispensation issued November 5, 1825, and chartered September, 1826.

Note. At the second rneedng of the Grand Encampment, Proceedings of September 16, 1810, p. 6, say: "Resolved, That a charter of recognition be granted to the encampment of Colchester in Connecticut."

At the conclave held in Pittsburg, 1898, the tabular statement for that year shows eleven subordinate commanderies.

Note. - The report of the General Grand Recorder for 1880, in tabular statement, p. 136, under Grand Commandery of Connecticut, says: "Organized July, 1796."

Dakota Territory.

Dakota, No. 1, at Deadwood; constituted August 14, 1881.

Cyrene, No. 2, at Sioux Falls; dispensation was granted August 14, 1881, and was formed November 22, 1881; chartered August 23, 1883.

February 25, 1882, dispensation was granted to De Molay, No. 3, at Yankton; formed March, 1882; chartered August 23, 1883.

March 23, 1883, dispensation granted to Tancred, No. 4, at Bismarck; formed April 12, 1883; chartered August 23, 1883.

Fargo, No. 5, at Fargo; dispensation issued June 24, 1883.

Delaware.

The first commandery formed in Delaware was St. John's, No. 1, at Wilmington; dispensation dated March 10, 1868; chartered September 18, 1868.

District of Columbia.

The first commandery organized in the District of Columbia was Washington, No. 1, in Washington City, December 31, 1824; chartered January 14, 1825.

Columbia, No. 2, received a dispensation January 18, 1863, and a Charter September 7, 1865.

Potomac, No. 3, in Georgetown, received a dispensation March 4, 1870, and a Charter September 22, 1871.

De Molay, in Washington City, received a dispensation February 19, 1872, and a Charter December 3, 1874.

This commandery is mounted.

Orient Commandery, in East Washington, received a Charter August 29, 1895, and was constituted October 19, 1895.

Four of these commanderies, viz.: No. 1, No. 2, No. 4, and No. 5, met in convention January 14, 1896, and organized the Grand Commandery of the District of Columbia by authority of a Warrant of the Grand Encampment dated December 2, 1895.

Potomac, No. 3, united with the Grand Commandery at its Organization under the Warrant, January 4, 1896.

Florida.

The Grand Commandery was organized August 15, 1895, by a Warrant dated August 1, 1895.

The following commanderies were organized:

Coeur de Lion, No. 1, at Warrington; dispensation June 20, 1868; Charter * 1868; renewed December 3, 1874.

Damascus, No. 2, Jacksonville; dispensation May 18, 1870; chartered September, 1871.

De Molay, No. 3; dispensation March 17, 1851

Olivet, No. 4; dispensation * 1889.

Pulaski, No. 5; dispensation February 21, 1893

Plant City, No. 6; dispensation March 10, 1895.

Georgia.

The Grand Commandery was organized April 25, 1860, by authority approved September 16, 1859.

Georgia Encampment, No. 1, at Augusta, received a dispensation dated in 1823, and chartered May 5, 1823.

St. Omar, No. 2, at Macon; dispensation granted July 26, 1848, and chartered September 11, 1850.

St. Aldema, at Columbus; dispensation dated December 1, 1857.

Coeur de Lion, at Atlanta; dispensation dated May 14, 1859, and chartered September 17, 1859.

Idaho.

The following commanderies have been instituted in Idaho Idaho, No. 1, at Boise City; dispensation May 24, 1882; formed September 13, 1882; chartered August 23, 1883.

Lewiston, No. 2, at Lewiston; chartered August 11, 1892.

Moscow, No. 3, at Moscow; chartered August 11, 1892.

Gate City, No. 4, Pocatello; chartered August 29, 1895; instituted December 14, 1895.

Illinois.

The Grand Commandery was organized October 27, 1857, by authority of the Grand Encampment June 27, 1857, and duplicated September 15, 1857.

The subordinate commanderies were:

Apollo, No. 1, at Chicago; by dispensation 1844 to 1847, and chartered September 14, 1847. The tabular statement in Proceedings for 1856, p. 358, is indefinite.

Belvidere, No. 2, Alton; by dispensation March 25, 1853, and chartered November 1, 1853.

Central, or Centre, No. 3, at Decatur; by dispensation July 26, 1856; extended October 24, 1856; and by order of Grand Encampment continued until the ensuing session of the State Grand Commandery.

Peoria, No. 4, at Peoia; by dispensation July 25, 1853, and Charter September 19, 1853.

Freeport, No. 5 at Freeport; by dispensation June 10, 1857, and Charter September 16, 1859.

Indiana.

The Grand Commandery of Indiana was organized May 16, 1854, by authority of the Grand Encampment April 24, 1854.

The commanderies in Indiana were :

Roper, No. i, at Indianapolis; by dispensation May 14, 1848, and Charter October 16, 1860.

Greensburg, No. 2, at Greensburg; by dispensation January 25, 1851, and Charter September 19, 1853.

La Fayette, No. 3, La Fayette; by dispensation April 2, 1852, and Charter September 19, 1853.

Fort Wayne, No. 4, at Fort Wayne; by dispensation May 13, 1853, and Charter September 19, 1853.

Indian Territory.

The Grand Commandery was instituted by authority of the Grand Encampment December 17, 1895, the Warrant being issued November 28, 1895, at Muscogee.

The subordinate commanderies were :

Muscogee, No. 1, at Muscogee; by dispensation dated December 6, 1892, and Charter *

Chickasaw, No. 2, at Purcell; by dispensation dated May 31, 1894, and Charter August 29, 1895, and constituted October 29, 1895.

McAllester, No. 3 at McAllester; by dispensation dated July 14, 1894, and Charter August 29, 1895, and ccnstituted October 14, 1895.

Iowa.

The Grand Commandery of Iowa was organized June 6, 1864, by authority of the Grand Encampment September 19, 1859.

The subordinate commanderies were:

De Molay, of Iowa, No. 1, at Muscatine; by dispensation March 14, 1855, and Charter September 10, 1856.

Palestine, No. 2, at Iowa City; by Charter at once, September 15, 1856.

Siloam, No. 3, at Dubuque; by dispensation February 9, 1857, and Charter September 16, 1859.

Des Moines, No. 4, at Des Moines; by dispensation July 10, 1857.

Kansas.

The Grand Commandery was constituted December 29, 1868, by Warrant from the General Grand Master, Sir William Sewall Gardner, December 2, 1868. The subordinate commanderies were:

Leavenworth, No. 1, at Leavenworth; dispensation issued February 10, 1864; chartered September 6, 1865.

Washington, No. 2, at Atchison; dispensation issued June 5, 1865; chartered September 6, 1865.

Hugh de Payen, No. 3, at Fort Scott; dispensation issued April 13, 1867; chartered September 18, 1868.

De Molay, No. 4, Lawrence; dispensation issued March 10, 1868; chartered September 18, 1868.

Kentucky.

The Grand Commandery was constituted October 15, 1847, by Warrant from the Grand Encampment.

The subordinate commanderies were:

Webb, No. 1, at Lexington; by Charter at once, January 1, 1826.

Louisville, No. 2, at Louisville; by dispensation January 2, 1840, and by Charter September 17, 1851.

Versailles, No. 3, at Versailles; by dispensation April 26, 1842, and Charter 1844.

Frankfort, No. 4, Frankfort; by Charter September 15, 1847.

Montgomery, No. 5, at Mt. Sterling; dispensation[239] some time between 1842 and 1847; by Charter September 15, 1847.

There is no note of a dispensation issued to Frankfort Encampment, but in the account current of the G.G. Recorder we find that Frankfort Encampment, Kentucky, paid for dispensation $90, also that Montgomery Encampment did the same, and as in the latter case the tabular statement, p. 358, mentions that dispensation as between 1842 and 1847, Frankfort Encampment may have been in the "same boat." We have been forcibly impressed, in reading over these old records, how very careless the General Grand Officers and also the recorders and committees were in omitting important dates in their reports, which omissions have cost this writer many, many weary hours in hunting up such data as would enable him to supply these important dates for the benefit of the future student of Masonic history.

Louisiana.

The Grand Commandery of Louisiana was organized by the Warrant of the Grand Encampment February 12, 1864.

The Invincibles, at New Orleans, was organized between 1826 and 1829, and a Charter was issued some time in 1829.

Indivisible Friends, No. 1. This encampment was chartered by the Grand Encampment of New York in 1826. Jurisdiction was transferred to the General Grand Encampment in 1838 and accepted.[240]

Jacob de Molay, No. 2, New Orleans; dispensation April 15, 1850; continued by order Seyember 12, 1850, and chartered April 25, 1851.

Maine

The Grand Commandery was constituted May 5, 1852, for the State of Maine.

---

[239] Front Proceedings of Grand Encampment, 1847, we copy this: "Resolved, That the Report of the Committee of Dispensations and New Encampments be so amended as to permit Frankfort and Montgomery Encampments to join in the petition for the formation of a Grand Encampment in the State of Kentucky." Which was rejected.

[240] Note at bottom of p., 358, Proceedings of General Grand Encampment, 1856.

Portland Encampment, No. 2, is the first one on the printed list of 1856 at Portland; dispensation issued between 1842 and 1847, and chartered September 14, 1847.

St. John's, No. 3, at Bangor; dispensation February 18, 1850, and chartered September 17, 1850.

We can not find any evidence in the body of the Proceedings of No. 1, but the "Register" at end of 1847 and 1850 Proceedings gives "Maine," No. 1, at Portland, * 1844, and chartered September 14, 1847.

Maryland.

The Grand Commandery was constituted January 23, 1871.

The first commandery instituted was Maryland, No. 1, at Baltimore. This encampment was first chartered by the Grand Encampment of Pennsylvania May 2, 1814, and it appears on the record of 1832 of the Grand Encampment of the United States.

A resolution was passed admitting it under the jurisdiction of the General Grand Encampment, and directing that its Charter be endorsed by the General Grand Officers.[241]

Baltimore, No. 2, Baltimore; by dispensation June 17, 1859, and Charter September 16, 1859.

We shall now follow the history of the Knight Templar Order in Maryland by Sir Knight Edward T. Schultz, to whom the whole world of Masonry is indebted for his four volumes of the history of Masonry in that State. The result of this labors to himself has been almost total blindness, brought about by his incessant application in search of the facts connected with Masonry in Maryland.

Sir Knight Schultz says:

"The writer has for many years given much time and attention to the investigation of the origin of Encampment No. 1 of this city, and while he has been fortunate in obtaining documents which clearly establish the date of its organization, and many interesting facts in reference to its early history, he has not, he regrets to state, anything but theories to offer in regard to the source whence it emanated."

He had been furnished by the Grand Recorder of the Grand Commandery of Pennsylvania, Bro. Creigh, with certified copies of several documents in his office, written in 1814 and 1815, by the officers of Encampment No. 1 of Maryland to the Grand Officers of the Grand Encampment of Pennsylvania, which had been recently formed and in

---

[241] Proceedings of General Grand Encampment, 1832, p. 32.

which formation Encampment No. 1 had participated and was then a constituent.

Here follow copies of several old documents under seal to prove the facts set forth.

In one of these documents is a Charter of "recognition" which allowed their claim to an original organization prior thereto - dated in 1790 - as the letter from Archbishop Dobbin says: "I am induced to state that this Encampment insists in receiving its number and rank according to the date of its institution, the complete organization of which took place in the year 1790." Consequently we must class Maryland among the early jurisdictions where Templary had its origin.

This Charter of "recognition," we must observe, was issued to "Encampment of Knight Templars, No. 1, Maryland," thus showing that the demand made by the encampment, to have in rank and number agreeable to the date of its institution, was admitted to be a valid claim by the Grand Commandery of Pennsylvania, and thereby the year 1790 was fully recognized to be the date of the complete organization of Encampment No. 1, of Maryland.

Sir Knight Schuhz shows by documents that this encampment has had a continued existance from 1790 to the present day, and is yet known by the same name.

There is a facsimile of a Templar diploma shown and a copy of its text in print which shows that this Encampment No. 1 was in 1802 attached to Washington Lodge, No. 3, as Royal Arch Chapters and Encampments of Knights Templars in those early days were generally, if not wholly, held under warrants of Master Masons' Lodges,

In Webb's Monitors of 1802 and 1805 are shown three encampments in Maryland, viz.: Nos. 3, 13, and 24, and Sir Knight Schultz thinks they were Washington Lodge, No. 3; Concordia, No. 13; and Zion Lodge, No. 24; the first two located in Baltimore, and the last in Havre de Grace, Cecil County.

There is shown also another facsimile diploma issued by Encampment No. 1 to Philip P. Eckel, which Sir Knight Schultz thinks indicates that the encampment had severed its connection with Lodge No. 3 and had an independent organization, and says it must have been certainly as early as 1807, from a Masonic notice in the City Directory for that year, viz.: "Maryland Encampment No. 1, Knights Templars, meets on the second Tuesday in every second month."

The copper-plate from which this diploma was printed is in the Archives of Maryland Commandery.

It was designed by Philip P. Eckel and engraved by John Bannerman.

An old lady named Elizabeth Sadds, living in Baltimore in 1881, aged ninety-four years, informed Sir Knight Schultz that she knew Bannerman well; that he came from Scotland in 1773 and was the first engraver who lived in Baltimore, and he died in 1809.

The seal is the same on all the documents and was used until about 1814, when a new seal was made (which is shown).

This latter seal was used until 1854, when the name was changed to its present title, "Maryland Commandery, No. 1." Sir Knight Schultz has only theories to suggest as to the source from which the encampment was originally formed.

From traditions among the old members of the commandery it was supposed that the orders came from San Domingo with immigrants from that island.

He says: "We for a long time were inclined to believe that the encampment originated in the Rose Croix Chapter 'La Verite,' which was brought to Baltimore by the refugees from San Domingo; but the discovery of the 1802 diploma would indicate that, at that time at least, the Encampment was held under the authority of a Master Mason's Lodge."

Sir Knight Schultz refers to the list of degrees published by Cole and mentioned by us in Chapter LI.[242] In this list we enumerated the orders of the Red Cross, Knights Templar, and Knights of Malta, that were said to have been conferred by the Sublime Lodges, at Charleston, New York, and Newport in 1816.

Sir Knight William B. Hubbard, who was Grand Master of Templars, said: I suppose that we owe the origin of Templar Masonry in the United States to a distinguished Sov.'.Ins.'. of the Scottish Rite."[243] Bro. A.G. Mackey thought that the Orders of Knighthood were introduced through the A.'.A.'.R.'., not the A.'.A.'.S.'.R.'., for that system dates only from 1801, when it is well known that the Templar and Red Cross had both been worked as early as the South Carolina patent shows, in 1783.

Bro. Robert Macoy, in his sketch of the Knights Templar of New York, says:

"After a very careful examination of this important subject, we are impressed with the conviction that the introduction of the Order into this country was brought about somewhat in this wise: That a few

---

[242] Ch. LI. of this work, p. 1310
[243] Letter to T.S. Gourdin.

Sir Knights, having received the Order in England, or Ireland and having immigrated to this country, met together, as they became known to each other, by appointment, in a secluded place in New York and other parts of the country; and after testing each other by the best evidence in their possession, organized themselves into 'encampments' or 'conclaves,' and assumed control of 'territorial jurisdiction,' conferred the Orders, elected officers, issued diplomas, etc." "For the present, or something more reliable than any 'statement' yet presented can be accepted, we can offer nothing better as authentic history for the introduction of the Order of Knights Templar upon this Continent; nor do we deem it derogatory to the legitimacy of the 'transmission' or of the merits of the system of Templarism, to admit these conclusions.

During the early period of the institution there was no organized body that possessed absolute authority to issue warrants, hence it was recognized as legal for any number of Sir Knights, having the inherent righl to assemble in a secure place, apply the essential tests to each other, open an encampment, receive petitions and create Knights Templar."

Sir Knight Schultz concurs, somewhat, in the theories of Sir Knight Macoy, which he thinks "most worthy of acceptance," and says: "In every instance in which there is a mention of the Templar degree being conferred in this country prior to the year 1800, it is in connection with a Master Mason's Lodge.

St. Andrew's, of Boston, and St. Andrew's Lodge, of Charleston, as has been stated, conferred the Order - the former in 1769 and the latter in 1783.

The early encampments in Pennsylvania, Bro. Creigh says, were held under warrants of a Master's Lodge; and Encampment No. 1, of Maryland, as shown by the first diploma, was attached to Washington Lodge, No. 3."

After the organization of the Supreme Council of the A.'. A.'. S.'.R.'. at Charleston, in 1802, the Inspector-General took charge of all the degrees having no governing head, and as was stated by Cole, above referred to, "the Sublime Lodges at Charleston, Albany, and Providence conferred as many as fifty-five degrees."[244]

Subsequent to 1800, "Encampments were formed by Knights who received the Orders from an Inspector, or High Grade Mason."

At the constitution of the Grand Encampment of New York, Elias Hicks, Orator of the day, said: "The numerous Encampments of

---

[244] Freemason's Library," 1826, p. 317.

Knights Templar now existing within this State being self-created bodies, are consequently governed by their own private and individual law, acknowledging no superior authority, because, in fact, none heretofore existed.[245]

Sir Knight Schultz concludes, therefore, that Encampment No. 1 was organized in the same manner as those in New York were.

At the convention for the organization of the Grand Encampment in Pennsylvania, which met February 15, 1814, Sir Henry S. Keating was the delegate from Encampment No. 4, of Baltimore, Md.; who, on the election of Officers, which followed, was made G.St.B. Under the provision adopted therefor, a Charter of Recognition was granted to Encampment No. 1, of Baltimore, which has been referred to in this chapter.

After the organization of the General Grand Encampment of the United States, in New York City, June 20, 1816, Encampment No. 1, of Baltimore, came under its jurisdiction, but not until November 29, 1832, and an endorsement was made on the Charter of Recognition received from the Grand Encampment of Pennsylvania in 1814.

Sir Knight Schultz claims that Encampment No. 1 "is the oldest existing body of Knights Templar upon the American Continent"[246]

After Baltimore Commandery, No. 2, was chartered, there was no other commandery formed until Monumental, No. 3, of Baltimore, was organized by virtue of a dispensation issued by the Grand Master of Templars May 16, 1866.

At the next triennial conclave, September, 1868, at St. Louis, a Charter was granted, and on November 6, 1868, the commandery was duly constituted.

July 12, 1870, resolutions were adopted to organize a Grand Commandery of the State. This occurred January 23, 1871.

Jacques De Molay, No. 4, of Frederick City, was organized by virtue of a dispensation issued November 23, 1867, by Sir Henry L. Palmer, Grand Master of Templars, which occurred March 2, 1868.

At the triennial conclave of the Grand Encampment of the United States, September, 1868, a Charter was ordered, and continued until the formation of the State Grand Commandery, when it came under its jurisdiction.

Grand Master William Sewall Gardner issued a dispensation March 2, 1869, to form Crusade Commandery, No. 5, of Baltimore, and

---

[245] Schultz, "History," vol. i., p. 367.

[246] Ibid., p. 376. MELROSE ABBEY

April 26, 1869, the first meeting was held. The Officers were selected, all of whom were members of Maryland Commandery.

Three chartered commanderies met in convention by their representatives in Baltimore, Md., December 12, 1870, and elected Grand Officers.

The Grand Master was duly notified and requested to grant his Warrant for the formation of the Grand Commandery of Maryland.

The three commanderies were: Maryland, No. 1, Baltimore; Baltimore, No. 2, Baltimore; Monumental, No. 3, Baltimore.

The Warrant of the Grand Master was dated January 3, 1871.

January 23, 1871, the Cdand Commandery was then dedicated in ancient form to St John the Almoner.

The first Grand Conclave of the New Grand Commandery was held January 23, 1871.

May 11, 1871, Crusade Commandery, No. 5, of Baltimore, was constituted, under Charter granted by the Grand Commandery May 10, 1871.

Antioch Commandery, No. 6, of Cumberland, by dispensation issued August 26, 1871, was organized August 27, 1871.

A Charter was issued, and January 14, 1873, the commandery was duly constituted.

Palestine Commandery, No. 7, at Annapolis, was organized April 14, 1873, a dispensation having been issued by Grand Commander Mann.

A Charter was granted May, 1873. June 2, 1873, this commandery was duly constituted.

Beauseant Commandery, No. 8, received a dispensation May 27, 1875, to form a commandery in Baltimore, and was organized June 15, 1875.

A Charter was granted May 10, 1876, and the commandery was duly constituted May 11, 1876.[247]

Massachusetts and Rhode Island.

The Grand Encampment of Massachusetts and Rhode Island was formed May 6 1805, which was the first Grand Encampment to be organized in the United States, according to the authorities in Massachusetts, which statement has been challenged by the Templars in Pennsylvania, who claim that the very first Grand Encampment was organized in Philadelphia May 12, 1797, as will be shown under that head.

---

[247] Schultz, "History of Masonry in Maryland," vol. iv., p. 659.

Sir William Sewall Gardner, M. E. Grand Master of the Grand Encampment of Massachusetts and Rhode Island, at the semi-annual meeting in Boston, May 5, 1865, in his address said: "This day completes the sixtieth year of our existence as a Grand Encampment and marks an epoch in our history. "On the 6th of May 1805, Sir Thomas Smith Webb, of Providence; Sir Henry Fowle, of Boston; Sir Jonathan Gage, of Newburyport, with other Templar Masons, assembled in the Masonic Hall at Providence and formed this Grand Encampment." "There they assembled and laid the foundation of Templar Masonry, as we recognize it to-day." "This Grand Encampment was the germ of Templar Masonry as now organized in the United States, and the ritual as adopted here has been taken as the true Templar Work throughout the jurisdiction of the Grand Encampment of the United States.

I am aware that in Pennsylvania there was a Grand Encampment in the early part of this century, and that it professed to confer the Order of the Temple.

It is impossible to tell now what its ritual was, but there is evidence tending to show that it was entirely different from that taught by this Grand Body.".......

Perhaps no person in the United States had more to do with the formation and renovation of this ritual than Sir Henry Fowle.

His judgment, therefore, upon the ritual as exemplified by the Grand Encampment of Pennsylvania in 1816 in his presence, is of great weight, and leads to the conclusion that the work as used by that Grand Body, whereon it originated, was entirely different from that in use in this jurisdiction.

"We have then for our gratification, not only the fact, which is now universally conceded, that this Grand Encampment is the oldest Grand Body of Masonic Knighthood upon this continent, but also that it has furnished the ritual which is now used in all the bodies, both Grand and Subordinate, within the United States.

"The English Order, from which our fathers in this Grand Encampment derived the elements of our ritual, is termed the 'Masonic Knights Templar's Conclave' in open and avowed confession of the dependence of the Order upon the Masonic institution.

I need but allude to the ritual to convince you that it was built upon Masonry, and that the form and manner of our work are eminently Masonic.

In its teachings and its ceremonials, this Order of the Temple which we confer is but Masonry Christianized; a complete acknowledgment of and a full belief in the divine Mission of the risen Messiah, engrafted upon the Masonic forms, precepts, and ritual."

"It is worthy of notice, from the establishment of this Grand Encampment to the present time, it has been one of the most conservative bodies of Knighthood in the United States."

Mexcio.

A Warrant was issued to organize a commandery called "Popocatapetl," No. 1, for the Federal Districts of Mexico, dated September 1893.

Michigan.

The Grand Commandery of Michigan was instituted by the Grand Master of the General Grand Encampment, in person, who installed the Grand Officers January 11, 1858.

The first Warrant was issued February 13, 1857.

The first commandery organized was Detroit, No. 1, at Detroit; by dispensation November 1, 1850, and Charter September 19, 1853.

Then followed Pontiac, No. 2, at Pontiac; by dispensation March 25, 1852, and Charter October 27, 1853.

Eureka, No. 3, at Hillsdale; by dispensation February 13, 1854, and Charter September 10, 1856.

Peninsular, No. 4, at Kalamazoo; by dispensation March 3, 1856, and Charter September 10, 1856.

Monroe, No. 5, at Monroe; by dispensation March 29, 1856, and Charter September 12, 1856.

De Molay, No. 6, Grand Rapids; by dispensation May 9, 1856, and Charter September 12, 1856.[248]

Peninsular, No. 4, it appears from the record,[249] declined to place herself under the Grand Commandery of the State and regularly sent her returns and dues to the General Grand Recorder, acknowledging no other superior than the Grand Encampment from which she received her Charter on September 10, 1856.

The controversy was referred to the Committee on Jurisprudence, which thoroughly examined the whole matter and the principles of State-Sovereignty in a report and offered the following:

---

[248] Creigh, "History of Knight Templars," ch. v., pp.501 and 502.

[249] Proceedings of General Grand Encampment, 1859, p. 39.

"Resolved, That the Grand Commandery of Michigan, from the date of its formation has of right exercised sole and exclusive jurisdiction over all subordinates in that State.

"Resolved, That all dues paid by Peninsular Commandery, No. 4, to the Grand Recorder of this Grand Encampment, occurring since the formation of the Grand Commandery of Michigan, be paid to the Grand Recorder of that body."[250] Which resolutions were adopted.

The following was then adopted:

"Resolved, That at the formation of a State Grand Commandery, it is the right as well as the duty of every subordinate in the State, whether Chartered or under Dispensation, to enroll itself under such State Grand Commandery, and respect and obey its laws and regulations."[251]

Minnesota.

The Grand Commandery of Minnesota was constituted October 23, 1865. The following were the subordinate commanderies :

Damascus, No. 1, at St. Paul by dispensation July 12, 1856, and Charter September 10, 1856.

Coeur de Leon, at Winona; dispensation issued May 13, 1864; chartered September 6, 1865.

Mankato, at Mankato; dispensation issued April 5, 1865 chartered September 6, 1865.

Zion, at Minneapolis; dispensation issued May 19, 1863 chartered September 6, 1865.

Mississippi.

The Grand Commandery of the State of Mississippi was constituted January 21, 1857. The order to establish the Grand Commandery was first issued December 5, 1856, and renewed December

22, 1856. The subordinate commanderies were :

Mississippi, No. 1, at Jackson; by dispensation July 5, 1844, and Charter September 12, 1844.

Magnolia, No. 2, at Vicksburg; by dispensation October 10, 1850, and Charter January 4, 1854.

Lexington, No. 3, at Lexington; by dispensation July 22, 1856, and Charter September 1, 1856.

---

[250] Ibid., p. 53.
[251] Ibid., p. 56.

Missouri.

The Grand Commandery for the State of Missouri was constituted May 2, 1860.

Approved September 16, 1859.[252]

St. Loius No. 1, at St Louis; no dispensation; chartered September 17, 1847.

Weston, No. 2; dispensation March 9, 1853, and chartered September 10, 1853.

Lexington, No. 3; dispensation September 30, 1853, and chartered September 10, 1856.

Montana.

The Grand Commandery of Montana was constituted May 14, 1888.

Constituent commanderies:

Virginia City, No. 1, at Virginia City; dispensation August 27, 1860; chartered September 23, 1868.

Helena, No. 2, at Helena; dispensation January 21, 1869; chartered September 21, 1871.

Montana, No. 3, at Butte; by dispensation June 26, 1878, and chartered August 20, 1880; constituted June 24, 1881.

Damascus, No. 4, at Miles City; by dispensation March 8, 1886; formed March 16, 1886, and chartered September 23, 1886.

Nebraska.

The Grand Commandery of Nebraska was constituted December 27, 1871 (statement of 1895). (Statement of 1880 has 28th.)

The first commandery was Mount Calvary, No. 1; organized uly 24, 1865; chartered September 6, 1865.

The second was Mount Olivet, No. 2, at Nebraska City; organized January 25, 1867; chartered September 18, 1868.[253] In the Proceedings of the nineteenth triennial of the General Grand Encampment for September 15, 1871,[254] it is recorded under "Proxies to constitute New Commanderies," " V.'. E.'. Sir George W. Belt constituted and installed the officers of Mount Olivet Commandery, No. 2, Nebraska City, January 25, 1868." In the Proceedings of 1868,

---

[252] Proceedings General Grand Encampment, 1859, p. 50.
[253] Proceedings General Grand Encampment, 1871, P. 28.
[254] Ibid., p. 30.

September 18,[255] it is recorded that a Charter was ordered to be issued to Mount Olivet, No. 2, Nebraska City (September 18, 1868).

Here appears to be a discrepancy, as a Charter was granted after the commandery was constituted (January 25, 1868).

The third commandery was Mount Carmel, No. 3, at Brownsville; organized July 22, 1870; chartered September 21, 1871.

The fourth was Mount Moriah, No. 4, at Lincoln; organized February 17, 1871; chartered September 21, 1871.

Nevada.

The first commandery organized in Nevada was De Witt Clinton, No. 1, at Virginia, February 4, 1867, and chartered September 18, 1868; constituted and officers installed, January 8, 1869.

The second was Eureka, No. 2, at Eureka; dispensation granted June 6, 1880; chartered August 18, 1880, and constituted October 15, 1880.[256]

New Hampshire.

The Grand Commandery of New Hampshire was constituted September 28, 1897.

The first subordinate encampment which was warranted was Trinity, No. 2, located at first at Hanover, March 24, 1824.[257] It was dormant for some time, and was re-chartered September 19, 1853 and removed to Manchester.

De Witt Clinton, No. 1, Portsmouth; Charter January, 1826.[258]

Mount Horeb, No. 4, Hopkinton; Charter May 21, 1826; became dormant in 1856.

North Star, No. 3, Lancaster; dispensation May 2, 1857; chartered September 16, 1859.

St. Paul, No. 4, at Dover; dispensation November 7, 1857 chartered September 16, 1859.

---

[255] Ibid., p. 65.
[256] The General Grand Encampment approved the formation of a State Grand Encampment for New Hampshire September 14, 1859 (see p. 50 of the Proceedings General Grand Encampment, 1859) ; but it was never formed until 1897.
[257] Proceedings General Grand Encampment, 1826, p. 12.
[258] Ibid., 1853, p.192.

Mount Horeb, No. 5, at Concord; dipensation May 31, 1859. As above shown the original Charter was issued May 21, 1826, and was restored September 16, 1859.[259]

New Jersey.

The Grand Commandery of New Jersey was constituted February 14, 1860, by the approval of the General Grand Encampment dated September 16, 1859.

The first subordinate commandery was Hugh de Payens, No. 1, at Jersey City; by dispensation March 12, 1858, and Charter September 16, 1859; constituted November 25, 1859.

St. Bernard, No. 2, at Hightstown ; by dispensation March 27, 1859, and Charter September 16, 1859; constituted October 12, 1859.

Helena, No. 3, at Burlington; by dispensation September 16, 1859, and chartered September 16, 1859;[260] constituted October 12, 1859.

New Mexico.

The first commandery organized in New Mexico was Santa Fe, No. 1, at Santa Fe; dispensation granted May 31, 1869 organized Ma 31, 1869, and Charter September 21, 1871.

The next was Las Vegas, No. 2, at Las Vegas; dispensation April 10, 1882; chartered August 23, 1883.

Pilgrim, No. 3, at Albuquerque; dispensation April 4, 1883 chartered August 23, 1883.

McGorty, No. 4, at Deming; dispensation July 13, 1886; chartered September 23, 1886.

Aztec, No. 5, at Raton; dispensation November 16, 1892; chartered August 29, 1895, and constituted December 20, 1895.

Rio Hundo, No. 6, at Reswell; dispensation June 17, 1895 Charter August 29, 1895; constituted November 30, 1895.

New York.

The Grand Encampment of New York was formed at origine, June 18, 1814.[261]

There is no history of the regular formation of this Grand Encampment.

---

[259] Proceedings General Grand Encampment, p. 358, in note to table (K).
[260] The record shows that the dispensation and Charter were issued on the same day - Proceedings, 1859, p. 358.
[261] Ante, pp. 1390, 1391.

In the history of the organization of the General Grand Encampment we have shown how the formation occurred.

We are reminded of the remark of an old negro, who said: "Poor Marse Greely, he never had no father or mother, 'kase he said hisself that he was a 'self-made man.'" Nevertheless, he was the great editor of the great State of New York. Moreover, the Templars of that State can refer to another illustrious example, viz., "Melchizedek, King of Salem, the Priest of the Most High God, who met Abraham returning from the slaughter of the kings and blessed him.

Without father, and without mother, without descent (pedigree), having neither beginning of days, nor end of life."[262]

The commencement of the Templar Order in New York is involved in great obscurity; yet there were several bodies, having no authority whatever, which were organized at an early date.

Sir Knight Robert Macoy bestowed great labor in endeavoring to arrive at the very first history of the Order in New York.

In the volume of Proceedings of the Grand Commandery, there is a history of the Templar Order in New York State, prepared by the Grand Recorder.

In a subsequent report he states that "Several of the Grand Recorders, committees, and reporters have embodied valuable historical hints in their several papers, which throw light upon the origin of Templary, . . . but none thus far have satisfactorily supplied the link that separates the Templars of the Crusades from the modern Templars or Templarism as it exists in the United States, England, and Canada."

Sir Knight Macoy said that "Sir Knights anywhere in the United States could and probably did meet and increase their numbers or dignify their worthy companions by the authority of inherent rights, keeping few and probably no records.

We are certain that those who lived and labored in the days referred to have passed to their final rest and have left few traces behind."

Sir Knight Parvin, on commenting upon Sir Knight Macoy, says: "And yet the few traces they have left did not confirm the position assumed by Sir Knight Macoy, but rather go to prove that the Sir Knights made in those days were made in Lodges or Chapters working under Lodge Warrants, except possibly in a few instances, where the degree of Knight Templar was conferred by officers of some of the bodies of the Ancient and Accepted Scotch Rite."[263]

---

[262] Heb., ch. vii., vs. 1, 3.
[263] History of Masonry," p. 539.

In this we agree with Sir Knight Parvin.

Sir Knight Macoy, in his efforts to prove priority for New York in Templary, supports his statement as to the existence of the Order prior to 1785, quotes from old newspapers published in New York City, verified by reference to the reprint of the Grand Lodge Proceedings from 1781 to 1815, published in 1876, by authority of the Grand Lodge.[264]

This is shown in the order of procession on St. John's Day (December 27, 1785), providing that Knights Templars with drawn swords were to be in the procession.

Also from the "Independent Journal," December 28, 1785, is a notice of "the proceedings of the anniversary of St. John the Evangelist," and that it gave the same programme or form of procession as was provided by the Grand Lodge; and then states, "that whilst the members of the fraternity celebrated the natal days of their patron saints, Sir Knights as a body seldom appeared in public."

Sir Knight Macoy says further: "We refer to what was known as Old Encampment, Grand Encampment, and sometimes as Morton's Encampment, of which General Jacob Morton was for many years Grand Master.

The date and circumstances under which this Grand Encampment was established are not definitely known.

The general belief is that it was the body of Knights Templars that participated in the celebrations of St. John's Day, December 27, 1785, June 24, 1789, and again in 1795.

The first published list of this Commandery appeared in 1796, when Jacob Morton was Grand Master.

The body continued to hold stated meetings until 1810, when it disappeared.

Gen'l Jacob Morton was admitted an honorary member of the Grand Encampment of the State in 1815."

Reference is also made in these transactions of the Grand Lodge to the attendance of the "Knights Templars in the form as directed by their presiding officer," etc., at the observance of "the solemn funeral rites in commemoration of our illustrious Brother, George Washington, with a procession," etc.

At the first conclave after the formation of the Grand Encampment of the State, in June, 1814, the Grand Orator "delivered a discourse in which he gave a historical sketch of the foundation of the Order of Knights Templars, in a style calculated to excite the liveliest

---

[264] Reprint of Proceedings of New York, December 21, 1785, p. 42.

interest, which was manifested by reiterated applause; and in order, at the same time, to perpetuate the motives that led to the establishment of this Grand Encampment as the ground-work of our future operations.

He concluded by giving the following concise account of the proceedings and the ceremonial that took place at its formation by the Sov.'. Grand Consistory of Chiefs of Exalted Masonry for the United States of America, its Territories and Dependencies, at their Asylum, held in the City of New York, on the 22d day of the month Shebath, of the Hebrew year, 7813, corresponding with the eleventh month, A.L. 5813; January A.D. 1814, and the foundation of our order the 694th year, and at which most, if not all, the members here present assisted.

"The numerous Encampments of Knights Templars now existing within this State, being self-created bodies, are consequently governed by their own private and individual laws, acknowledging no superior authority, because, in fact, none heretofore existed."[265]

The consistory itself which authorized this Grand Encampment was a self-constituted body of the Cerneau creation without any authority, and pirated degrees which never belonged to the Ancient and Accepted Rite, and thue is no evidence whatever that Cerneau or any of the members of that consistory had ever received the Templar or Red Cross degree.

At this conclave De Witt Clinton was chosen Thrice Illustrious Grand Master, who was not present; and by reference to all the Proceedings from 1814 to 1826 we do not find him as being present at a single conclave, although he was re-elected at every election until his death, which occurred in 1828.

At the conclave held May 22, 1815, Columbian Encampment, No. 5, was voted to have a Charter of Recognition, and it was also, voted "that the numerical characteristics 1, 2, 3, 4, be kept in reserve for the several encampments already established within this State, and in the order which they now respectively stands should they or any of them apply for a renewal of their Charters under the Grand Encampment."[266]

At the conclave held May 4, 1816, a Charter was granted upon the petition of "a collective body of Sir Knights Templars, Royal Arch Masons and Members of the Sov.'. Grand Council of Princes of the Royal Secret for the State of Louisiana, sitting at New Orleans, authorizing them to open and to hold, in a regular and authentic manner, an encampment of Sir Knights of the Red Cross, Most Holy and Illustrious Knights of Malta, Knights of the Mediterranean Pass and

---

[265] The pot called the kettle black
[266] Proccedings of Grand Encainpinent of New York, from 1814 to 1859, p.14.

Invincible Knights Templars, to be under and subject to the jurisdiction of that Grand Encampment and who had formed themselves into a provisory association under the title of Louisiana Encampment, No.__, until the pleasure and sanction of the Supreme Body be known and obtained.

This was known as No 6.

At the conclave held June 9, 1816, a delegate was chosen to represent the Grand Encampment in the convention of representatives from the Grand Encampments of the several States in the Union, to be held at Philadelphia on Tuesday next, and Thomas Lowndes was selected.

The history of that coovention has already been written in Chapter LIII.

At the annual conclave held June 29, 1816, Columbian Encampment, was the first encampment to be represented in any conclave.

A Charter was also issued for an encampment of Knights Templars and Appendant Orders, sitting at New Orleans.

By a special conclave the Grand Recorder was instructed to correspond with Sir Thomas Smith Webb, Deputy General Grand Master, requesting copies of the Constitution of the General Grand Encampment of the United States, for the purpose of so modifying the Constitution of this Grand Encampment that it may conform thereto."

At the annual conclave a committee reported and submitted a form of new constitution and it was adopted.

The preamble sets forth:

"The Grand Encampment of the State of New York having by its representatives assisted to form the General Grand Encampment of the United States of America, and having acknowledged the supreme authority of the same, did, on the 11th day of December, A.D. 1820, in full session, upon report of a committee appointed to revise the former constitution, adopt the former constitution for its future government."[267]

From the minutes of the special conclave held on Trinity Sunday, June 17, 1821, for the purpose of installing the Grand Officers, after which a resolution was adopted to transmit certain copies of the constitution to different parties, the only subordinate encampments mentioned are Columbian, No. 5, in New York, and Indivisible Friends, No. 6, in New Orleans, which No. 6 was originally chartered as Louisiana Encampment.

---

[267] Proceedings Grand Encampment of New York, P. 28.

Copies were also sent to the encampments at Albany and Stillwater, in that State, which had not yet united with the Grand Encampment.[268]

At the special conclave held February 8, 1823, upon application therefor, a Warrant was issued to Utica Encampment, No. 7, at Utica.[269] At a special conclave February 18, 1823, a Warrant was ordered to be issued, upon application therefor to Temple Encampment, No. 2, at Albany.[270]

At the special conclave held August 16, 1823, upon application therefor, a Warrant was issued to form Morton Encampment, No. 4, in the city of New York.

This encampment was regularly installed by the Grand Encampment August 18th following.

At the special conclave held September, 1824, upon application therefor, a Warrant was issued to LaFayette Encampment, No. 7, in the city of Hudson.

At the annual conclave there were present the representatives or proxies of Columbian, No. 1; Utica, No. 3; Morton, No. 4; and LaFayette, No. 7. At the annual conclave held December 16, 1825, warrants were issued to Plattsburg Encampment, No. 8, at Plattsburg; to Cherry Valley, No. 9, at Cherry Valley, and Genesee, No. 10, at Le Roy.

At the annual conclave held June 9, 1826, a Warrant was issued to Watertown Encampment, No. 11, at Watertown, to which a dispensation had been granted previously (no date mentioned).

At the special conclave held September 18, 1826, an order was passed to authorize a dispensation to be issued to form an encampment in the village of Rochester.

At the annual conclave field June 8, 1827, there were represented: Columbus, No. 1; Temple, No. 2; Utica, No. 3; Morton, No. 4; LaFayette, No. 7; Plattsburg, No. 8, Cherry Valley, No. 9; Genesee, No. 10; Watertown, No. 11.

A Warrant was issued to New Jerusalem Encampment, No. 13, in Ithaca.

A Warrant was also issued to Monroe Encampment, No. 12, a dispensation leaving been granted to this encampment in Rochester, ordered September 16, 1826.

Genesee Encampment was authorized to change its location from Le Roy to Batavia.

---

[268] Ibid., p. 34.
[269] Ibid., p. 41.
[270] Ibid., p. 42.

At a special conclave held February 20, 1808, resolutions were adopted on the death of their distinguished Chief, De Witt Clinton.

At the annual conclave held June 6, 1828, a Warrant was ordered to be issued to Clinton Encampment, No. 14, in Brooklyn, a dispensation having been previously issued.

We have now brought the history of this important Grand Encampment down from its doubtful origin to the death of the distinguished Chief, who was also the Head and Mainstay of the General Grand Encampment until his death, and our limits in this chapter will not permit us to proceed any further, and we close by observing that no single Grand Commandery has exerted greater influence for good and the prosperity of Templar Masonry than the Grand Commandery of the Empire State.

"Esto perpetua."

North Carolina.

The Grand Commandery of North Carolina was constituted May 10, 1881.

The first official notice of Templarism is found in the Proceedings of the Grand Encampment of the United States, September 19, 1826, where it is reported that a Charter had been granted, among many orbers, to Fayetteville Encampment, at Fayetteville, December 21, 1821.[271]

In the report of the General Grand Recorder at the tenth meeting, held September 14, 1847,[272] he stated that a dispensation had been issued to that Encampment, but whether a Charter was granted he is unable to say.

"Certain it is, the encampment is known to have ceased all operations many years ago, although it is said a Charter was known to have existed."

The General Grand Recorder also stated:[273]

"Some time in 1845 a Sir Kright from Richmond, Virginia, and another from another State, not now recollected, assisted by a most respectable Sir Knight of Wilmington, North Carolina, who, it is said, had seen the Charter which had there been consumed by fire, held a meeting and conferred the degrees of Knighthood upon so many Royal Arch Masons as seemed to them sufficient to form an Encampment;

---

[271] Proceedings of General Grand Encampment, 1826, p. 20)
[272] Ibid., 1847, p. 114.
[273] Ibid., p. 147.

and, having done so, they proceeded to elect officers and to organize an encampment.

This being done, the Recorder of that body so formed wrote to the undersigned, requesting that another Charter might be furnished them.

Being informed that all their proceedings were irregular, it is believed they proceeded no further, but he can not assert with certainty that such is the fact"

Fayetteville Encanmpment, at Fayetteville, was originally chartered December 21, 1821; as before stated.

Wilmington Encampment, at Wilmington, was chartered originally at an early date, but there is no record in the Proceedings of the General Grand Encampment except in 1874, where it is said the dispensation was renewed March 18, 1872.

The following was adopted at the conclave of the General Grand Encampment September 16, 1850.

"Resolved, That the letter of P.W. Fanning, dated Wilmington, North Carolina, September 8, 1850, with its enclosure, being referred to the General Grand Recorder, to reply to the same, and with the view of authorizing the Sir Knights of Wilmington and Fayetteville to resume their labors as Encampments subordinate to this General Grand Encampment; and that the Most Excellent General Grand Master is empowered, in his discretion and upon examination into the merits of the case, the authorizing of a charter in the place of the one lost, without other than the Recorder's fee as to him may appear just and expedient."[274]

Charlotte, No. 2, at Charlotte; dispensation was issued June 14, 1875, and chartered August 30, 1877.[275]

Durham, No. 3, at Durham; was constituted October 14, 1880.

North Dakota.

The Grand Commandery of North Dakota was constituted June 16, 1890.

Ohio.

The Grand Encampment of the State of Ohio was constituted October 24, 1843.

The General Grand Encampment voted for the constitution of the Grand Encampment September 17, 1841.[276]

---

[274] Proceedings of General Grand Encampment, 1850, p. 150.
[275] Ibid., p. 192.

The first subordinate encampment was established at Worthington by dispensation June, 1818, and chartered September 16, 1819.

The second was Miami, at Lebanon; by Charter May 14, 1826.

The third was Clinton, No. 1, at Mount Vernon; by dispensation 1826 and 1829, and was represented in the General Grand Encampment in 1829.

The fouth was Lancaster, No. 2, at Lancaster.

There does not appear on record any dispensation, but a Charter was granted December 9, 1835.

The fifth was Cincinnati, No. 3; by dispensation December, 1839, and Charter September 17, 1841.

The sixth was Massillon, No. 4, at Massillon; by dispensation July 5, 1843, and Charter September 12, 1844.

The seventh was Mount Vernon, No. 5, at Mount Vernon; by dispensation July 22, 1843, and Charter September 12, 1844, which was originally Clinton, No.1.

Oklahoma.

The Grand Commandery of Oklahoma was constituted by authority of the Grand General Encampment February 10, 1896.

Warrant to form Grand Commandery dated November 8, 1895.[277] The subordinate commanderies were :

Guthrie, No. 1, at Guthrie; by dispensation November 17, 1892, and Charter December 22, 1892.

Oklahoma, No. 2, at Oklahoma; by dispensation October 7, 1892, and Charter November 12, 1892.

Ascension, No. 3, at El Remo; by dispensation May 8, 1893, and Charter August 29, 1895, and was instituted December 3, 1895.

Oregon.

The Grand Commandery of Oregon was constituted April 13, 1887.

Ivanhoe, No. 2, at Eugene City; by dispensation April 6, 1883, and chartered August 23, 1883.

Temple, No. 3, at Albany; by dispensation June 5, 1886, formed July 8, 1886, and chartered September 24, 1886.

Pennsylvania.

---

[276] Ibid., 1841, p. 79.
[277] Proceedings of General Grand Encampment, 1898, p. 62.

The commencement of the Templar Order in Pennsylvania was at an early day, and a contest was vigorously prosecuted between the Templars of Massachusetts and Rhode Island and Pennsylvania as to when a Grand Commandery was formed and in which jurisdiction.

We shall quote from Sir Alfred Creigh's work on Templarism in Pennsylvania to show what he has written on that point in his reply[278] to Sir Wm. S. Gardner, of Massachusetts, in his address at the semi-annual meeting in Boston, May 5, 1865.[279]

"The history of Templarism in Pennsylvania is one of peculiar interest to every Sir Knight of the Order, whether enrolled under our banner, or waging war in sister jurisdictions in defence of innocent maidens, helpless orphans, destitute widows, and the Christian religion.

To Pennsylvania and Pennsylvania alone are we indebted for the first Grand Encampment which was ever constituted in the United States.

She therefore has no competitor for the honor, the glory, and the immortality which is emblazoned upon her Templar history; and the 12th day of May, 1797, when the Convention met in Philadelphia, composed of delegates from Nos. 1 and 2 of Philadelphia, No. 3 of Harrisburg, and No. 4 of Carlisle (whose respective organizations took place from 1793 to 1797),[280] should be held as sacred as the 4th of July, 1776 - the one having given birth to the Orders of Christian Knighthood, and the other to our political existence.

It required sober thought, sound judgment, mature reflection, discriminating mind, and far-seeing perception in the Sir Knights composing that convention as they were about to inaugurate a system of Christian Ethics which would have an influence for weal or for woe upon the dissemination of the principles of Christian Knighthood.

The idea was happily conceived, and the Sir Knights who risked their Masonic and Templar representation upon its success have rendered the name of Pennsylvania eternal in the annals of Templarism."

Sir Knight Creigh then enters into a statement of some historical and other dates to show that the four subordinate encampments which organized the Grand Encampment were regularly constituted prior to the formation of the Grand Body.

---

[278] "Templarism in Pennsylvania," 2d series, p. 504.
[279] Ibid., p. 502.
[280] It is very remarkable that in those ancient times the years never had any months or days.-EDITOR.

But, however, he finds that from the published By-Laws of Nos. 1 and 2, of Philadelphia, that on December 21 1812, these two united as No. 1, and from this encampment and also No. 2, of Pittsburg, was formed a second Grand Encampment, on February 16, 1814, with the addition of delegates from Rising Sun Encampment, No. 1, of New York; Washington Encampment, No. 1, of Wilmington, Del.; and Baltimore Encampment, No. 1, Baltimore, Md.

The style of the second Grand Encampment was the "Pennsylvania Grand Encampment with Masonic jurisdiction thereunto belonging." The second Grand Encampment existed until June 10, 1824, or at least its Grand Master, Sir Anthony Fannen, exercised his authority as such, for on that day he issued a dispensation to the officers of St. John's Encampment, No. 4, which was instituted June 8, 1819, "to dub and make John E. Schwartz a Sir Knight of our most illustrious Order of Knights Templar." The original of No. 1, of 1794, kept up a complete and unbroken organization until June 13, 1824, and No. 2 was merged into it December 27, 1812, as above noticed.

St John's, No. 4, after the parent body had ceased in 1824, still existed and recognized as her superior the source of all Masonic authority within the State, the R.W. Grand Lodge of Pennsylvania.

It was upon this Rock that the delegates of the Pennsylvania Grand Encampment of 1814, and the delegates of the New England States which assembled in convention on June 16, 1816, in Philadelphia, split, and the Pennsylvania Grand Encampment charged the other delegates with seceding from the convention, while the New England delegates (consisting of Sir Knights Webb, Fowle, and Snow) reported that the reason why Pennsylvania would not enter into the union for a General Grand Encampment were: 1st, " That the Encampments in Pennsylvania avow themselves as being; in subordination to and under the Grand Lodge of Master Masons;" and 2d, "Their unwillingness to the arrangement or order of succession in conferring the degrees," as practised by the New England States," especially to the Mark and the Excellent Master, as unnecessary and not belonging to the system of Masonry." The delegates of the New England States then adjourned to meet on June 25, 1816, in New York, and there formed the present General Grand Encampment of Knights Templars of the United States.

After 1824 all the subordinate encampments ceased to labor except St John's No. 4, and she, with views as above expressed, continued to be loyal to the Grand Lodge until February 12, 1857.

In May, 1852,[281] St. John's, No. 4; Philadelphia, No. 5; Union, No. 6; and De Molay, of Reading, established a Grand Encampment, under the authority of the Grand Lodge of Pennsylvania, but the Grand Lodge on February 16, 1857, resolved (very wisely, if very late) that they had no authority over the degrees of Knighthood, but that its legitimate sphere was the primitive degrees of Ancient Craft Masonry; a union was therefore effected, and both Grand Encampments of Pennsylvania since 1857 acknowledge as their legal head the Grand Encampment of Knights Templars of the United States.

Prior to April 12, 1854, the subordinate encampments had no governing head. Their charters were derived from the General Grand Encampment of the United States, or by the authority of the Grand Lodge of Pennsylvania.

Pittsburg Encampment, No. 1; Jacques De Molay (of Washington), No. 2; and St. Omer's (of Uniontown, but afterward of Brownsville), No. 3, all were chartered by the General Grand Encampment.

Hubbard Commandery, of Waynesburg, was under Dispensation from the same body. St. John's Encampment, No. 4, derived her Charter from the Grand Encampment of 1814; Philadelphia Encampment, No. 5; Union Encampment (of Philadelphia), No. 6; and De Molay (of Reading), No. 7, were under the Grand Lodge of Pennsylvania.

It was firmly believed and maintained by the Brethren of Pennsylvania that the R. W. Grand Lodge of Pennsylvania was the source of all Masonic authority within her geographical limits, and they were sustained by reference to the fact that Templar Encampments were held under Blue Lodge Warrants; that in Ireland the Grand Encampment was formed as early as 1818, yet several encampments continued to work under their old lodge warrants, as was also the fact in Scotland and in Canada.

All encampments thus constituted in Europe were considered legal.[282]

A Warrant was issued by the General Grand Master of the General Grand Encampment, authorizing the formation of a Grand Encampment of Pennsylvania.[283] A convention met at Brownsville April 12, 1854, and organized the present Grand Commandery of

---

[281] We suppose again, May had no days then!
[282] Templarism in Pennsylvania," 2d series, p. 20.
[283] Ibid., p. 77.

Pennsylvania, subordinate to the Grand Encampment of the United States.[284]

The other encampments met in Philadelphia May 10, 1854, and organized a Grand Encampment, and after the adoption of a constitution and election and installation of officers, instructed the Grand Recorder to notify the Grand Lodge of their organization.[285]

After some time, committees of conferences having been appointed by both bodies[286] and duly considered the condition of Templary with two contending rival bodies, good counsel prevailed.

The supremacy of the General Grand Encampment was acknowledged[287] and the union was finally accomplished, which was officially proclaimed by R. E. Sir W. W. Wilson, Grand Commander of the Grand Commandery, June 1, 1857, and subsequently by M. E. Sir William B. Hubbard, Grand Master of the Grand Encampment of the United States.[288]

South Carolina.

It is claimed for South Carolina that the Templar Order was first duly organized in that State as shown in the old patent which we have previously described in Chapter LI., pages 1377-78.

In the work by Theodore S. Gourdin, from which we have quoted, we derive the principal sources of our information, and also from the address of the Grand Master of Templars to the Grand Encampment August, 1883, as well as from Companion Albert G. Mackey's History of Freemasonry in South Carolina, are we indebted for what is now considered a very near approach to the period of the introduction of the Order of the Temple, and we may, with some degree of exactness, say that an encampment did exist prior to the date of the patent referred to, which was issued August 1, 1783.

As this document has been fully described, we need not here dwell upon it, and rest the case.

The following are the commanderies now in that State, which are subordinate to the General Grand Encampment :

South Carolina, No. 1, whose original Warrant was destroyed by fire in 1843, and a dispensation was issued May 17, 1843.[289]

---

[284] Ibid., p. 127.
[285] Ibid., p. 118.
[286] Ibid., 1st series, pp. 131-35.
[287] Ibid., 2d series, p. 135.
[288] Templarism in Pennsylvania, 1st series, p. 22.
[289] Proceedings General Grand Encampment, 1844, p. 81.

On September 29, 1823, a Charter of Recognition was issued, as the encampment had been working for many years prior to the organization of the General Grand Encampment.[290]

Columbia No. 2, at Columbia; dispensation June 11, 1875; chartered August 30, 1877.[291]

A previous Charter of Recognition had been issued January 24, 1824.[292]

Spartanburg, No. 3, at Spartanburg; dispensation granted October 1, 1891; chartered August 29, 1895.

Note. - There was an encampment named LaFayette at Georgetown chartered March, 1825,[293] but there is no further notice of it in the Proceedings and it is not now in existence.

---

[290] Ibid., p. 21.
[291] Ibid., 1877, p. 192.
[292] Ibid., p. 20.
[293] Ibid., p. 20.

South Dakota.

The Grand Commandery of South Dakota was constituted May 14, 1884; being within the boundaries of the State of South Dakota, it continues under the name and style of the Grand Commandery of South Dakota.[294]

Tennessee.

The Grand Commandery of Tennessee was constituted October 11 1859.

Approved September 16, 1859.
The subordinate commanderies were:
Dispensation.
Dispensation
Chartered Nashville, No. 1, at Nashville... Between 1844-47.
September 14, 1847 Yorkville, No. 2, at Yorkville.... July 10, 1857.
September 17, 1859 De Molay, No. 3, at Columbia.... December 20, 1859.
September 16, 1859 Cyrene, No. 4, at Memphis........ March 27, 1859.
September 16, 1859

Texas.

The Grand Commandery of Texas was constituted January 18, 1855.

A Warrant had been issued by the General Grand Master to form and establish this Grand Encampment December 31, 1853.[295]

The subordinate commanderies were San Filipe de Austin, No, 1, at Galveston, by Charter December 10, 1835.

Ruthven No. 2, Houston; by dispensation February 2, 1848, and Charter September 11, 1850.

Palestine, No. 3, at Palestine; by dispensation May 16, 1853, and Charter September 19, 1853.

Utah.

The following subordrate conmmanderies were organized in Utah under warrants from the General Grand Encampment:

Utah, No. 1, at Salt Lake City; dispensation granted December 20, 1873, chartered December 3, 1874.

---

[294] Proceedings General Grand Encampment, 1892, p. 41.
[295] Ibid., 185, p.248.

El Monte, No. 2, at Ogden; had a dispensation granted October 22, 1885, which was opened November 11, 1885; chartered September 23, 1886.

Vermont.
The Grand Encampment of Vermont was constituted August 14, 1851.[296]

December, 1850, consent was given to three encampments to form a Grand Commandery.

Vermont, at Windsor; chartered February 23, 1821.

Green Mountain, at Rutland; chartered March 12, 1823.

Mount Calvary, at Middlebury; chartered February 24, 1824.

Burlington, No. 2, at Burlington; dispensation June 28, 1849 chartered September 17, 1850.

LaFayette, No. 4, at Berkshire; dispensation November 9 1850; old Charter endorsed October 27, 1853.

Calvary, at Middlebury; old Charter of Mount Calvary renewed

Virginia.
The Grand Encampment of Virginia was constituted November 27, 1823.

The history of the old encampments is very interesting, but is too lengthy for our pages. (See Proceedings of General Grand Encampment.) The subordinate encampments in the State were:

Richmond, at Richmond; chartered May 5, 1823.

Warren, at Harper's Ferry; chartered July 4, 1824.

Winchester, at Winchester; chartered July 4, 1824.

These three encampments were erased September 17, 1847.[297]

Wheeling, No. 1, at Wheeling; dispensation issued August 31, 1838, and afterward extended six months.

It appears from all that can be learned in the Proceedings of the General Grand Encampment from 1823, that the Grand Encampment of Virginia, which in the Proceedings is only recorded as having been organized "prior to 1826," did not continue very long.

The encampments at Richmond, Harper's Ferry, and Winchester, two of which held charters of recognition, and one of constitution from the General Grand Encampment, the report of a

---

[296] The Table in Proceedings of General Grand Encampment for 1895 says June 27, 1824

[297] Proceedings of General Grand Encampment, 1847, p. 110.

committee in 1847[298] says: "About 1826 these three Encampments formed a Grand Encampment for the State, which, in that year, was represented in the General Grand Encampment (Sir James Cushman).[299]

"Nothing further is known of this Grand Encampment, but it is presumed to have ceased to exist soon after its organization; for it appears that in 1858 a dispensation, and subsequently a Charter, was granted by this General Grand Encampment to a commandery to be located at Wheeling in that State.

Matters continued in this condition until this 11th of December, 1845, when delegates from sundry Encampments, including the three owing their allegiance to the General Grand Body, met at Richmond, and having resolved that it was impossible to revive the extinct Grand Encampment, proceeded to form a new one for the State.

"Such is a brief Statement of the facts.

Your Committee are of the Opinion that when the original Grand Encampment of Virginia ceased to exist, jurisdiction over the State reverted to this body.[300]

"And this seems to have been the view entertained in 1838, when this General Grand Encampment established an Encampment at Wheeling.

"They are also of the opinion that immediate jurisdiction over, at least, the three Subordinate Encampments, which derived their authority from this body, also reverted to its original source.

This being true, there was no power vested in the Subordinate Encampments in Virginia to organize a Grand Encampment without the consent of the General Grand Encampment as provided by this Constitution.

This consent or approval was never obtained or even asked for.

"It follows therefore, that the body now existing, and styling itself the Grand Encampment of Virginia, is irregular and unauthorized.

It refuses alilegiatice to this General Grand Encampment, and denies its authority in the State of Virginia."

In 1871, at the Tiennial Encampment, a memorial from the Grand Commandery of Virginia was presented by Sir Knights W. B, Isaacs and R. E. Withers "Asking leave to withdraw from the jurisdiction of the Grand Encampment of the United States." The memorial is quite too lengthy for our pages.

This was referred to a committee of three.

---

[298] Ibid., 1847, p. 119
[299] Proceedings of General Grand Encampment, 1826, p. 9.
[300] Proceedings, 1871, pp. 175 to 180.

This committee made a lengthy report, in which they answered the reasons for a separation as set forth in the memorial, and presented the following:

"Resolved, That the Grand Encampment entertaining for the Grand Commandery of Virginia the most courteous and friendly feeling of fraternal brotherhood, and being anxious to preserve intact the knightly array of the constituent Grand Commanderies and to continue to preserve the good, well-being, and perpetuation of 'Templar Masonry,' does decline and refuse 'to allow the Grand Commandery of Virginia, in peace, in honor, and in recognition, to withdraw from the jurisdiction of the Grand Encampment' as prayed for in its memorial.

Respectfully submitted by the Committee, "THEODORE S. PARVIN, "CHARLES W. WOODRUFF, " RICHARD F. KNOTT."

N.B. - Subsequently Sir Knight Isaacs was made the General Grand Recorder, and Sir Knight Withers the General Grand Master, of the General Grand Encampment.

Washington Territory.

The Grand Commandery was organized June 2, 1887.

Washington Commandery, No. 1, at Walla Walla; dispensation issued April 19, 1882, and a Charter was granted August 23, 1883.

Seattle, No. 2, had a dispensation issued February 22, 1883, and was chartered August 23, 1883.

Cataract, No. 3, at Spokane, had a dispensation issued to it July 30, 1885, and was organized August 14, 1885; and chartered September 23, 1886.

Ivanhoe, No. 4, at Tacoma; a dispensation was issued March 23, 1886; formed April 27, 1886, and chartered September 23, 1886.

West Virginia.

West Virginia was a part of the State of Virginia until June 20, 1863. As we have shown under Virginia, the Grand Encampment was organized November 27, 1823, and from October, 1824, under various changes, and frequently being dormant for years, and having no communion with the majority of Templars of the General Grand Body, that Grand Encampment, now Commandery, has existed as under and by virtue of the constitution of the Grand Encampment of the United States.

It has exercised exclusive jurisdiction over the territory now included in the State of West Virginia, with a single exception under the constitution of the Grand Encampment of the United States.

The Grand Commandery of Virginia continued to exercise jurisdiction over it the same as theretofore.

In the list of its subordinate commanderies, the Grand Commandery of Virginia classed Wheeling, No. 1; Palestine, No. 9, at Martinsburg; Star of the West, No. 12, at Morgantown, and in 1868 a dispensation was issued by the Grand Commander of Virginia for a new commandery at Monongahela,[301] all in West Virginia.

After the formation of West Virginia State the Grand Encampment did not claim the commanderies therein as its immediate subordinates, nor exercised any power in West Virginia hostile to the jurisdictional claim of the Grand Commandery of Virginia.[302] The Grand Commandery of West Virginia was organized by P.G.M. James H. Hopkins, February 25, 1874. In the history of the Grand Commandery of Virginia we have shown the subordinate commanderies which were located in the present State of West Virginia, viz., Warren, at Harper's Ferry; Winchester, at Winchester; and Wheeling, No. 1, at Wheeling.

Wisconsin.

The Grand Commandery of Wisconsin was organized October 20, 1859.

Wisconsin, No. 1; dispensation, no date found, and Charter granted September 11, 1850.

Note. - We have been unable to find any reference in the Proceedings of the General Grand Encampment prior to 1859 of any other encampment in Wisconsin.

Wyoming.

The Grand Commandery of Wyoming was organized by authority of the General Grand Encampment September 23, 1886, and constituted March 8, 1888.

---

[301] Proceedings, 1871, p. 55.
[302] Ibid., P. 56.

The constituent commanderies were:

Place	Dispensation.
Charter Wyoming, No. 1 Cheyenne	March 5, 1873. December 3, 1874
Ivanhoe, No. 2 Rawlins	February 9, 1885. February 16, 1885 September 23, 1886
Immanuel No. 3 Laramie	May 1, 1886. May 18, 1886. September 23, 1886

CHAPTER LIX

HISTORY OF COLOURED MASONRY IN THE UNITED STATES

The action taken by the Grand Lodge of the State of Washington, wherein the legality of the organization of Prince Hall Lodge was duly recognized, renders it proper that, in the history of Masonry in the United States, some notice should be taken of that lodge and its successors in the present work.

In our examination of this matter we have found the subject so well treated by the Grand Master of the Grand Lodge of Massachusetts, Brother William Sewell Gardner, in an address delivered before that Grand Lodge, in 1870, that we shall use the same as a foundation, and largely as the structure of this article, for the reason that he has fully and thoroughly covered the entire ground and answered all the arguments employed by the fiends of that famous body of negro Masons, within the years 1898 and 1899 in almost every Grand Lodge in the United States, by the Grand Masters, and committees appointed, to respond to the action of the Grand Lodge of Washington in 1898, who have clearly set forth their views, in opposition to the recognition of negro Masonry in this country.

The views set forth in this address have been referred to by most of those writers and there is nothing new for the present writer to urge in opposition to recognition.

In his own response in the report on correspondence in the "Annual Proceedings of the Grand Lodge of the District of Columbia," for the year 1898, one point insisted upon by him was, that the charters of the Grand Lodge of England issued to Military Lodges did not authorize said lodges to make Masons of citizens in any country where there were already duly constituted lodges under Grand Lodge jurisdiction.

The argument used was, that a lodge could not go beyond the letter and terms of the Charter by whose authority it worked.

We laid this down as a necessary and fundamental principle, and we have been pleased to notice very many of our correspondents agree with us in that position; and finding that Grand Master Gardner uses the same point, we have thought it best to follow out his address as being more comprehensive and more strictly adhering to the true history of the first introduction of this foul blot upon the escutcheon of our Masonry, all through its succeeding ramifications, and subsequent discoloring of our fair fame and otherwise pure record in the United States.

It is due to our Brethren in Washington to say, that when it became known to the Craft at large in that State that the movement, on the part of their leading men, thus to drag in the dust the proud banner of Masonry had aroused the ire of every Grand Lodge in the country, at the succeeding Communication in June, 1899, the obnoxious resolutions were annulled and former harmonious and cordial relations have been restored.

We now proceed to use Brother Gardner's admirable address to give a true history of Prince Hall Lodge:

Address.

BRETHREN: In the Grand Lodge of New Hampshire, at its session held at Manchester on the 18th of June, 1869, "the Committee on Foreign Correspondence offered their report, and, on motion, it was voted, That the reading of the report be dispensed with, and that it be published with the printed proceedings."

In this report the following statements are made:

"In Massachusetts there was no legal Grand Lodge till the Union in 1792."

"The American doctrine of Grand Lodge jurisdiction has grown up since" the establishment of the African Lodge at Boston, by authority of a Charter from the Grand Lodge of England, "and is not elsewhere fully received even now; besides, there was then no Grand Lodge of Massachusetts, or in that State, whose rights could be interfered with; for, notwithstanding the claim to antiquity of that Grand Lodge, it was not formed till 1792, and the two Provincial Grand Lodges, before existing in that Colony, both expired in 1775 by the death of their Provincial Grand Masters.

The Massachusetts Grand Lodge did not pretend to meet after the death of Warren, and although St. John's Grand Lodge did have some sort of meetings, probably no law that ever existed in Masonry anywhere would hold such meetings regular."

If this report had been read to the Grand Lodge of New Hampshire, its venerable Past Grand Masters, Israel Hunt and Horace Chase, then present, could have informed the Committee on Foreign Correspondence that they were treading upon dangerous ground, and alluding to a delicate subject.

The Grand Lodge of New Hampshire was organized on the 8th of July, 1789, by four Deputies from St. John's Lodge of Portsmouth, chartered by the Massachusetts "St. John's Grand Lodge" June 24, 1734, and one Deputy from Rising Sun Lodge of Keene, chartered by the "Massachusetts Grand Lodge" March 5, 1784 - five Deputies from two Lodges.

All Masonic authorities claim that, to organize a legitimate Grand Lodge, there must be present the representatives of "not less than three Lodges holding Charters or Warrants from some legal Grand Lodge."

All the Lodges in New Hampshire existing prior to the year 1790, with the single exception of St. John's of Portsmouth, received their Charters from the "Massachusetts Grand Lodge."

St. Patrick's was chartered and established at Portsmouth, March 17, 1780.

It continued in existence until the latter part of the year 1790, when it ceased working, most of its members joining St. John's Lodge, which was revived about that time.

It never acknomledged the jurisdiction of the Grand Lodge of New Hampshire.

November 8, 1781, the "Massachusetts Grand Lodge" chartered a Lodge at Cornish, then claimed to be a part of Vermont, but now set off to New Hampshire.

It met at Cornish a few times, and when Cornish was decided to be in New Hampshire, it moved to Windsor, Vt., on the opposite side of the Connecticut River, and took the name of Vermont Lodge, No. 1.

Rising Sun, of Keene, well known as the Lodge which gave Masonic light to Thomas Smith Webb, was chartered by the "Massachusetts Grand Lodge" March 5, 1784.

It surrendered its Charter to the Grand Lodge of New Hampshire August 3, 1792, and received a new one with the same name, and rank No. 3.

The "Massachusetts Grand Lodge" granted a Charter for a Lodge at Charlestown by the name of "Faithful Lodge, No. 27," February 22, 1788.

This Charter was surrendered to the Grand Lodge of New Hampshire April 30, 1800, and a new one given, by which it was styled "Faithful Lodge, No. 12."

Dartmouth Lodge, of Hanover, received a Charter from "the Massachusetts Grand Lodge" December 18, 1788, and was the last Lodge chartered by this Grand Lodge in New Hampshire.

Its dissolution took place before it acknowledged the jurisdiction of the Grand Lodge of that State.

The Grand Secretary, Horace Chase, says, that when the Grand Lodge of New Hampshire was formed, July 8, 1789, "as appears from the record there were but three Lodges in the State, viz., St. John's and St. Patrick's at Portsmouth, and Rising Sun at Keene."

However irregularly organized the Grand Lodge of New Hampshire may have been the "Massachusetts Grand Lodge" disclaimed jurisdiction in that State thereafter.

It is unnecessary to state that this Grand Lodge, since 1789 to the present time, has been on the most friendly and fraternal relations with our sister Grand Lodge of New Hampshire, and that it will require something more than unauthorized and unconfirmed statements of a Committee on Foreign Correspondence to unsettle these pleasant relations.

Nevertheless, when it is pretended before a body of such great respectability as the Grand Lodge of New Hampshire, that, in 1784, when it is said the "African Lodge" in Boston obtained its Charter in England, there was no existing Grand Lodge in Massachusetts, for the purpose of proving the then and present legitimacy of the African Lodge, and of adding the weight and influence of the Grand Lodge of New Hampshire to this pretense, it is due to ourselves, and to the Craft universal, that the truth should be fully known and fearlessly spoken.

The time is propitious to meet this false pretense, and I need but resume the history of the "Massachusetts Grand Lodge" where it was left at its Centennial on the recent Feast of St. John the Evangelist.

The system of Provincial Grand Lodges originated in the Grand Lodge of England in 1726, and arose from the necessity of having, in the distant colonies of Great Britain where Masonry has extended, some authority and power, not only to control and govern the Craft, but also to establish new Lodges in the Provinces.

The Provincial Grand Master was appointed by commission of the Grand Master, wherein the extent of his powers was set forth, and by virtue of which he convened his Grand Body.

In the language of early days, this commission was styled a Deputation, and this word conveys the true idea of the Provincials' position.

It was a Deputy Grand Lodge, with its various Deputy Grand Officers, convened by the power and authoity of the Provincial Grand Master as the Deputy of the Grand Master.

It possessed no sovereign power.

The Lodges under the jurisdiction of the Provincial Grand Master were not necessarily registered in his Grand Lodge.

They were returned to England, registered in the Grand Lodge there, and classified as we do our Lodges at the present day, as belonging to a certain District or Province.

The Provincial Grand Master had power to appoint a Deputy and commission him, who in the absence, sickness, and disability of his chief, assumed his functions.

The Grand Wardens and other officers he also had the exclusive right to appoint, although sometimes he nominated brethren to these offices and permitted the Grand Lodge to elect them.

Each Lodge in the Province had the right of representation in the Provincial Grand Lodge, by its Master and Wardens or by a regularly appointed representative, and the expenses of the Grand Body were assessed upon the various subordinates.

The right of appeal existed from every act and decision of the Provincial Grand Master or Grand Lodge, to the Grand Master of England, thus making the Provincial and his Grand Lodge subordinate to the power by which they were created.

The allegiance of the Lodges and of the Craft was to the Grand Lodge of England, and to the Provincial Grand Lodge and Grand Master, through the parent Body.

There was no direct allegiance to the Provincial from the Craft.

It was a temporary power which he held ex gratis, and of which he could be deprived at the pleasure of the Grand Master by whom he was appointed.

Thus it will be seen that the Provincial Grand Master was appointed for the convenience of the administration of the affairs of the Grand Lodge of England in distant parts, in the same manner that our District Deputies are appointed at the present time.

The powers, however, in the one case, were more extended than they are in the other.

The means of communication with London were not so easy and rapid as now, and the distance from the Grand East required that some officer should be stationed here, who should be invested with authority for sudden emergencies and instant action.

The Provincial Grand Master having been regularly commissioned and installed, could not resign his trust to his Provincial Grand Lodge.

That Body had no power to accept it.

His resignation must be made to the Grand Master from whom he received his commission.

The Provincial Grand Lodge was the creation of the Provincial Grand Master, and was wholly under his direction and control.

He appointed its officers, and summoned the representatives of the Lodges to assemble in Grand Lodge.

In this Grand Lodge there was no inherent power, save what it derived from the Provincial Grand Master, by virtue of his delegated authority, thus making it the very reverse of a Sovereign Grand Lodge, the Grand Master of which derives his authority from the Sovereign Body by whose votes he is elected to office, and over which he presides.

The Grand Master appointing his Provincial, could annul the commission at his will and pleasure.

The officer being created by the pleasure of the Grand Master of England, all the adjuncts, appointees, and creations of the office depended upon the same pleasure, and existed during the will of the appointing power. If a Provincial Grand Master was removed, and his commission recalled, and the Grand Master declined to appoint his successor, it is clear that the Provincial Grand Lodge established by virtue of such commission would cease to exist.

Such a Grand Lodge never possessed any vitality which would survive the life of the commission appointing the Provincial Grand Master.

The death of the Provincial would also lead to the same result.

The commission to him from the Grand Master would lose all its force upon his decease.

Whatever act the Provincial performed, he did by virtue of the commission to him.

His Deputy Grand Master and Grand Wardens, appointed by trim, and not by the Grand Master of England, nor by his confirmation, derived their power and character as Grand Officers from the Provincial, and when the Provincial expired, their tenure of office expired also.

To show that these conclusions are correct, I will refer to the authorities.

The office of Provincial Grand Master was established by the Grand Lodge of England, as has already been stated, in 1726, and the first Deputation was granted May 10, 1727.

Preston says of the office, at this date: "A Provincial Grand Master in that district over which he is limited to preside, and being invested with the power and honor of a Deputy Grand Master in his Province, may constitute Lodges therein, if the consent of the Masters and Wardens of three Lodges already constituted within his District have been obtained, and the Grand Lodge in London has not disapproved thereof. He wears the clothing of a Grand Officer, and ranks, in all public assemblies, immediatetly after Past Deputy Grand Master. He must, in person or by deputy, attend the quarterly meetings of the Masters and Wardens of the Lodges in his District, and transmit to the Grand Lodge, once in every year, the proceedings of those meetings, with a regular statement of the Lodges under his jurisdiction."

Speaking of the year 1737, he says: "The authority granted by patent to a Provincial Grand Master was limited to one year from his first public appearance in that character within his Province; and if at the expiration of that period, a new election of the Lodges under his jurisdiction did not take place, subject to the approbation of the Grand Master, the patent was no longer valid.

Hence we find, within the course of a few years, different appointments to the same station; but the office is now permanent, and the sole appointment of the Grand Master."

In Entick's Constitutions of 1756 there is a section entitled "Of Provincial Grand Masters," which is as follows:

"Art. 1. The office of Provincial Grand Master was found particularly necessary in the year 1726; when the extraordinary increase of the Craftsmen, and their traveling into distant parts, and convening themselves into Lodges, required an immediate Head, to whom they might apply in all Cases, where it was not possible to wait the Decision or Opinion of the Grand Lodge.

"Art. 2. The appointment of this Grand Officer is a Prerogative of the Grand Master: who grants his Deputation to such Brother of Eminence and Ability in the Craft, as he shall think proper: not for life, but during his good Pleasure.

"Art. 3. The Provincial thus deputed, is invested with the Power and Honor of a Deputy Grand Master; and during the continuance of his Provincialship, is entitled to wear the Clothing, to take rank as the Grand Officers, in all publick Assemblies, immediately after the past Deputy Grand Masters: and to constitute Lodges within his own Province.

"Art. 4. He is enjoined to correspond with the Grand Lodge, and to transmit a circumstantial Account of his Proceedings, at least once in every Year.

At which Times, the Provincial is required to send a List of those Lodges he has constituted for the general Fund of Charity: and the usual demand, as specified in his Deputation, for every Lodge he has constituted by the Grand Master's Authority."

The Constitutions of the United Grand Lodge of England have been more particular in specifying the powers, duties, and prerogatives of the Provincial Grand Master and Grand Lodge.

I will refer to a single Section of these Constitutions:

"The Provincial Grand Lodge emanates from the authority vested in the Provincial Grand Master, and possesses no other powers than those specified.

It therefore follows that no Provincial Grand Lodge can meet but by the sanction of the Provincial Grand Master or his Deputy; and that it ceases to exist on the death, resignation, suspension, or removal of the Provincial Grand Master, until some Brother is duly appointed or empowered to perform the functions of Provincial Grand Master, by whose authority the Provincial Grand Lodge may be again established."

In Scotland this office was created in 1738, and the first nomination made abroad in 1747.

In November, 1757, R.W. Col. John Young was appointed Provincial Grand Master over all the Lodges in America holding of the Grand Lodge of Scotland, and in 1768 James Grant, Governor of the Province of East Florida, was appointed Provincial Grand Master of North America, Southern District.

The commissions were issued "to continue in force until recalled." In 1800 a series of regulations for the government of these officers were sanctioned by the Grand Lodge, previous to which time it is presumed that they were governed by the same rules and regulations as in England.

More recently, the "Laws and Constitutions of the Grand Lodge" have provided that the "meeting of the Provincial Grand Lodges shall not be interrupted by the death or retirement of the Provincial

Grand Master, unless the Grand Lodge shall not deem it expedient within the space of one year to appoint another.

A Provincial Grand Lodge not assembling for the space of two years, also becomes dormant, and has no power again to call meetings, unless empowered by the Provincial Grand Master, or by the order of the Grand Lodge or Grand Committee" - "When a Provincial Grand Lodge becomes dormant the Lodges in the District come under the immediate supervision of the Grand Lodge and Grand Committee."

These new rules and regulations were made to prevent the disruption of the Provincial Grand Lodges, which was inevitable upon the decease of the Provincial Grand Master.

In Ireland the same system has existed as in England and Scotland.

The present Constitutions provided that, "if the Provincial Grand Master die, resign, or be removed, the authority of the Provincial Deputy Grand Master shall continue for six months after, or until a successor to the Provincial Grand Master be appointed, but such authority of the Provincial Deputy Grand Master shall not continue longer, unless he be re-appointed."

If these authorities support the position taken, and if the conclusions arrived at are correct, it follows beyond all controversy that when Provincial Grand Master Joseph Warren expired on Bunker Hill, June 17, 1775, the Provincial Grand Lodge, of which he was the essence and life, expired also, and with it all the offices of which it was composed.

The Lodges established by him, and by the Grand Lodge of Scotland, were not affected thereby, as has already appeared.

They were, or should have been, registered in Edinburgh, and owed their allegiance to the Grand Lodge there.

The conclusion of the Eulogy pronounced by Br. Perez Morton at the re-interment of Joseph Warren, April 8, 1776, was devoted to the subject of independence, which was then agitating the Colonies.

Some of the language made use of by him upon this occasion seems to foreshadow the Masonic independence of Massachusetts, which was soon to follow. "Now is the happy time," said he, "to seize again those rights which, as men, we are by nature entitled to, and which by contract we never have, and never could have, surrendered."

On the 4th of July following, "The Declaration of Independence" was, by order of Congress, engrossed and signed, by which the United Colonies declared themselves to be free and independent States.

The effect of this declaration upon the Colonies I need not allude to; Massachusetts, by virtue of its claim, became a free, independent, sovereign State and the spirit of freedom and independence of Great Britain became infused into every organization and society which before this were bound and dependent.

It was an absolute revolution, by which a dependent colony became revolutionized into an independent State.

The idea of a permanent union of the States had then hardly been broached.

They had united for defence against a common foe, and had set themselves up as independent States, not only independent of Great Britain, but independent of each other.

Isolated from all the world, they each stood forth free, independent, sovereign States.

The Institution of Freemasonry, which numbered among its firmest adherents such revolutionists as Webb, Revere, Morton, and a host of others who followed in the footsteps of Warren, could not long withstand the influence of freedom, and Massachusetts set the example of a revolution in Masonic government, which has been followed successfully by every State in the Union.

It has become the American system, or, as the committee of New Hampshire call it, "The American Doctrine of Grand Lodge Jurisdiction," respected and recognized by the Masonic Fraternity the world over.

It had its birth on Bunker Hill, when the patriot Warren poured out his life's blood:

"The Patriot Grand Master, who fell in his might- The second of three - in defence of the right!"

"The American Doctrine of Grand Lodge jurisdiction," briefly stated, is this: "Three regularly-chartered Lodges existing in any State or Territory have the right to establish a Grand Lodge therein. Such Grand Lodge, when lawfully organized, has sole, absolute, and exclusive jurisdiction over the three degrees of Craft Masonry; over the Lodges and their Members; and over all Masons, unaffiliated as well as affiliated, in such State or Territory.

No other Grand Lodge whatever can lawfully interfere with this jurisdiction, and can neither establish Lodges in such State, nor continue any authority over Bodies which it might properly have exercised prior to the organization of such Grand Lodge therein."

By the erection of a Grand Lodge in such State, all Masonic powers over what is popularly called Blue Masonry are merged in it, and henceforth it exists therein supreme and sovereign over a jurisdiction which it can neither divide nor share with any other Masonic Grand Body in the world.

The several States of the United States of America, the Territories, when legally organized as such by Congress, and the District of Columbia, are each recognized as separate and independent jurisdictions in which Grand Lodges may be established.

This is the American doctrine, most religiously and masonically adhered to by the Craftsmen of the United States, and which our brethren upon the other side of the Atlantic must accede to, recognize, and support.

After the Declaration hereinafter referred to, made by the Massachusetts Grand Lodge, December 6, 1782, treaty stipulations were entered into by the several Grand Lodges then in existence, in confirmation of the action of Massachusetts.

The following preamble and resolutions were adopted by the Grand Lodge of New York:

"Whereas, The Grand Lodge of the State of Massachusetts have by a communication, dated the 4th of January last, suggested to this Grand Lodge the propriety of adopting a resolution declaring that no Charter or Dispensation for holding a Lodge be issued by any Grand Lodge to any number of Masons residing out of the State wherein the Grand Lodge is established, be it therefore

"Resolved and declared by this Grand Lodge, that no Charter or Dispensation for holding a Lodge of Masons shall be granted to any person or persons whatever, residing out of this State and within the jurisdiction of any other Grand Lodge."

The Grand Lodges of the United States have uniformly resisted every encroachment upon the jurisdiction of the several Grand Lodges."

The Feast of St. John the Evangelist, in 1776, was celebrated, and the record shows that a Grand Lodge was held by thirty-three brethren, Joseph Webb presiding as Deputy Grand Master.

A Grand Lodge was called by the Deputy of Warren, February 14, 1777, to hear the petition for a Charter at Stockbridge, of brethren in Berkshire County.

This proposition aroused the brethren to a realizing sense of their status and condition as a Grand Lodge.

They were doubtful of its power, as then organized, to grant the Charter prayed for.

The petition was accordingly laid over to Friday evening, March the 7th next, and it was " Voted, That the Deputy Grand Master should send a summons to all the Masters and Wardens under the jurisdiction to assemble on the 7th March, in order to consult upon, and to elect, a Grand Master for this State, in the room of our late worthy Grand Master Warren, deceased."

On the 7th of March the brethren met, and adjourned until the following evening. March 8, 1777, the following brethren assembled, representing St.

Andrew's Lodge, of Boston, Tyrian Lodge, of Gloucester, and St. Peter's Lodge, of Newburyport:
R.W. Joseph Webb, D.G.M., of St. Andrew's Lodge, Boston.
Paul Revere, S.G.W., of St. Andrew's Lodge, Boston.
Thomas Crafts, J.G.W., of St. Andrew's Lodge, Boston.
John Lowell, G. Treas., of St. Andrew's Lodge, Boston.
Nat. Peirce, G. Sec. pro tem., of St. Andrew's Lodge, Boston.
Thomas Urann, S.G.D., of St. Andrew's Lodge, Boston.
Edward Proctor, J.G.D., of St. Andrew's Lodge, Boston. Moses Deshon, P.M., of Tydan Lodg, Gloucester.
Philip Marett, G. St'd, of Tyrian Lodge, Gloucester.
S.W. of St Andrew's Lodge Boston.
Wintrop Grey, G. St'd, of Tyrian Lodge, Gloucester.
S.W. of St Andrew's Lodge Boston.
Wm. Greenough, M., of St Peter's Lodge Newburyport.
The brethren then unanimously elected a Grand Master, Grand Wardens, and other Grand Officers.
Joseph Webb was chosen Grand Master.

The Grand Lodge then acted upon the petition for a new Lodge at Stockbridge, and granted the same; this being the first act of the Independent Grand Lodge.

Massachusetts Lodge, of Boston, was not represented at this meeting; but, on the 18th of December, 1778, it petitioned the Grand Lodge, "setting forth that the exigency of the times would not admit of their assembling sooner, and praying said Lodge may retain the rank they formerly held under the Grand Lodge," which was granted.

All the Lodges under the old Provincial Grand Lodge of Warren, with the exception of Massachusetts, united in forming the independent Grand Lodge, and they forthwith yielded allegiance to it.

However, but few of the Lodges in Massachusetts at this time, were in a condition to hold meetings, by reason of "the exigency of the times."

The record of the meeting setting up the Independent Grand Lodge contains no account of the motives and incentives which gave rise to this action.

Grand Master Joseph Webb sent the following letter to the Grand Lodge of Georgia, which has recently been discovered by R.W. Br. I.E. Blackshear, Grand Secretary of that State:

"BOSTON, March 2, 1787.

"To the Right Worshipful, the Grand Master, Dep. G.M., G. Wardens, and Brethren of the Grand Lodge of Savannah in Georgia, greeting.

"GENTLEMEN AND BRETHREN: Having lately seen the Southern papers, that you had at last assumed to your selves the undoubted right of Forming a Grand Lodge in your State, I Congratulate you on so Important an acquisition, and wish you all the success imaginable: we, in this Common Wealth, assumed the same so early as 1777, since w'ch I find Pennsilvania and N. York have adopted; but how they have proceeded at Charleston or Virginia I have not as yet heard.

I hold a correspondence with those 2 Lodges, and should be glad of the same with you, and all in the Union at least.

Since our adopting, we have had 25 Lodges under the jurisdiction (tho' some of them Charters of Dispensation, in Connecticut, Vermont, N. Hampshire), until they appoint a G. Lodge of their own.

Inclosed, I have taken the freedom to send you the Regulations of our G. Lodge, w'ch you'l please to accept as a small token of my Respect.

So, wishing the Grand Lodge in particular, and those under your jurisdiction in general, all that Universal Benevolence, Brotherly Love, and Truth : Adieu! I remain with sincerity, your unknown tho' affectionate Brother and H'ble Serv.

"JOS. WEBB, G.M. Com. Wealt Massachusetts." (Received 27th April.)

Josiah Bartlett, afterward Grand Master, in an address before the Grand Lodge, said:

"How to assemble the Grand Lodge with regularity, was now made a serious question, as the commission of the Grand Master had died with him, and the Deputy had no power independent of his nomination and appointment.

"Communications for the consideration of this subject were held at different times, till the 8th of March, 1777, when, experiencing the necessity of preserving the intercourse of the brethren, and the want of a proper establishment to soften the rigors of an active and distressing war, they proceeded to the formation of an Independent Grand Lodge, with 'powers and preyogatives to be exercised on principles consistent with and subordinate to the regulations pointed out in the Constitutions of Ancient Masonry,' and our late worthy and Most Worshipful Brother, Joseph Webb, Esquire, whose amiable deportment and fidelity in the duties of his important office now claim our grateful remembrance, was duly elected Grand Master, and proceeded to install his officers, and organize the Grand Lodge."

Thaddeus M. Harris, who compiled the Constitutions in 1792, referring to this act of independence, quotes the above extract from Bartlett's address, and, in a foot-note, says that "the general regulations from Entick's Constitutions were adopted and practiced; except that the Grand Master and Wardens were elected by a ballot at large.

The other officers were appointed by the Grand Master."

The record itself, of December 6, 1782, recies the facts:

"Charters were not only granted for establishing Lodges in Massachusetts, but also in other States.

But anticipating that the independent government organized in this State would be followed by the Craft elsewhere, it was determined that all Charters granted without the limits of Massachusetts should be in force only until a Grand Lodge was formed in such State or Country where such Lodges were held.

Upon these conditions Lodges were established in New Hampshire, Vermont, Connecticut, and New York, prior to December, 1782."

"In October, 1778, it was voted that a Charter be granted to a traveling Lodge in the American army, to make Masons, pass, and raise, in this State, or any of the United States of America, where no other Grand Master presides.

But in any other State where there is a Grand Master constituted by the brethren of these United States, they are to inform him, and receive his sanction."

In September, 1780, the Grand Master "laid before the Grand Lodge a letter dated Philadelphia, August 19, 1780, signed William Smith, Grand Secretary, inclosing a printed list of the several Lodges in Pennsylvania under that jurisdiction, and advising that they had, in that Grand Lodge, thought it expedient to make choice of a Grand Master General, for the thirteen United American States; that they had nominated His Excellency General George Washington, and requesting the opinion and approbation of this Grand Lodge thereon."

"Circular letters were sent to the several Lodges under the jurisdiction requesting the attendance of the Masters and Wardens at the Grand Lodge, for the purpose of considering this proposition.

Brother Perez Morton was strongly in favor of the project, but the Grand Lodge Voted, That any determination upon the subject cannot, with the propriety and justice due to the Craft at large, be made by this Grand Lodge, until a general peace shall happily take place through the continent, inasmuch as the sentiments of the various Grand Lodges in the United States upon this question could not be made known under the peculiar circumstances of public affairs."

On the 10th of July, 1782, it was "Voted, That a committee be appointed to draw resolutions explanatory of the powers and authority of this Grand Lodge, respecting the extent and meaning of its jurisdiction, and of the exercise of any other masonic authorities within its jurisdiction." Brothers Perez Morton, Paul Revere, John Warren, James Avery, and John Juteau were appointed upon the committee.

A special meeting of the Grand Lodge was called to receive the report, September 30, 1782, when it was read and referred to the next meeting.

December 6, 1782, in a full Grand Lodge, it was considered.

This interesting report, omitting the formal introduction, is as follows:

"The Commission from the Grand Lodge of Scotland granted to our late Grand Master, Joseph Warren, Esquire, having died with him, and of course his deputy, whose appointment was derived from his nomination, being no longer in existence, they saw themselves without a head, and without a single Grand Officer, and of course it was evident that not only the Grand Lodge, but all the particular Lodges under its jurisdiction, must cease to assemble, the brethren be dispersed, the penniless go unassisted, the Craft languish, and ancient Masonry be extinct in this part of the world.

"That in consequence of a summons from the former Grand Wardens to the Masters and Wardens of all the regular constituted Lodges, a Grand Communication was held to consult and advise on some means to preserve the intercourse of the brethren.

"That the Political Head of this country, having destroyed all connection and correspondence between the subjects of these States and the country from which the Grand Lodge originally derived its commissioned authority, and the principles of the Craft, inculcating on its professors submission to the commands of the civil authority of the country they reside in, the brethren did assume an elective supremacy, and under it chose a Grand Master and Grand Officers, and erected a Grand Lodge with independent powers and prerogatives, to be exercised, however, on principles consistent with and subordinate to the regulations pointed out in the Constitution of Ancient Masonry.

"That the reputation and utility of the Craft, under their jurisdiction, has been most extensively diffused, by the flourishing state of fourteen Lodges constituted by their authority within a shorter period than that in which three only received Dispensations under the former Grand Lodge.

"That in the history of our Craft we find that in England there are two Grand Lodges, independent of each other; in Scotland the same, and in Ireland their Grand Lodge and Grand Master are independent either of England or Scotland.

It is clear that the authority of some of their Grand Lodges originated in assumption, or otherwise they would acknowledge the head from whence they derived.

"Your committee are therefore of opinion that the doings of the present Grand Lodge were dictated by principles of the clearest necessity, founded in the highest reason, and warranted by precedents of the most approved authority.

"And they beg leave to recommend the following resolutions, to be adopted by the Grand Lodge and engrafted into its Constitutions:

"I. That the brethren of the Grand Lodge, in assuming the powers and prerogatives of an independent Grand Lodge, acted from the most laudable motives and consistently with the principles which ought forever to govern Masons, viz., the benefit of the Craft and the good of mankind, and are warranted in their proceedings by the practice of Ancient Masons in all parts of the world.[303]

II. That this Grand Lodge be hereafter known and called by the name of 'The Massachusetts Grand Lodge of Ancient Masons,' and that it is free and independent in its government and official authority of any other Grand Lodge or Grand Master in the universe.

"III. That the power and authority of the said Grand Lodge be construed to extend throughout the Commonwealth of Massachuseas and to any of the United States, where none other is erected, over such Lodges only as this Grand Lodge has constituted or shall constitute.

---

[303] See Calcot, p. 107; "Masons' Pocket Companion," p. 92, London edition.

"IV. That the Grand Master for the time being be desired to call in all Charters which were held under the jurisdiction of the late Grand Master, Joseph Warren, Esquire, and return the same with an endorsement thereon, expressive of their recognition of the power and authority of this Grand Lodge.

"V. That no person ought or can, consistently with the rules of Ancient Masonry, use or exercise the powers or prerogatives of an Ancient Grand Master or Grand Lodge, to wit: To give power to erect Lodges of ancient Masonry, make Masons, appoint superior or Grand Officers, receive dues, or do anything which belongs to the powers or prerogatives of an ancient Grand Lodge within any part of the Commonwealth of Massachusetts, the rightful and appropriated limits to which the authority of this Grand Lodge forever hereafter extends."

The foregoing report was signed by Perez Morton, Paul Revere, John Warren, and James Avery.

It "was read paragraph by paragraph, and, after mature deliberation thereon, the same was accepted and ordered to be recorded in the proceedings of the Grand Lodge," where it now appears, signed by "Jos. Webb, Grand Master." A majority of the members of St. Andrew's Lodge objected to this report, although, at a Grand Lodge held March 1, 1782, a petition from its Master, Wardens, and members was presented, "praying that the Grand Lodge would grant them a Charter by the 'name of Saint Andrew,' they retaining their rank and precedency as heretofore in said Grand Lodge," which was unanimously granted.

"In 1768 John Rowe was appointed Provincial Grand Master of the St. John's Grand Lodge." He held the office until August 4, 1787, when he died.

After 1775 this Grand Lodge held no meeting until called together to attend the funeral of Grand Master Rowe.

In July, 1790, the Grand Officers assembled and voted to elect new officers, but no higher officer than a Senior Grand Warden was chosen.

The Massachusetts Grand Lodge, as early as 1787, had taken action upon the question of a union, and had appointed a committee to consider it.

"It is evident that the St. John's Lodge preserved its organization as such for the purpose of completing the contemplated union.

It granted no Charters, nor did it assume any of the powers of a Charter to St. John's Lodge, Boston, for the purpose of uniting the first and second Lodges into one.

The Grand Lodge record contains no reference to it, nor was there any record kept of the Grand Lodge doings for that year."

"Thus by the record, and by contemporaneous history, it is fixed beyond all question and doubt that the 'Massachusetts Grand Lodge' on the 8th of March, 1777, by a revolution and by assumption of the powers, duties, and responsibilities of a Grand Lodge, became a free, independent, sovereign Grand Lodge, with a jurisdiction absolute, exclusive, and entire throughout the Commonwealth of Massachusetts, and a provisional jurisdiction in other States and countries.

By this revolution and assumption, from that day to this, the Grand Lodge of Massachusetts, without interruption, has exercised all the plenary powers of a Grand Lodge.

It has held Regular and Special Meetings, elected and installed its Grand Masters and other Grand Officers, kept full and complete records of its doings, granted Warrants for new Lodges, erected and erased Lodges, compelled and received the allegiance of its subordinates and their members, and has been in correspondence with and recognized by the other Grand Lodges of the world.

From the 8th of March, 1777, to the day of this Quarterly meeting, the full and just - complete term of ninety-three years, there has never been any successful opposition to its claim of sovereignty.

From time to time it has gathered into self every opposing element possessing even a colorable title to legitimacy which it found within the borders of its jurisdiction."

"In the State of Massachusetts there have been three Lodges chartered by Grand Lodges of foreign jurisdictions, and but three - St. Andrew's, chartered in 1756, by the Grand Lodge of Scotland, and now one of our subordinates; Ancient York Lodge, No. 169, of Boston, chartered prior to 1772, by the Atholl Grand Lodge of England, and had but a brief existence; and the African Lodge, of Boston.

"It is claimed that in 1775 the persons named in the Charter of the African Lodge were made Masons in a traveling Lodge attached to one of the British regiments then stationed at Boston, and that they 'were soon after organized as, and dispensated into a Lodge,' before the death of Warren, to whom they applied for a Charter.

That they were made Masons may be true.

That they received a Dispensation for a Lodge there is not the least proof of, nor the slightest shadow of pretence for.

Dispensations for Lodges, as preliminary to granting a Charter, were not made use of in those days. But more than all, there was no authorized power here to grant such Dispensation save Provincial Grand Masters Rowe and Warren.

A traveling Lodge, although attached to a British regiment, could not authorize these persons to assessable as a Lodge.

Nor was it ever pretended that such Dispensation existed until recently.

This claim is nowhere stated directly, and contains so little foundation that it is not worth considering."

The Massachusetts Grand Lodge, at its Session October 1, 1773, after mature deliberation, decided that neither the Lodge at Castle william, nor any other traveling Lodge, "has any right to make Masons of any citizen."

There is no doubt that, on the 6th of March, 1775, the day after Warren delivered his celebrated oration in the Old South Church, where he was menaced by British troops, Prince Hall and thirteen others received the three degrees in a traveling Lodge attached to one of the British regiments in the army of General Gage, by whom Boston was then garrisoned; that Prince Hall and his associates met as a Lodge thereafter in Boston, without any warrant or authority, until May, 1787.

Application was sent to England for a Charter in 1784.

The letter of Prince Hall, dated March 1, 1784, accompanying the petition to the Grand Lodge of England for the Charter of the African Lodge, says - "I would inform you that this Lodge hath been founded almost eight years." "We have had no opportunity to apply for a Warrant before now, though we have been importuned to send to France for one, yet we thought it best to send to the fountain head, from whence we received the light, for a Warrant."

A Charter was granted September 29, 1784.

It did not arrive at Boston for nearly three years, and was received April 29, 1787, and, on the 6th of May following, Prince Hall organized the "African Lodge," at Boston, ten years after the Massachusetts Grand Lodge had asserted its freedom and independence; ten years after the American doctrine of Grand Lodge jurisdiction had been established.

"Without any other authoity than that contained in the Warrant for said Lodge, Prince Hall, the Master thereof, it is said, on the 22d of March, 1797, granted a Dispensation, preliminary to a Warrant, to certain persons in Philadelphia.

Soon afterwards Prince Hall established a Lodge at Providence, R.I. African Lodge, of Boston, continued to act as a subordinate Lodge until 1808, when, with the assistance of the Lodges at Philadelphia and

Providence, established as above stated, it organized a Grand Lodge at Boston, which Body granted Charters to several subordinates, not only in Massachusetts, but in several other States."

The African Lodge declared its independence in June, 1827, and published its Declaration in a newspaper printed at Boston.

"It is unnecessary to argue the masonic and legitimate effect of this Declaration.

It was a surrender of their Charter, and a public declaration that from thenceforth they ceased to act under it, or to recognize its validity or the authority from whence it was derived.

If the 'African Lodge' had any 'existence at this time, by force of this Declaration its existence came to an end."

A National Grand Lodge was formed in 1847; and, says the petition of Lewis Hayden and others to the Grand Lodge of Massachusetts, set out on page 132 of the Proceedings for 1869: "The African Lodge of Boston, becoming a part of that Body, surrendered its Charter, and received its present Charter, dated December 11, 1847, under the title of Prince Hall Grand Lodge of Free and Accepted Masons for the Commonwealth of Massachusetts, and by which authority we this day exist as a Masonic Body."

The Lodge prospered, but after the death of Prince Hall, December 4, 1807, aet. 72, it became dormant, and ceased.

Upon the union of the Grand Lodges of England, in 1813, African Lodge, which had been registered as No. 459 and as 370, "was removed from the list," and was never after recognized by the United Grand Lodge.

The Declaration of 1827 complains "that the members of African Lodge could open no correspondence with the Grand Lodge of England, and that their communications and advances were treated with the most studied neglect."

"Boyer Lodge, No. 1, was organized at New York City by the African Lodge or the Prince Hall Grand Lodge.

The members of this Lodge applied to the Grand Lodge of New York for recognition in 1812, 1829, and again in 1845.

Grand Secretary James Herring made a report in 1846 which contains a letter from Brother Charles W. Moore, Grand Secretary of the Grand Lodge of Massachusetts, which throws some light upon the condition of the African Lodge in Boston at this time.

"Why this Charter was granted without the consent of the Lodges in Massachusetts, and without any correspondence concerning the propriety of the step, is a question which can be answered by every

American who remembers the bitter hostility existing in England at that date towards the successful rebels against the crown of Great Britain.

This Charter, in common form, conferring no extraordinary powers upon the petitioners, authorizing them to hold a Lodge, enter, pass, and raise Masons, and no more, was undoubtedly granted by the Grand Master of England, and under it the petitioners commenced Work.

The successors of the persons named in that Charter have magnified the powers granted by it, have construed it to confer upon them Grand Lodge powers, have set up by virtue of it Grand Lodges, and finally a national Grand Lodge, with subordinate Staions and Lodges, and have established an 'American doctrine of Grand Lodge jurisdiction' peculiar to themselves, distinct and separate from any other Grand Lodge government known to man.

Their National Grand Body 'claims and exercises masonic authority over these United States, with full power and authority to settle all masonic difficulties that may arise among the Grand Lodges of these States.'"

The original Charter, granted September 29, 1784, under which the successors of the persons named have claimed to act from April, 1787, to the year 1847, and which was the only plausible authority by which they hope to be justified in their proceedings, was not only surrendered by operation of masonic law, June 18, 1827, by reason of the Declaration then made, but on the 11th of December, 1847, was actually in set form of words, and with premeditation, abandoned and surrendered, and if they now possess the parchment upon which it was written, it is kept only as a curious relic of the past, emasculated of its virility.

The first difficulty has been complicated with a National Grand Lodge, State Grand Lodges, and subordinate Lodges, so that it wail not be easy to escape from the triple bonds with which they have been bound.

This is purely a question of Grand Lodge jurisdiction which was settled and determined, September 17, 1797, by Massachusetts Grand Lodge, when it incorporated into its Constitution this Section:

"The Grand Lodge will not hold communication with, or admit as visitors, any Masons, residing in this State, who hold authority under, and acknowledge the supremacy of, any foreign Grand Lodge."

In some form of language the same feature has existed in their Constitutions from 1797 to this day, and is as follows:

"No Lodge of Ancient, Free and Accepted Masons can legally assemble in this Commonwealth under a Warrant granted by any foreign masonic power." Which is a question of Grand Lodge jurisdiction.

"The Institution of Freemasonry is universal.

It stretches from East to West, from North to South, and embraces within itself the representatives of every branch of the human family.

Its carefully-tyled doors swing open, not at the knock of every man, but at the demand of every true and worthy man, duly accepted, whatever his religion, his race, or his country may be.

This Grand Lodge stands upon the high vantage ground of this catholic society, and recognizes the great principles which must necessarily underlie an Institution which has a home on the continents and on the islands of the seas."

"When that celebrated play of Terence, styled the 'Self-Tormentor,' was first introduced upon the Roman Stage, before the great amphitheatre crowded with Senators, knights, citizens, and men of rank, some of whom had been found worthy of a Roman triumph, and Chremes, in his reply to Menedemus, repeated these words,

'Homo sum; humani nihil a me alienum puto' (I am a man; nothing which relates to man is alien to me), the vast assemblage rose up, impelled by a common sentiment, and rent the air with reiterated plaudits.

The memory of that scene has not yet faded away.

The words of Chremes have not yet ceased to reverberate.

We bear upon the Masons' arms of Massachusetts, and have inscibed upon our Grand Lodge banner, the motto,

'Humani nihil alienum.'" (Man everywhere our brother.)

True Copy of the Charter of the African Lodge.

"Effingham, A.G.M. To all and every Right Worshipful and loving Brethren, we, Thomas Howard, &c., &c., &c., Earl of Effingham, Lord Howard, Acting Grand Master under the authority of His Royal Highness Henry Frederick, Duke of Cumberland, &c., &c., &c., Grand Master of the Most Ancient and Honorable Society of Free and Accepted Masons, sends Greeting:

"Know ye, that we, at the humble petition of our right trusty and well beloved brethren, Prince Hall, Boston Smith, Thomas Sanderson, and several other brethren residing in Boston, New Zealand, in North America, do hereby constitute the said brethren into a regular Lodge of Free and accepted Masons, under the title or denomination of the African Lodge, to be opened in Boston, aforesaid; and do further, at their said petition, hereby appoint the said Prince Hall to be Master, Boston Smith, Senior Warden, and Thomas Sanderson, Junior Warden, for opening the said Lodge, and for such further time only as shall be thought proper by the brethren thereof, it being any future election of officers of the Lodge, but that such election shall be regulated agreeably to such By-Laws of the said Lodge as shall be consistent with the general laws of the society, contained in the Book of Constitutions; and we hereby will and require you, the said Prince Hall, to take special care that all and every the said brethren are, or have been, regularly made Masons, and that they do observe, perform, and keep all the rules and orders contained in the Books of Constitutions; and further, that you do, from time to time, cause to be entered in a book kept for that purpose an account of your proceedings in the Lodges, together with all such rules, orders, and regulations as shall be made for the good government of the same; that in no wise you omit once in every year to send to us, our successors Grand Masters or to Rowland Holt, Esq., our Deputy Grand Master, for the time being, an account in writing of your proceedings, and copies of all such rules, orders, and regulations as shall be made as aforesaid, together with a list of the members of the Lodge, and such a sum of money as may suit the circumstances of the Lodge and reasonably be expected towards the Grand Charity.

Moreover, we hereby will and require you, the said Prince Hall, as soon as conveniently may be, to send an account in writing of what may be done by virtue of these presents.

"Given at London, under our hand and seal of Masonry, this 29th day September, A.L. 5784, A.D. 1784.

By the Grand Master's Command.

"ROWLAND HOLT, D.G.M., Witness WILLIAM WHITE, "Grand Secretary."

The "Massachusetts Centinal," printed at Boston, in its issue of May 2, 1787, has the following document:

"AFRICAN LODGE, "BOSTON, May 2, 1787.

By Captain Scott, from London, came the Charter, &c., which his Royal Highness the Duke of Cumberland, and the Grand Lodge, have been graciously pleased to grant to the African Lodge, in Boston.

As the brethren have a desire to acknowledge all favors shown them, they, in this public manner, return particular thanks to a certain member of the Fraternity who offered the so generous reward in this paper, some time since, for the Charter, supposed to be lost; and to assure him, though they doubt of his friendship, that he has made them many good friends."

"Signed PRINCE HALL."

Extract from an Address of John V. De Grasse, before the "Prince Hall Grand Lodge" June 30, 1858: "Although, brethren, our Charter was granted in London, September 17, 1784, we did not receive it until April 29, 1787, through the neglect and almost culpable carelessness of Brother Gregory, who did not take it from the Office of the Grand Secretary, where it had remained over two years." "On the 29th of April the Charter and a beautiful bound book of the Constitutions were delivered to Prince Hall."

Declaration of Independence Published in a newspaper at Boston, June, 1827.

GREETING: "AFRICAN LODGE, NO. 459.

"GREETING: "Be it known to all whom it may concern, That we, the Master, Wardens, Members of the African Lodge, No. 459, City Of Boston (Mass.), U.S. of America, hold in our possession a certain unlimited Charter, granted September 29, A.L. 5784, A.D. 1784, by Thomas Howard, Earl of Effingham, Acting Grand Master under the authority of his Royal Highness Henry Frederick, Duke of Cumberland, &c., &c., &c., Grand Master of the Most Ancient and Honorable society of Free and Accepted Masons.

Be it further known, that the Charter alluded to bears the seal of the Most Worshipful Grand Lodge at London, England, and was presented to our much esteemed and worthy brethren and predecessors, Prince Hall, Boston Smith, Thomas Sanderson, and several others, agreeably to a humble petition of theirs, sent in form to the above Grand Lodge.

Be it remembered that, according to correct information as regards this instrument and the manner in which it was given, it appears to have been confined exclusively to the Africans, and to certain conditions.

Whether the conditions have been complied with by our ancestors, we are unable to say; but we can add that, in consequence of the decease of the above-named Brother, the institution was for years unable to proceed, for the want of one to conduct its affairs agreeably to what is required in every regular and well-educated Lodge of Masons.

It is now, however, with great pleasure we state that the present age has arrived to that degree of proficiency in the art, that we can at any time select from among us many whose capacity to govern enables them to preside with as much good order, dignity, and propriety as any other Lodge within our knowledge.

This fact can be proved by gentlemen of respectability, whose knowledge of Masonry would not be questioned by any one well acquainted with the art.

Since the rise of the Lodge to this degree of proficiency, we concluded it was best and proper to make it known to the Most Worshipful Grand Lodge from whence we derive our charter, by sending written documents and monies, to fulfil the agreements of our ancestors, giving information of the low state to which it had fallen, its cause, &c., with its rise and progress; and also soliciting favors, whereby we might be placed on a different and better standing than we had heretofore.

And notwithstanding this has long since been done, and more than sufficient time has elapsed for returns, yet we have never received a single line or reply from that Hon. Society.

In consequence of that neglect, we have been at a stand what course to pursue.

Our remote situation prevents us from making any verbal communication whatever.

Taking all these things into consideration we have come to the conclusion that with what knowledge we possess of Masonry, and as people of color by ourselves, we are, and ought by rights, to be free and independent of other Lodges.

We do, therefore, with this belief, publicly declare ourselves free and independent of any Lodge from this day, and that we will not be tributary, or be governed by any lodge than that of our own.

We agree solemnly to abide by all proper rules and regulations which govern the like Fraternity, discountenancing all imposition to injure the Order, and to use all fair and honorable means to promote its prosperity, resting in full hope that this will enable us to transmit it in its purity to our posterity for their enjoyment.

"Done at the Lodge, this the 18th June, A.L. 5727, A.D. 1827.

"In full testimony of what has been written, we affix our names:
"JOHN T. HILTON, R.M.W., "THOMAS DALTON, Sen. Ward., "LEWIS YORK, Jun. Ward., "J.H. PURRON, Secretary."

Letter from John Hervey, Grand Secretary of the United Grand Lodge of England.

FREEMASONS' HALL, LONDON, W.C., 11th November, 1868.

"DEAR SIR AND R. W. BROTHER: I am in receipt of your favor of the 20th ult., making enquiries respecting a Warrant granted in 1784 to a certain Prince Hall.

I have caused a most diligent search to be made in our books here, and the only reference I can find is in the Calendar for 1785, when a Lodge appears to have been working under the English Constitution, at Boston, under the No. 459, and called the 'African Lodge.' It afterwards became 370, and, I presume, had ceased working, as at the Union, in 1813, it was removed from the list.

"To reply to your questions categorically

"1st. I can find no record in 1775 of any Dispensation; but as the G. L. Books were not then kept, as they are now, with accuracy, such may, nevertheless, have existed.

"2d. It was struck off the list in 1813, but I can find no trace of any return having been made, and consequently imagine it must have ceased working long before, although retained on the list.

"3d. I should say most decidedly, that the said 'Prince Hall' was never appointed D.G.M., or had power to grant warrants for the establishment of Lodges in your country.

Henry Price, of Boston, was P.G.M. for America from 1775 to 1804, after which year his name disappears from the lists.

"It is quite clear that the Lodge referred to is not working under the English Constitutions, and that the parties holding the Warrant can have no right to it, and are not a regular Lodge, unless empowered to meet under your Constitutions.

I am, dear Sir and Brother, yours, truly and fraternally, "JOHN HERVEY, Grand Secretary CHARLES W. MOORE, Deputy Grand Master, Grand Lodge of Massachusetts.

Extract from the Report of James Herring, Grand Secretary, to the Grand Lodge of New York, June 2, 1846.

The undersigned, having requested the R.W. Charles W. Moore, Grand Secretary of the Grand Lodge of Massachusetts, to endeavor to see the Charter of the so-called African Lodge, of Boston, and, if possible, obtain a copy thereof, begs leave to incorporate the following extract from Br. Moore's letter, dated JULY 26, 1845 :

"I called, agreeably to your request, on Mr. Hilton - who, I believe, is the Master of the African Lodge in this city - stated to him the object of my visit, and asked permission to see the Charter of his Lodge.

He informed me that there was a difficulty between his and Boyer Lodge, of long standing, that they had nothing to do with that Lodge, nor would they have, until the difference referred to was settled.

He further stated, that they were entirely independent of the white Lodges; asked no favors of them; and would have nothing to do with them; nor would they admit a white Mason, if he should present himself as a visitor.

In the course of his conversation he distinctly said that he had been 'told by them people' (meaning Boyer Lodge) to have no communication with anybody on the subject of their recognition by the Grand Lodge of New York.

He also positively and repeatedly refused to allow me to see the Charter of his Lodge, or to give me any information in relation to its history or present existence.

It is proper for me to add, that my conversation with him was kind and gentle. I explicitly stated to him that I did not call officially, but as a friend, and at your request, with a view to ascertain whether Boyer Lodge was a regular constituted Lodge, such as the Grand Lodge of New York could recognize. . . .

"The African Lodge has never been recognized by the Grand Lodge of this Commonwealth.

Applications have several times been made by its members for admission to our Lodges, but they have generally, if not always, been refused.

Mr. Hilton stated to me that he had once, through the influence of a friend, gained admission into one of our out-of-town Lodges.

If so, the Brother who introduced him laid himself open to censure, and would have been dealt with, had the circumstance come to the knowledge of the Grand Lodge.

That the course of our Grand Lodge, in reference to the African Lodge, is not the result of prejudice, it is only necessary for me to say, that, within the last month, a colored Brother from England has visited, and been kindly received, in one of our city Lodges.

"Such is the state of the case, so far as I am able to communicate it.

The argument does not belong to me; but you will permit me to inquire, whether your Grand Lodge is prepared to recognize any real or pretended Lodge, existing within another jurisdiction, before it had been recognized by the Grand Lodge of that jurisdiction? Again, does your Grand Lodge allow other Grand Lodges to establish Lodges within its jurisdiction? and is it ready to recognize Lodges so established?

"These three questions have been, by repeated decisions of this Grand Lodge, answered in the negative; and, according to the treaty stipulations entered into by the Grand Lodges of this continent, soon after the revolution, and the uniform resistance of any encroachment upon the sole jurisdiction of the several Grand Lodges down to the present time, these questions can be answered only in the negative.

"The undersigned would further state, that the legality of the Body, called Boyer Lodge, No. 1, has been already twice reported on by Committees of this Grand Lodge on the 3d of March, 1812, and on the 4th of March, 1829.

In the latter report, the main facts were correctly stated and able arguments sustained, and the conclusion drawn that Boyer Lodge, No. 1, can be regarded only as a clandestine Lodge.

The undersigned can arrive only at the same conclusion, it being established beyond doubt that the African Lodge, at Boston, was illegally established by the Grand Lodge of England within the jurisdiction of the Grand Lodge of Massachusetts; that its name has been long stricken from the roll of the Grand Lodge of England; that its assumed authority to grant Warrants was unmasonic and fraudulent; and further, that the statement contained in the memorial of said Boyer Lodge, that it had been 'regularly and legally constituted and installed as a Master Mason's Lodge, with a legal Warrant or Charter,' is totally unfounded.

All of which is respectfully submitted,
"JAMES HERRING,
"Grand Secretary."
NEW YORK, June 2, 1846.

In June, 1855, one Peter G. Smith, of Montpelier, Vt., visited Boston, and "joined a Lodge of Masons." Upon returning to Montpelier, he attempted to visit a regular Lodge, but was refused admission.

Mr. Smith then wrote to Boston, and received the following reply:

"No. 60 SOUTHAC STREET, BOSTON, September 6, 1855.
"PETER G. SMITH, ESQ.

"MAY DEAR SIR AND BROTHER: Yours, bearing date August 14, came duly to hand. You say that the Grand Master of Vermont says that the colored Masons had their Charter taken from them, and that they are now working without a Charter.

We reply that the charge is no doubt innocent, but it is nevertheless false from beginning to end.

The original Charter is now in our possession, and always has been, and we worked under it until some time after the war between this country and Great Britain, when the colored Masons held a Convention and declared themselves independent, the same as the white had already done before.

This was done on account of the difficulties of making the returns to the mother country.

There has always been the best feelings, and our brethren all visit the Lodges, not only in England, but in all parts of the world.

"If the Grand Master of Vermont wishes any more light, we are prepared to give it to him; or if he has a curiosity, he can see the original Charter.

Yours fraternally,
"J. S. ROCK,

"Corresponding Grand Secretary of Prince Hall Grand Lodge."

To this letter Philip C. Tucker, Grand Master of Vermont, replied in a communication to Peter G. Smith as follows:

"VERGENNES, September 22, 1855.
"MR PETER G. SMITH, Montpelier.
"SIR: I received yours of yesterday, enclosing a letter to you from Mr. J.S. Rock, of Boston, this morning.

"As to the Lodge of colored men existing in Boston, calling itself 'Prince Hall Grand Lodge,' and such Lodges as acknowledge its jurisdiction, I have to say that my understanding on the subject is this:

"I suppose it to be true that on the 20th day of September, 1784, a Charter for a Masters' Lodge was granted to Prince Hall and others, under the authority of the Grand Lodge of England, and that the Lodge then chartered bore the name of 'African Lodge, NO. 459,' and was located at Boston.

If any other Charter was ever granted, at any other time, by the Grand Lodge of England, or any other Grand Lodge, to the colored persons of that city, it has never come to my, knowledge.

"I suppose it to be also true that African Lodge, No. 459, did not continue its connection for many years with the Grand Lodge of England, and that its registration was stricken from the rolls of that Grand more than fifty years ago.

"I suppose it further to be true that this Lodge, NO. 459, and all others which have originated from it, have always held themselves aloof, and have always refused to acknowledge any allegiance to the Grand Lodge of the Commonwealth of Massachusetts.

"I also suppose it to be true that, on the 18th day of June, 1827, this same Lodge, No. 459, issued a Declaration, and had it published in some of the Boston papers, signed by John T. Hilton, Thomas Dalton, Lewis York, jr., and J.H. Purron (claiming to be Master Wardens, and Secretary thereof), which Declaration contained the following language: 'We publicly declare ourselves free and independent of any Lodge from this day, and we will not be tributary, or governed by any Lodge than that of our own.'

"And I still further suppose it to be true that, in the month of July, 1845, R.W. Charles W. Moore; the Grand Secretary of the Grand Lodge of Massachusetts, had a personal interview with Mr. Hilton, then Master of this said Lodge, NO. 459, in which interview Mr. Hilton said, that they (the members of said Lodge) were 'entirely independent of all white Bodies, asked no favors of them, and would have nothing to do with them; nor would they admit a white Mason, if he should present himself as a visitor.'

"All these things are of record, and cannot, I think, be denied in any quarter.

From them I form the following opinions:

"First.

Even if a Charter for a subordinate Lodge, to be located within the United States, could be lawfully granted by the Grand Lodge of England, after the close of the American Lodges, its vitality would necessarily expire when the grantor substantially revoked the grant by striking it from its records, and thus disavowing all connection with the grantee.

"Second. 'That the mere retention of a Charter, after its legal revocation, cannot preserve or retain any right, power, or authority in the original grantees or their successors, where the right to revoke is reserved, as it always is in all Grand Lodges, in the grantor.

"Third.

Even if African Lodge, NO. 459, had a lawful masonic existence June 18, 1827, the Declaration of that date was both unmasonic and revolutionary, and placed that Body as effectually beyond recognition by either the Grand Lodge of Massachusetts or any other Grand Lodge in the United States, as was the French Lodge of Virginia, or the German Lodges of New York.

"Fourth.

Had African Lodge, NO. 459, been in all things a lawful Lodge, after the Declaration of its first officer, of July, 1845, that 'it would not admit a white Mason if he should present himself as a visitor,' it would have been both humiliating and degrading to have allowed the doors of the white Lodges to stand open for a reciprocity of courtesies which were thus gratuitously and roughly declared inadmissible, in advance of any request, offer, or wish to establish them.

"I have the highest masonic authority in Massachtiseas for denying 'the brethren' of the Lodge in question 'all visit the Lodges,' so far as the Lodges of Massachusetts are concerned.

A Past Grand Master of the Lodge of the Commonwealth, writing at Boston, in 1848, says: 'There are no Lodges of colored Masons in this city or any other part of the United States that are recognized and acknowledged by the Grand Lodge of Massachusetts, or to our knowledge, by any other regularly-constituted Grand Lodge in this country.

It (the African Lodge) was never recognized by the Grand Lodge of this State, nor has there been any masonic intercourse between the two Bodies.'

"The same Brother, writing at the same place, in 1846, says, in referring to that Lodge: 'Applications have several times been made by its members for admission to our Lodges, but they have generally, if not always, been refused.' Again he says, 'That the course of our Grand Lodge in reference to African Lodge is not the result of prejudice, it is only necessary for me to say that, within the last month, a colored Brother from England has visited, and been kindly received in one of our city Lodges.'

"I believe I am correct in stating that the two following propositions are recognized as sound masonic law in this country:

"First.

That no Grand Lodge of any State can regularly recognize a subordinate Lodge existing in another State, or its members, until such subordinate Lodge is recognized by the Grand lodge of the State in which it exists.

"Second.

That no Grand Lodge, either in these United States, or any other country, can legally establish a subordinate Lodge in any other State where a regularly-constituted Grand Lodge exists.

"From these views you will readily perceive why the Masonry of the United States does not and cannot either recognize 'Prince Hall Grand Lodge,' or its subordinates, or their members, as regular.

To our understanding, the whole of these organizations are irregular and unmasonic, and exist adverse to masonic regulations and law. If, as Mr. Rock asserts, members of these Bodies are admitted to 'visit Lodges in England and all parts of the world,' that admission probably arises from the fact that the history and masonic positions of these Bodies are not so well understood elsewhere as they are in the United States.

"Mr. Rock expresses an inclination to 'give the Grand Master of Vermont more light' on this subject.

As he signed himself 'Corresponding Secretary of Prince Hall Grand Lodge,' I suppose him to possess all the light' which the subject has in it; and whatever that light may be able to reflect upon me of the truth of the past or the present, will always receive the respectful attention it may deserve from

"Your Humble Serv't, "PHILIP C. TUCKER, "Grand Master of the Grand Lodge of Vermont.".

Communication from the Grand Secretary of the United Grand Lodge of England FREEMASONS' HALL, LONDON, W. C., "May 5, 1870.

"WILLIAM SEWALL GARDNER, ESQ., Most Worshipful Grand Master of Massachusetts.

"M.W. SIR AND BROTHER: I would have replied earlier to your esteemed letter of the 12th March, had not the information you required necessitated a longer search than could be prosecuted at the moment.

I regret that I can afford so little information, as our records, excepting, as to the proceedings of our own Grand Lodge, were not kept in the accurate manner as is now the general practice.

As you are already aware, the Warrant for the African Lodge was granted in 1784, and was numbered 459; but the fee for the Warrant, 4 pounds 4s., does not appear in our Grand Lodge accounts until the 4th April, 1787.

The following remittances were received for the Charity Fund from the African Lodge, viz.:

"November 25, 1789, 2 pounds 2S. 11d.
"April 18, 1792, 1 pound 1S. 0d
"November 27, 1793, 1 pound 5S. 6d.
"November 22, 1797, 1 pound 5S. 0d.

"In 1793 its number was altered to 370, and continued so numbered in our Calendar until 1812, when, on the re-numbering consequent on the union of the two Grand Lodges, the African Lodge was omitted.

"I send you enclosed a verbatim copy of all the documents I can discover relating to the Lodge; but the petition for the Lodge is not forthcoming.

Should any other documents present themselves, which is somewhat unlikely, I will send you copies, and have the honor to remain, M.W. Sir and Brother,

"Yours fraternally,
"JOHN HERVEY,
"Grand Secretary."

Copies referred to in the above letter:

"RIGHT WORSHIPFUL SIR: We now, send you an account of the Lodges proceeding since we sent our last, which was in August last, together with ten dollars for the Fund of the Grand Charity, by Captain Scot, which he saith he hath delivered to the Grand Secretary, but he hath no recept with him for the money.

We have initiated into the Lodge this year Samovel Beean, a black man, and the Reverend Mr. John Merrand, a black Minister from home, but last from Beech Town in Nova Scotia.

We shall make a colletchen on St. John's Day next, which we shall send by the first carefull hand; the Lodge in general behaves veriwell in there Station, so that there no just complantes made against them.

I hope I may allways have the plesevr of sending a good account of the African Lodge.

After whiching all Happyness to our Royal Grand Master, and all the Officers and Members of the Grand Lodge, I beg leve to subscribe myself your most obedient humble servent and Brother, PRINCE HALL."

"BOSTON, November 9, 1789.
"To the Most Worshipful WILLIAM WHITE, ESQ., G. S.

"DEAR SIR: These comes to acquant you that we have sent sundrey, letters to our Right Worshipful Rowland Holt, Esq., and to your Worship according to my order in the Charter; and with those we sent you datted Auegust 2, 1788, we sent Ten Dollars for the Grand Charity but have not had a anser wether you had receved them or not, and the Lodge is uneasey with me on that acount, as I paid the money to Mr. Bengmen Greene, Jun., one of Captain James Scotts Merchants, and receved his recepte for the money to be sent to him with the Letters for you, as I did not now were to derecte them to you, and if you receved them that must be the Reson; therefore, Sir, be so good when you send an ansear to this you would send me some word were to derect them, that you may have them, which we hope will be by the Berrer hearof.

I have sent you a sermon, preched on St. Johns Day by our Brother John Marrant, for our Grand Master, and another for you, which I hope you will recevn.

Our Brother Sanderson is Dead.

All the rest of our Br are in health.

So no at pesent.

But must beg leve to subscribe myself your vere humble servent and Br., "PRINCE HALL."

"To the Right Worshipful, the Grand Master, Wardens, and Members of the Grand Lodge of England.

"We your petitioners, Sampson H. Moody, Peter Howard, Abraham C. Derendemed, John I. Hilton, James Jackson, Zadock Low, Samuel G. Gardner, Richard Potter, Lewis Walker, and other Companions Who have been regularly Exalted to the Sublime Degree of Royal Arch Masons.

"Our worthy and well beloved Brethren Prince Hall, Boston Smith, Thomas Sanderson, and several Brethren having obtained a Warrant from your Honourable Body, on September 29, 1784, A.D., A.L. 5784, when, under the Government of Thomas Howard, Earl of Effingham, Lord Howard, &c., &c., &c., acting Grand Master Under the authority of his Royal Highness Henry Frederick, Duke of Cumberland, Grand Master of the Most Ancient and Honourable Society of Free and Accepted Masons.

"This Warrant allowing us to confer but the three Degrees, and Finding it injurious for the benefit of our Body by having no legal authority to confer the other four degrees.

And understanding that the seven degrees is given under the Warrants from the Grand Lodge, we, therefore, humbly solicit the Renual of our Charter to ourtherise us Legally to confer the same, as we are now getting in a flourishing condition.

It is with regret we communicated to you that, from the Decease of our Well Beloved Brethren who obtain'd the Warrant we have not been able for several years to transmit Monies and hold a regular Communication; but, as we are now permanently established to work conformable to our Warrant and Book of Constitutions.

We will send the Monies as far as circimstances will admit, together with the money, for a new Warrant.

Should your Honourable Body think us worthy to receive the sarae.

We remain, Right Worshipful and Most Worshipful Brethren,
"With all Due Respect, Yours fraternally, "(Signed) SAMSON H. MOODY, W.M.,"PETER HOWARD, S. W., "C. A. DERANDAMIE, J. W.
"Given under our hands at Boston, in the year of our Lord 1824, January 5th (5824).
"WILLIAM J. CHAMPNEY, "Secretary"

CHAPTER LX

THE ANTI-MASONIC EXCITEMENT

GENERAL history of Masonry in the United States would be incomplete if a notice of the anti-Masonic episode were left out; we shall, therefore, devote a few pages to this subject.

There have been, generaly diffused among the people, very erroneous ideas in regard to the sudden disappearance of one William Morgan, of whom it was said, that in consequence of a threatened publication of an exposure of the secret work of Freemasonry, he was either murdered or kidnaped and conveyed surreptitiously out of the country, and was never heard of afterward.

It was an undeniable fact that he suddenly disappeared from the State of New York, and there is no satisfactory evidence that he was ever seen by anyone again.

Volumes have been published, both by anti-Masons and Masons, in, apparently, a vain effort to establish the charge on one side, that he was either murdered or transported out of the country, and, on the other side, that he came to no harm from the Masons, who were accused of his "sudden taking off."

The latest publication was prepared by Past Grand Master Jesse B. Anthony, 33 degree, of New York,[304] who availed himself of the excellent account by Hon. Josiah H. Drummond, Past Grand Master of the Grand Lodge of Maine, and the pamphlets published, several years since, by Past Grand Master Rob.

---

[304] "History of Masonry and Concordant Orders," p. 514.

Morris, of Kentucky, who spent much time and money in the State of New York, and other writers who had investigated all the circumstances connected with the affair.

Our limits in this work do not admit of so extended an examination as that of Brother Anthony; nevertheless, it will be necessary, for a proper understanding of the case, to devote considerable space to a clear statement of all the ascertainable facts, and leave all speculations and conjectures to our readers.

William Morgan, it is said, was from Virginia;[305] born in 1775 or 1776; was a stone mason by trade.

In 1821 he resided near York in Upper Canada and was engaged as a brewer.[306]

His brewery being destroyed by fire, from thence he found his way to Rochester, N.Y., and worked at his trade as a stone mason, and in 1823 went to Batavia.[307]

In the "Letters to John Qudncy Adams" it is related that "he was a hard drinker and his nights, and sometimes his days also, were spent in tippling-houses, while occasionally, to the still greater neglect of his family, he joined in the drinking carousals of the vilest and most worthless men; and his disposition was envious, malicious, and vindictive."

Some persons doubt if he ever was regularly made a Mason; but it is nevertheless true that, after reaching Batavia, he was admitted as a visitor in Wells Lodge of that place.

After this he was made a Royal Arch Mason in Western Star Chapter, at Le Roy, N.Y., May 23, 1825.

His name was on the first petition for the establishment of a Royal Arch Chapter in Batavia.

Some others seeing his name on the petition, declined signing it, and a new one was gotten up, leaving his name off.

After the chapter was organized, upon his application for membership he was rejected.[308]

There was at that time a weekly newspaper the - "Republican Advocate," conducted by one David C. Miller.

---

[305] H. Brown's "Narrative, Batavia, New York, 1829," P. 15.
[306] Ibid., p. 16.
[307] Ibid., p. 16.

[308] Ibid., p. 17.

It is said he had been initiated in a lodge in Albany, N.Y., but owing to his noted character, ascertained thereafter, he had been refused advancement.[309]

These two worthies, and companions in dissipation, both impecunious and greatly in financial difficulties, concocted the scheme to divulge what they knew of Masonry.[310] Morgan having advanced further in the degrees, was to furnish the information, and Miller was to do the editing, printing, and publishing.

This scheme, by some means, became known to the Masons.

No doubt, in the drunken orgies of Morgan he had boasted of his contemplated revenge.

Articles also crept into the paper;[311] one of which was publicly read in a bar-room in 1826, which stated: "There will be issued from the press in this place, in a short time, a work of rare interest to the uninitiated, being an exposition of Ancient Craft Masonry, by one who has been a member of the institution for years.

Morgan having had some transaction in Canandaigua with the tavern-keeper - we think it was simply borrowing some clothing, and having failed to return the articles, a warrant was taken out for larceny, upon which his arrest followed, and he was carried to Canandaigua by a posse; among them were several conspicuous Masons. He was acquited of the charge, because he had borrowed the clothing, and had not stolen them.

He was again arrested for a debt to another tavern-keeper, and upon confession of judgment he was sent to jail.

Miller was also arrested, September 12, 1826, and carried to Le Roy;[312] he was discharged, as the plaintiff did not appear in time.[313]

A few days previous to Miller's arrest, a warrant in behalf of the plaintiff (Johns) was issued by a justice of the Peace residing in Le Roy against Miller and John Davids, his partner in the printing office, for the purpose of collecting money before then advanced by Johns in the prosecution of their undertaking.

The officer in whose hands the warrant was placed for execution was a constable of the town of Stafford, who, having learned that the office of Miller was strictly guarder and that he was fully

---

[309] Ibid., p. 15.
[310] Ibid., p. 15.
[311] Ibid., p. 18.
[312] H. Brown's "Narrative, Batavia,, New York, 1829," P. 54.
[313] Ibid., p. 56.

determined to resist all attempts to serve any process upon him, engaged a number of assistants.

On September 12th he and his posse, who were followed by a large number of people, went to Batavia to make the arrest.

So many strangers, without any ostensible business, making their appearance in Batavia, aroused the most fearful apprehension among the citizens.

Miller received a note early in the morning from some unknown person that an effort would be made to take by force the papers intended for publication.

He showed this note to a few of the citizens of the town, some of whom were Masons, and asked their opinion.

They advised him to look upon the matter as idle rumor, as to attempt such a measure was impracticable and foolish.

So many unknown persons, however, suddenly making their presence known, and as if by concert, those who had advised him to take no notice of the warning; received by Miller began to fear that it was indeed a preconcerted plan to carry out the intention of obtaining, by violence if necessary, the aforesaid papers.

The magistrates were all absent from the village, and this also increased the suspicions. Very soon a number of the citizens, Masons as well as others, offered their services to prevent any violence.

Morgan had gone from Batavia the day before this in the charge of an officer, but no news of him had yet been received.

Consternation and apprehension pervaded that small community, but as nothing further transpired, order and quietness soon prevailed.

Soon after this the constable, with a single individual accompanying him, went to the office to arrest Miller and Davids with a civil process.

The office was fortified by "two swivels," fifteen or more guns, and six pistols, all being loaded, but was at that time undefended, except by Miller, Davids, and a son of Miller.

The assistant arrested Davids, who called for a pistol; the constable arrested Miller. Both of them submitted and were carried through an armed crowd of their friends to a tavern across the street.

A very large number of persons, nearly fifty, were there assembled.

They gave no sign of any hostility whatever, and in conversation with others showed that no intention on their part existed of any violence or wrong.

Subsequent disclosures, however, clearly showed that in the minds at least of a few an intention had existed of obtaining possession of the "papers" by force if necessary.

Those Masons in Batavia to whom this design had been communicated severely condemned such intention, which was conceived in folly and would be fraught with mischief and ruinous in consequences.

These views having been communicated to the leaders, the whole scheme was abandoned.

The absence of the justices was caused by their being subpoenaed as witnesses in a trial at Bethany on that day.[314]

From the evidence produced it was clearly shown that certain indiscreet and overzealous Masons did inaugurate a scheme to get rid of Morgan and prevent the publication of his pretended "exposure." He was conveyed out of the State, by his own consent, from a fear that someone would murder him.

A promise was made to take care of his wife and children, and with $500 in hand he was taken into Canada.

There were a great many incidents connected with the expedition to transport him out of the State, which we deem it unnecessary to mention in detail.

This affair created wonderful excitement in allthe New England States and in New York and Pennsylvania, among the Masons particularly; it extended, in a milder form, southwardly, and reached as far as the District of Columbia, but its effects, morally and politically, south of the famous historical "line of Mason and Dixon," was very slight indeed.

In New York, Pennsylvania, and Vermont, however, the loyal members of the Craft sustained their integrity against political, religious, and social persecutions.

A new political party was organized, and that party made a national issue at the next presidential canvass in 1832, and William Wirt was their candidate for the office of Chief Magistrate, and the canvass resulted in his receiving the electoral vote of Vermont, the only State to cast their votes for him. We are glad to announce that when Masonry again revived and came forth from that terrible time of persecution, under the leadership of that grand and magnanimous MAN, Philip C. Tucker, as we have shown in preceding chapters, he brought order out of confusion and re-established Masonry in all its branches.

---

[314] The above account is condensed from Brown's "Narrative," pp. 51 - 55.

At the present day there can not be found more enthusiastic Masons in any State of our Union, than now exist in the Green Mountain State.

The official examinations of parties who were directly or remotely connected with the abduction of Morgan, aroused and continued to excite the sentiments of hostility to the Masonic Institution; it was once well said that the "fice-dog always barks at what he does not understand," so with that similar class in ever community, they are always ready and constantly seeking opportunities to oppose what is beyond their linmited comprehension.

Charges were constantly found against those Masons who were suspected of any complicity in those affairs, and suits were brought against them for several years.

Among those who were arrested and imprisoned was Eli Bruce.

From 1827 to 1831 there was always some one or more confined in the jail at Canandaigua.

Eli Bruce was charged with the abduction of Morgan, and was acquitted, for it was not proved that anyone had been abducted.

De Witt Clinton was then Governor of New York, as well as one of the most prominent and distinguished Masons in the United States, and was of course eminently desirous of ascertaining the truth in all these matters.

He formulated certain questions to Eli Bruce, who was the High Sheriff of the County, as to his agency in these matters: Bruce declined to answer them and he was promptly removed from his office.

Governor Clinton, it is well known, both in his private and public utterances, condemned the whole transaction of the removal of Morgan.

The official account of Bruce's trial shows that complaint was made to the Governor, and Bruce was summoned to Albany in answer to the charges and show cause why he should not be removed. The reply by his counsel did not satisfy the Governor, and he was tried in the court at Canandaigua, in August, 1828.

He was convicted and sentenced to twenty-eight months in jail.

The execution of the sentence was postponed until May 13, 1829, upon his appeal, but on May 20, 1829, he was imprisoned until September 23, 1831. The evidence at the trial showed that Bruce understood that Morgan voluntarily consented to his removal and that a cell at Lockport was prepared for him until he could be carried to Canada.

He at first declined to have anything to do with the affair, but at last gave in, and, with the others, conveyed Morgan over the river to Canada.

Matters having been delayed for Morgan's removal, he was reconveyed to the State and concealed in the old magazine at Fort Niagara, until the time was suitable for his conveyance to the farm provided for him in Canada.

From that time Morgan, it appears, was never seen by anyone, and Bruce testified that he did not know when or how he disappeared.

Other parties were implicated, and upon trial of each, they were punished by imprisonment.

The anti-Masonic spirit was not satisfied with the punishment of those immediately concerned in this nefarious transaction.

Many conventions were held, and self-constituted Missionaries sprang up, like toadstools in a night, and scattered their venomous seed broadcast and found favorite soil, in the debased condition of many polluted minds, in which to foster these seeds of opposition to an Institution which, in all its principles and daily practices, had demonstrated its utter abhorrence to any such transactions as the Morgan affair, and also as being subversive of public order, private human rights, and the clearly enunciated precepts of Masonry - whose Theological virtues are Faith, Hope, and Charity, whose cardinal virtues are Temperance, Prudence, Fortitude, and Justice, whose principal Tenets are Brotherly Love, Relief, and Truth.

A convention of delegates from several Baptist churches was held at Le Roy, N. Y., January, 1827, and

"Resolved, That all such members as belong to Baptist churches and who also belong to the Society of Freemasons, be requested to renounce publicly all communication with that order, and if the request is not complied with in a reasonable time, to excommunicate all those who neglect to do so." If the present writer be permitted to publicly express his private opinion, it would be, that all such loyal members who refused to comply with so outrageous a resolution would, after the "excommunication," be immediately received into the church of an all merciful Savior, and welcomed out of so bigoted and benighted a congregation; as time has subsequently proved they were.

At the famous Lewiston Convention they published the following discoveries:

1. That the unhappy Morgan was taken to Newark, Upper Canada, gagged, bound, and blindfolded.

2. That he was then offered to the British Masons of that place, with the request that they should get him on board a British Man-of-War or turn him over to Brandt, the Indian Chief and a Mason, to be executed with savage cruelty.

3. That the Newark Lodge assembled on this proposition, and sent for Brandt, who came accordingly.

4. Brandt proved himself too noble of nature to have anything to do with so cowardly, inhuman, and wicked a transaction.

The savage hero disdained to do that which conwardly white monsters urged him to do.

5. The Newark Masons, thus rebuked by savage justice and magnanimity, likewise finally declined to take charge of the miserable victim.

6. The diabolical wretches, who had him in custody, brought him back as far as Fort Niagam, and then murdered him in cold blood, cutting his throat from ear to ear, cutting out his tongue, and burying him in the sand, and concluding the hellish rites by sinking the body in the lake.

Brandt denied the charge so far as it related to him, "false in one, false in all." The 6th is a clincher for mendacity - the whole statement is contrary to all the legal testimony in the case, and does not tally with a subsequent account of finding Morgan's body in the Niagara River, but was put forth by the political party of the day; and when Thurlow Weed was told that it did not prove to be Morgan's body, he said very pertinently, "It's good enough Morgan till after election."

September 11, 1830, a convention was held in Philadelphia.

A committee reported an address, stating that Morgan was murdered, notwithstanding that in all the legal proceedings there was not a single witness to prove that Morgan was murdered.

This address, however, demanded the suppression of the Institution of Masonry.

The following extract will show the spirit which prevailed:

"To this government Freemasonry is wholly opposed.

It requires submission to its own authority in contempt of public opinion, the claim of conscience, and the rights of private judgment.

It would dam up the majestic currents of improving thought, among all its subjects throughout the earth, by restricting beneficial communication.

In attempting to do this it has stained our country with a brother's blood, tempted many of our influential citizens into the most degraded forms of falsehood, and burst away with its powers undiminished, its vengeance provoked, and its pollution manifest, from the strong arm of retributive justice.

The means of overthrowing Masonry cannot be found in any, or in all our executive authorities.

They cannot be found in our judicial establishment

"The only adequate corrective of Freemasonry - that prolific source of the worst abuses is to be found in the right of election, and to this we must resort.

"There is therefore no impropriety in resorting to the elective franchise to correct the evils of Freemasonry.

"It, Freemasonry, ought to be abolished; it should certainly be so abolished as to prevent its restoration. No means of doing this can be conceived so competent as those furnished by the ballot boxes." We here see what prejudice, ignorance of the subject, and a spirit of persecution can effect upon the minds of men, when prompted by ambition for public office.

The first paragraph is a long tissue of falsehoods, as time proved those utterances to have been; not a sentence was predicated upon a single fact which had been or could be proven.

Every Mason will at once declare that every charge made in that address was maliciously false and mis-leading.

In 1836 a National Convention of anti-Masons was held in Philadelphia and nominated William H. Harrison for President, and Francis Granger for Vice-President, and this ended the political influence of that party.

The writer of this article was old enough to remember that contest and the prominent actors therein.

Their failure at that time did not dishearten most of the leaders, as very soon thereafter they became prominent leaders of the newly organized Anti-Slavery party, a subject with which we have nothing to do whatever.

All the Grand Lodges within the States affected by this untoward anti-Masonic persecution, passed such resolutions as to, and did, satisfy most people, that Masonry as an institution had nothing to do with the Morgan affair, but condemned the injudicious and unauthorized individuals who were participants, nor made any efforts to screen them from merited justice; nevertheless, the persecution of individuals continued, and many who were socially so situated as to render their lives unbearable, surrendered their memberships and withdrew from the Institution.

At length, in some of these States, particularly in Vermont, the lodges and other bodies ceased to hold their meetings, as has been shown in our different histories of those bodies.

In 1840 there were signs of renewal of activities in Masonic affairs; thirteen years of persecution had passed and there came a revival.

We learn from the authorities in New York that the lodge at Le Roy, Olive Branch, No. 39, never ceased its meetings, although located in the immediate neighborhood of the place where the whole difficulty originated, and is considered as the preserver of Masonry in Western New York during all those years of persecution and excitement.

Governor Clinton wrote to the Governors of Upper and Lower Canada asking that inquiry be made in regard to Morgan, and said in his letters:

"During the last year he (Morgan) put a manuscript into the hands of a printer at Batavia, purporting to be a promulgation of the secrets of Freemasonry.

This was passed over by the great body of the Fraternity without notice and silent contempt; but a few desperate fanatics engaged in a plan of carrying him off, and on the 12th of September last (1826) they took him from Canandaigua by force, as it is understood,[315] and conveyed him to the Niagara River, from which it is supposed that he was taken to his Britannic Majesty's dominions.

Some of the offenders have been apprehended and punished; but no intelligence has been obtained respecting Morgan since his abduction."

In response to this request of Governor Clinton, the Lieutenant-Governor of Upper Canada issued his proclamation:

"50 pounds Reward. - His Excellency the Lieutenant-Governor having received a communication from His Excellency the Governor of the State of New York, by which it appears that William Morgan who some years ago exercised the calling of a brewer in this place, and who has recently resided in Canandaigua, in the State of New York, was some time in the last year conveyed by force from that place, and is supposed to be forcibly detained in some part of this Province; any person who may be able to offer any information respecting the said William Morgan, shall, upon communicating the same to the Private Secretary of His Excellency the Lieutenant-Governor, receive the reward above offered.

"Government House, January 31, 1827."[316]

---

[315] The weight of evidence was that he went voluntarily. - EDITOR.
[316] "History of Masonry and Concordant Orders," P. 516.

The Grand Lodge of New York adopted the following:

"Whereas, It is alleged that an outrage has been committed on the body of William Morgan, and

Whereas, Proceedings in consequence of such allegations have been made in Courts of justice in relation to the subject, and

"Whereas, By reason of foul misrepresentation an effort has been made to impress the public mind with an opinion that the Grand Lodge and the Fraternity in general have attempted to screen, if not to protect, the perpetrators of this alleged outrage; therefore be it

"Resolved, That the Grand Secretary be instructed to ascertain from the public record a statement of the facts in relation to the persons said to have been Masons, charged and convicted of the abduction of Morgan,[317] and report to this Grand Lodge at its next annual communication."

A supplemental report was adopted (June 2, 1832):[318]

"That participating with the members of this Grand Lodge, and the Great Body of the Masonic Fraternity, in a feeling of deep abhorrence of the outrage, which was a violation alike of Masonic obligation and the law of the land, they (the Committee) have examined the papers submitted thereto with that attention which the importance of the subject demands.

The voluminous nature of the papers presented and the shortness of the time have, however, prevented them from investigating the subject as fully as they would desire, and further time was asked in which to formulate a report."

At the communication of the Grand Lodge of New York held March 7, 1832, Mordecai Meyers presiding, twelve experienced and capable members of the Grand Lodge, together with the Grand Officers, were appointed to visit all the Lodges in the City of New York, Brooklyn, and Staten Island, to arouse them to a sense of their duty, instruct the officers of said lodges in their work, to advise and encourage them to a strict adherence to the Constitution and Regulation of this Grand Lodge, and to inspect their books.

EXTRACTS from the "Proceedings of the Triennial Session of the Grand Encampment of Knights Templars for the United States of America assembled at the Asylum in Masonic Temple, in the City of Baltimore, in the State of Maryland, on Tuesday, the 19th of September, A.D. 1871 A.O. 753."

"Grand Master Gardner then read the following Address:

---

[317] "History of Grand Lodge of New York vol. iii., p 2.
[318] Ibid.

"Knights, Companions: On Thursday, the 29th of November, 1832, fourteen bold and valiant Knights assembled in the Masonic Temple in this city, and proceeded to open the General Grand Encampment of the United States.

The Rev. Sir Jonathan Nye, of New Hampshire, presided over the deliberations, and welcomed his associates by an affectionate and fraternal address.

The illustrious Sir James Herring, of New York, recorded the proceedings; while the venerable Prelate, Rev. Sir Paul Dean, of Massachusetts, implored the blessings of heaven upon the brave Knights and their doings. Of these fourteen good men, and true, two were from New Hampshire, five from the jurisdiction of Massachusetts and Rhode Island, one from Connecticut, two from New York, one from Maryland, and three from the District of Columbia.

"The General Grand Chapter met at the same time in Baltimore, that distinguished man and Mason, Edward Livingston, of Louisiana, being its presiding officer.

He was re-elected to the high office which he had so honorably filled for the preceding three years.

"No session of the National Grand Bodies, held before or since that time, has so attracted public attention as did this of 1832.

John Quincy Adams, ex-President of the United States, did not consider this meeting of a mere handful of men in Baltimore beneath his notice, or unworthy the abuse of his caustic pen; and page after page of his letters, then published in the newspapers of the day, since collected into a volume, attest the interest which that meeting occasioned.

"The period was indeed a peculiar one. For six years the excitement and frenzy of anti-Masonry had been gathering strength and fury, until at last, in a national convention of anti-Masons held here in the City of Baltimore, candidates were nominated for the two highest offices of the Republic.

The election took place in 1832, and William Wirt of Maryland, and Amos Ellmaker, of Pennsylvania, the nominees of the anti-Masonic, political party for President and Vice-President, received the seven electoral votes of Vermont, and no more.

The power of anti-Masonry culminated in 1832; and when the General Grand Encampment assembled here, in the waning days of autumn, and found the fires around which the national Council of anti-Masons had been held, and read by their uncertain and unsteady light the strength and weakness of Anti-masonry in the Union, they knew that the battle had been fought, and that the night of agony was over.

The hate and bitterness and fiendish hostility they knew would still remain - powerful in localities to infinite harm - but the Nation had repudiated antiMasonry, and had elected, as President, Andrew Jackson, an acknowledged, out-spoken, well-known Freemason; so well known that on the 23d of May, 1833, John Quincy Adams, in a published letter to Edward Livingston, then Secretary of State, paid a merited compliment to the Past Grand Master of Tennessee, in words intended to be severe and censurable.

"'The President of the United States,' said Adams, 'is a Brother of the Craft, bound by its oaths, obligations, and penalties, to the exclusive favors, be they more or less, of which they give the mutual pledge.

That in the troubles and difficulties which, within the last seven years, have befallen the craft, they have availed themselves of his name, and authority, and influence, to sustain their drooping fortunes, as far as it has been in their power, has been matter of public notoriety.

A sense of justice has restrained him from joining in their processions, as he has been importunately urged by invitations to do, but he has not withheld from them his support'"

Almost forty years have passed away since the National Grand Bodies assembled in Triennial Session in the City of Baltimore.

Behold the change! Those fourteen brave Knights have gone to their reward - not one of them now lives to rejoice at this triumphant return to Baltimore.

They sleep peacefully and serenely the last great sleep: peace to their ashes; honor to their names.

The railroad and telegraph now traverse populous States, then scarcely known.

The Union stretches from ocean to ocean, and holds in its fast embrace great States, whose territory was then unexplored.

From all parts of this wide extended country - from the Atlantic and the Pacific - from the great rivers, with their fertile valleys - from the mountain ranges, with their verdant slopes - from the rugged North and the sunny South - from the great West, whither the star of empire is taking its course, and from the sea-girt populous East - come up here to Baltimore to this Eighteenth Triennial Session of the Grand Encampment of the United States, in companies, in battalions, in regiments, thousands of true Knights, bearing the banners of the Cross, living witnesses of the truth of the resolutions passed by the General

Grand Encampment in 1832, that "Political Parties, in assailing the orders of Knighthood, aim a blow at all the free institutions of the country."

The institution which in 1832, was abused and maligned, its members insulted and degraded, and which could then gather in its National Convention but fourteen tried souls, has survived the abuse, the malignity, the insults, and degradation, and stands before you today in its wisdom, strength, and beauty.

In 1832 those fourteen Knights did not disturb the usual tranquillity of Baltimore, and their presence here was unrecognized.

Quiet in demeanor, unobtrusive in manner, they came with a firm determination to fully perform their devoirs to Temple Masonry.

In 1871 the authorities of Baltimore, with a liberality of sentiment and a heartiness of greeting which will be gratefully appreciated by every Templar of the United States, welcome us as guests of their municipality.

The Templar Knights throng the city - its houses, streets, and squares, and are received by brethren and citizens with a warmth of fraternal, generous hospitality, unbounded and catholic as the principles of Freemasonry.

PART FOUR
SYMBOLISM OF FREEMASONRY
CHAPTER I

SYMBOLISM OF FREEMASONRY

Introduction.

THE study of Symbols is so closely interwoven with Language that it is essentially necessary, in a treatise on Symbology, that we should begin with an examination into the Origin of language itself; for it is to be presumed that language, or rather speech, was the very first effort of man to make his wishes known to his fellow-man. The habitual use of certain words, applied to the same objects, produced the primitive language.

We shall not attempt to follow those who have supposed that language was derived from certain inorganic sounds predicated upon the "utterances of Animals," called "Bow-Wow" theory by Max Muller and others. Now we must remember that it has been clearly proven by distinguished philologists that "the whole of what we call the human mind is realized in language, and in language only. Our next task would be to try to discover the constituent elements of language, and watch, in their development, the true historical development of the human mind.[319]" It becomes requisite in order fully to understand "symbolisms," as applied to the Ancient Mysteries, the Religions of the World, and also to Speculative Masonry, that we should be more particular in tracing the genealogy of language, from its very commencement, so far as it is possible to do so, by consulting the works of those distinguished writers

---

[319] Max Muller, "Science of Thought," vol. i., p. 176.

of the present century, and more particularly within the last quarter of the century now about to close; and inasmuch as on this particular subject of language there is intimately associated that of the mind, which means "thought" and which, again, means "combination," no better work can possibly be referred to than the Science of Thought, by Max Muller in his recent two volumes, which we may constantly quote from wherever in that work we find that his authority will confirm our own ideas.

Muller is strictly a "scientist" in whatever line of thought he enters for examination, and upon this very subject he has shown the manner in which we may attain the truth, viz., by the " Constituent Elements of Thought," "Thought and Language," "Constituent Elements of Language," the "Origin of Concepts and Roots."

In the proper examination of any individual subject-matter the only true method of examination is by analysis; hence Muller does analyze, so as to show each and every element which enters into the composition of language. He says:

"Few words have been used in so many different senses as Thought. I mean by Thought the act of thinking, and by thinking

I mean no more than combining. I do not pretend that others have not the right of using Thought in any sense which they prefer, pro vided only that they will clearly define it. I only wish to explain what is the meaning in which I intend to use the word, and in which

I hold it ought to be used. ' I think' means to me the same as the Latin Cogito, namely Co-agito, ' I bring together,' only with the proviso, that bringing together or combining implies separating, for we cannot combine two or many things without at the same time separating them from all the rest. Hobbes expressed the same truth long ago when he said ' that all our thinking consisted in addition and subtraction.'"

"Humiliating as this may at first sight appear, it is really not more so than that the most subtle and complicated mathematical processes, which to the uninitiated seem beyond all comprehension, can be reduced in the end to addition and subtraction.

"Thinking may not seem so marvellous an achievement as we formerly imagined when we look up with vague admiration to the Mathematical Calculations of Newton, or to the Metaphysical $peculations of Kant; yet if what these thinkers achieved has been achieved by such simple processes as addition and subtraction, combining and separating, their work to the mind becomes in reality far more marvellous than it appeared at first. Much, however, depends on what we combine and separate, and we have therefore to consider what corresponds in thinking to the numbers with which the mathematician operates, what are, in fact, the known quantities that constitute the material of our thoughts, what are the elements which we bring together or co-agitate."

Muller then proceeds to distinguish in our knowledge four things "Sensations, Percepts, Concepts, and Names, and, while we can distinguish these, we must not suppose that they ever exist as separate entities; for no words are possible without concepts, nor can there be concepts without percepts, nor percepts without sensations. If we postulate sensations as the causes of percepts, percepts as the causes of concepts, and concepts as the causes of names, it would seem a very natural conclusion that sensations could exist previous to and therefore independent of percepts, percepts of concepts, concepts of words. And yet we have only to try the experiment in order to convince ourselves that, as a matter of fact, thought, in the usual sense of the word, is utterly impossible without the simultaneous working of sensations, percepts, concepts, and names, and that in reality the four are inseparable."

With these fundamental principles thus clearly laid down by Muller, we may discover how, at the earliest period in man's history, he very soon found a name for every fact which was presented to his observation. We shall follow the Author in his most interesting and conclusive arguments to prove the position which he has taken. The service of language is to convey our thoughts to one another.

There are various ways in which men can communicate with one another-by gestures, cries, words; make pictures to represent their ideas, characters or letters. These are signs, and in order to under stand in what manner they operate we must commence with such signs as are the most natural and simple. When parties meet who speak different languages they endeavor to make themselves understood by gestures which would most naturally indicate the idea wished to be conveyed

"This is the gesture-language, as we all know how to use it. But to see what a full and exact means of Communication it may be worked up to, it should be watched in use among the deaf and dumb, who have to depend so much upon it. To give an idea how far gestures can be made to do the work of spoken words, the signs may be described in which a deaf-and-dumb man once told a child's story in presence of the writer. He began by moving his hand, palm down, about a yard from the ground, as we do to show the height of a child-this meant it was a child he was thinking of.

Then he tied an imaginary pair of bonnet-strings under his chin (his usual sign for female) to make it understood that the child was a girl. The child's mother was then brought on the scene in a similar way. She beckons to the child and gives her two-pence, these being indicated by pretending to drop two coins from one hand into the other: if there had been any doubt as to whether they were copper or silver coins this would have been settled by pointing to something brown or even by one's contemptuous way of handling coppers which at once distinguishes them from silver. The mother also gives the child a jar, shown by sketching its shape with the forefingers in the air, and- going through the act of handing it over. Then by imitating the unmistakable kind of twist with which one turns a treacle-spoon, it is made known that it is treacle the child is to buy. Next, a wave of the hand shows the child being sent off on her errand, the usual sign of walking being added, which is made by two fingers walking on the table. The turning of an imaginary door-handle now takes us into the shop, where the counter is shown by passing the flat hands as it were over it. Behind this counter a figure is pointed out; he is shown to be a man by the usual sign of putting a hand to one's chin and drawing it down where the beard is or would be; then the sign of tying an apron around the waist adds the information that the man is the shopman. To him the child gives the jar, dropping the money into his hand, and moving her forefinger as if taking up treacle, to show what she wants. Then we see the jar put into an imaginary pair of scales which go up and down ; the great treacle-jar is brought from the shelf and the little jar filled with the proper twist to take up the last trickling thread; the grocer puts the two coins in the till, and the girl sets off with the jar; she sees a drop of treacle on the rim, wipes it off with her finger, and puts her finger in her mouth, how she was tempted to take more, how her mother found her out by the spot of treacle on her pinafore, etc."

The student anxious to master the principles of language will find this gesture-talk so instructive that it will be well to explain its workings more closely. "The signs used are of two kinds. In the first kind, things actually present are shown. Thus, if the deaf-mute wants to mention `hand,' or ` shoe,' he touches his own hand or shoe. Where a speaking man would say `I,' `thou,' `he,' the deaf-mute simply points to himself and the other persons. To express `red,' or 'blue,' he touches the inside of his own lip or points to the sky. In the second kind of signs ideas are conveyed by imitations. Thus, pretending to drink may mean 'water,' or 'to drink,' or 'thirsty.' Laying the cheek on the hand expresses 'sleep' or `bed-time.' A significant jerk of the whip-hand suggests either 'whip' or 'coachman,' or 'to drive,' as the case may be. A 'lucifer' is indicated by pretending to strike a match, and `candle' by the act of holding up the forefinger and pretending to blow it out. Also in the gesture-language the symptoms of the temper one is in may be imitated, and so become signs of the same temper in others. Thus the act of shivering becomes an expressive sign for 'cold'; smiles show 'joy,' 'approval,' 'goodness,' while frowns show 'anger,' 'disapproval,' 'badness.' It might seem that such various meanings to one sign would be confusing, but there is a way of correcting this, for when a single sign does nit make the meaning clear, others are brought in to supplement it. Thus, if one wants to express 'a pen,' it may not be sufficient to pretend to write with one, as that might be intended for 'writing' or 'letter'; but if one then pretends to write and holds up a pen, this will make it plain that the pen itself is meant."

"It has to be noticed that the gesture-language by no means matches sign for word with spoken language. One reason is that it has so little power of expressing abstract ideas.

The deaf-mute can show particular ways of making things, such as building a wall, or cutting out a coat, but it is quite beyond him to make one sign include what is common to all these, as we use the abstract term to 'make.' Even ' in' and ' out' must be expressed in some such clumsy way as by pretending to put the thing talked of in, and then to take it out. Next let us compare an English sentence with the sign by which the same meaning would be expressed among the deaf and dumb. It will at once be seen that many words we use have no sign at all corresponding to them. Thus, when we should say in words, ` The hat which I left on the table is black,' this statement can be practically conveyed in gestures, and there will be signs for what we may call 'real' words, such as hat, leave, black. But for what may be called the 'grammatical' words, the, which, is, there will be no signs, for the gesture-language has none. Again, grammars lay down distinctions between substantives, adjectives, and verbs. But these distinctions are not to be found in gesture-language, where pointing to a grass-plot may mean `grass' or `green,' and pretending to warm one's hands may suggest `warm' or to warm one's self, or even 'fire-place.' Nor (unless where artificial signs have been brought in by teachers) is there anything in the gesture-language to correspond with the inflection of words, such as distinguish goest from go, him from he, domum from domus. What is done is to call up a picture in the minds of the spectators by first setting up something to be thought about, and then adding to or acting on it, till the whole story is told. If the signs do not follow in such order as to carry meanings as they go, the looker-on will be perplexed. Thus, in conveying to a deaf-and-dumb child the thought of a green box, one must make a sign for 'box' first, and then show as by pointing to grass outside, that its color is `green.'

"This account of the gesture-language will have made it clear to the reader by what easy and reasonable means man can express his thoughts invisible signs."[320] So we may conclude that from these fundamentals, by which men formulated their special gestures, soon they became enabled to produce visible signs to represent "things," and, gradually, to sketch the same upon any plain surface, so that the ideas became permanently fixed to be understood by others for any given time, by which they were reminded of separate facts, or continuous narratives.

In due time, when religious rites were adopted, these written or engraved signs became symbols, and emblems, and were perpetuated from fathers to sons, along the track of time, and their engravings upon stone, either as monuments, tombs, obelisks, or temples, have existed from time immemorial to our day.

We may thus trace from the original elements of symbols the great variety of combinations which we find, in the representations of the various Deities, in all the ancient religions of the world, in which, did our limits permit, we might with great profit trace the gradual development from the simplest forms to the most abstruse and recondite representations of Deity.

"Wherefore, from hence it plainly appears that these Platonic and Egyptian pagans, who thus reduced their multiplicity of Gods to the divine ideas, did not therefore make them to be so many minds or spirits, really distinct from the Supreme God (though dependent on him, too), but indeed only so many partial considerations of one God, as being all things, that is, containing within himself the causes of all things. And accordingly we find that the Egyptian Theologers called their religious Animals symbols of the eternal ideas; so did they also call them symbols of God.

"Celsus applauds the Egyptian Theologers talking so magnificently and mysteriously of those brute animals worshipped by them, and affirming them to be certain symbols of God.

"But lastly, as God was supposed by these pagans not only to pervade all things, and to fill all things, but also he being the cause of all things, to be himself in a manner all things, so was he called also by the name of everything, or everything called by his name; that is, the several

---

[320] "Anthropology," by Tylor.

Max Muller, in his Treatise on Words, clearly shows from whence are derived certain words which, in our language, have become so common as to have lost their original technical sense.

Light.

The great object of Aryan desire derived through the Latin Lux, from the Greek Luknos, was nearly the same in Sanskrit, and the Moon, Lukina. So the seven Stars in the North, being the Seven "Shiners," became the "Great Bear," because the same word was used for shining, and a bear, whose hair was shining. We have the Greek Lukabos, a year, a revolution of Luc; Lukeios, an epithet of Apollo; Lukos, a Wolf with shining hair, from leukos, white or shining, and sacred to Apollo; Lucus, a grove, because planted around the high places of Luc; the English word Luck, because it indicates prosperity, is represented by Light.[325]

The Seven Stars, or Seven Rishis, were derived from Rishi, itinerant, from Ri, and Rish, to go. Arktos-Bear, Riksha-Bear. The Worship of Light passed to the causes of Light; first of the Sun, Moon, and Stars, then of Fire; then into more solid forms, to represent the flame, upright Stones, of Conical and pyramidal form, rough Stone or unhewn, as in Gaul and in Britain.

The Worship of individuals, either real or mythical, was transferred to animals, which were made to represent them; as, from the doctrine of transmigration, the Soul of Osiris had passed into a Bull, that animal became the Supreme object of Worship; as the Cat was for Diana, and the Cow for Isis. Now, writing Hieroglyphically contributes greatly to this Species of idolatry, and the Priests did then, as they have done ever since, in every form of worship, hold the power and the method of interpretation from all but those whom they chose to initiate into those mysteries, and concealed by this veil, so artfully thrown over their system, from all others.

Thus, the Hieroglyph for God was a Star, and the symbol of a Star was a Serpent, from whence proceeded the Universal Serpent Worship which extended over the whole World.

It would not be an unprofitable task to follow out to its legitimate conclusion the subject of the Serpent Symbol, but we shall only allude to some of the symbols in our further illustrations of this subject. It has been well settled that the serpent symbol was legitimately derived from the traditions of Paradise, so familiarly known

---

[325] Faber, 11 Mysteries Caberi," vol. i., p. 29.

and represented by all the Nations of Antiquity, and in their religious rites, it may be said, "The trace of the Serpent was over them all."

From this meager sketch it may be seen how religion, which was first pure, and an earnest outpouring of the heart to the Great and beneficent Creator, degenerated into gross idolatry.

We now pass from the general subject to the more special one of Hieroglyphical writings.

It is assumed that alphabetical Characters in their first condition were substantive emblems or simple representations of language.

From Shuckford, in his Connections of Sacred and Profane History, we learn that "the first language had but one part of speech, and consisted chiefly of a few names for creatures and things Mankind had to do with." Others do not concur in this, and say, " The art of thinking, which is the arrangement of our ideas from the perceptions of natural objects, cannot exist without some degree of reason ; and the various and abstruse combinations of reason will scarcely be produced without the use of words expressing qualities, action, or passion, as well as connectives to draw consequences or blend ideas which are relative, uniform, and rational."

Original names have invariably represented innate qualities as understood universally among those using a common language; whence the origin no man can determine, although it is attempted to show that animals received names which in their utterance would indicate some distinguishing trait or characteristic. It is, however, quite certain that the Oldest Alphabets, in their elements, represented substantive objects, as in Hebrew and Cognate Alphabets, viz., Aleph א, the Ox; Beth ב, a House or enclosure; Gammel ג, a Camel. Spineto[326] says: "The Original mode of Writing was the exact figure of the object, which, for the Sake of diminishing labor, became first simple drawing of the Outline, and ultimately an arbitrary Mark, which produced the three different modes of Writing among the Egyptians, generally designated by the appellations of hieroglyphic, demotic, and hieratic."

A great cause which advanced the Conventional system of Written signs or Characters was the imagery of primitive language.

One Author says: "Rhetoric, which springs naturally out of language, became a Science when reduced to a system; natural figures, untrammelled by the restriction of rules, became more expressive: Cain's inquisitive reply to the stern demand was, ` Am I my brother's Keeper?'

---

[326] Spineto, " Hieroglyphs," ix., 297.

Lamech says to his wives: 'Hear my voice, ye Wives of Lamech, and hearken unto my speech, for I have slain a Man to my wounding and a young man to my hurt. If Cain shall be avenged Seven fold, truly Lamech Seventy and Seven fold.'" In the Nabathean Alphabet, reputed to have been Antediluvian, if they wished to state in what manner a man died by a violent death, they used one of a variety of characters, representing 1st, By lightning. 2d, Guillotine. 3d, Serpent. 4th, Hatchet. 5th, Poison. 6th, Dagger. 7th, Cord. To express firmness of mind, personal strength and courage, some stately or majestic production of Nature was employed, as the Oak and Lion. A warrior was termed a Lion, or an Oak; on the contrary, an irresolute or weak man by a reed; insincerity by a Serpent, and fidelity by a dog.

OIE9'X

"Let us, for example, suppose that the letter B was called Bai and such a term primarily imported being or existing. We are told Bai was the Egyptian denomination for a branch of the Palm-tree, which tree was anciently regarded as an emblem of being, existence, or immortality; again, Horapollo says, Bai signifies a Hawk, the soul and the Wind, wherefore the Egyptians used the Hawk as a symbol for the soul.

"The Greeks called the palm-branch Baion, Bais, and Beta or Baita, the letter B, preserves the sound of Hebrew Beth or Egyptian Bat, but the idea of the name, in Greek from Bei baioo, to con firm, establish or place in a permanent state of existence. The Latins called this letter Be, nearly the simple name of the Bai or symbolical palm-branch. And Be in the Celtic conveys the same leading idea of existence. Irish Be is the term for life; Cornish signifies Be, Am, Art, is, existent."[327]

The Hebrew word for the Deity called the Tetragrammaton is also derived from the word "to be," "I am," "I will be," "I am all that exists." In Egyptian, the same word is used for the principal Deity.

The Origin of Hieroglyphics was simply picture-writing, and consisted in the representation of a drawing of any visible object connected with it. Improvements arose to obviate difficulties and meet the necessities of circumstances as they occurred, and in due season a regular system was ordained, and became conventional and determinate. Thus, certain symbols became known and established for certain characteristics ;   as, for instance, The Hawk, as an emblem of the Supreme Deity, because of its ; piercing sight and swiftness.

---

[327] Davis, of " Celt. Res.," p. 339, in Oliver's Lecture V., p. 64.

The Asp also, not being subject to old age, and moving without limbs. The Crocodile, because it has no tongue, which organ God has no occasion for.

At the period of the greatest perfection of Egyptian writing there were three kinds, viz., Epistolic, Hieroglyphic, and Symbolic. The Priests had a fourth, which was termed Hierogrammatic, which was known only to their order. Modern writers subdivide the above into

1, Pure Hieroglyphic, or picture;
2, Linear Hieroglyphic, or emblems;
3, Phonetic Hieroglyphic, or representations of sound; and
4, Demotic, or Epistolographic, or Enchorial[328] writing, for the uses of common life.

Symbolic writing was subdivided into three parts, viz., Curiologic, speaking literally; Tropical, a figure; and Allegorical, description of one thing, under the image of another.

This was for greater secrecy, each admitting of a different method of interpretation, which was communicated only to a few. In the Curiologic style, the moon was pictured by a crescent; Tropically by a Cat; Allegorically by the figure of Isis or a veiled female; The Sun by a disk; Tropically by an Ox, and Allegorically by a figure of Osiris.

The word Symbol, derived from Sumbolon (Symbolum), means that which represents, or is a sign of something expressing to the initiate a doctrine, thought, or principle; Emblem, from Em blema, first signified work inlaid, or raised ornaments, or Mosaic work; now it is made to mean the same as symbol.

A.D. 363, Yamblichus[329] says that he considered the mode of teaching by symbols most necessary, and that nearly all the Greeks cultivated it, as the Most Ancient and transcendentally honored by the Egyptians, and adopted by them in the most diversified Manner. "The first requisite of a symbol is, that it shall really mean something; that it shall be in its nature a proper and adequate sign and token of something ; and the second is, that this something shall be worth knowing and remembering."[330]

---

[328] Enchorios, place, country, popular, common, invented at a late period. They invented another system of Magical Communication which imbedded Cabalistic Secrets in comprehensive phrases, that were not only mysterious, but absolutely formidable to the ignorant. Soothsayers were Magic Alarm-posts; philters and dangerous compounds were treasure Chambers, etc.

[329] "Vita Pythagoras."
[330] Albert Pike

"The Origin of the science of Symbols is lost in the night of time, and seems to connect itself with the Cradle of Humanity; the most ancient Worships submitted to its law; the Arts of design, Architecture, Statuary, and Painting were born under its influence, and the primitive writing was also one of its applications."[331]

"Everything is Emblematic, everything is figurative, everything is more or less Hieroglyphic amongst the Ancients. They began in Chaldea by placing, or rather by giving to Some Constellations the name of the Ram, and of the Bull, either to signify the productions of these Animals during the Spring, or to pay a peculiar homage to the Deity, as soon as they began to depart from the religion of Noah. Fire was the symbol of the Deity among the Persians. The rising of Sirius or Dog-Star informed the Egyptians of the inundation of the Nile. The Serpent, holding its tail in its mouth, became the image of eternity. The whole of nature was disguised and emblematically represented by the primitive inhabitants of our globe. If we place all the symbols and emblems which we have received from Antiquity under the inspection of a Man of sense, or even of a scholar who had never heard of them, he will not be able to explain any of them. It is a figurative and emblematic language which requires a particular study before it can be understood."[332] One of the most beautiful of the Ancient figures is that of Timaeus of Locri, who describes Deity to be " a Circle whose centre was everywhere and whose circumference nowhere."[333]

"The philosophy of the Egyptian Priests was abstruse and hidden; enveloped in fable, and allegory, and exhibiting only dark hints, and obscure resemblances to truth, and thus much even the priests themselves insinuate to us, in many instances, particularly in those sphinxes which they seem designedly to have placed before their Temples, as types of the enigmatical nature of their theology; of this nature was the inscription engraved upon the base of Minerva's statue at Sais, whom they look upon the same as Isis, viz.: ' I am everything that has been, that is, and that shall be; Nor has any Mortal ever yet been able to discover what is under my Veil.'"[334]

The name of AMUN-AMN is interpreted by Manetho to signify "Concealment," or something which is hidden. Osiris is designated under the hieroglyphs of an eye and a scepter, the former denoting his

---

[331] Portal, " Symbols des Egyptiens."
[332] Spineto, "Lectures on Elements of Hieroglyphics."
[333] Albert Pike. Plutarch,
[334] De Isidi et Osiride," died A.D. 140.

providential Wisdom, as the latter does his power, they being the two most distinguishing Characteristics of Deity. Also of symbols - " Under which the Mystics endeavored to lead their Votaries to the Knowledge of divine truth, and, though some of these are more clear and explicit than others, yet are they not any of them without hazard; for whilst some persons by wholly mistaking their Meaning and application, have thereby plunged themselves into superstition, others, that they might avoid so fatal a quagmire, have unawares dashed themselves upon the rock of Atheism."

It was principally among the East Indians, Egyptians, and Syrians that the most extraordinary emblems were consecrated to religion.

A South Sea Island Missionary tells how once being busy carpentering, and having forgotten his square, he wrote a message to his wife for it, with a piece of charcoal on a block, and sent it by a native, who, amazed to find that the block could talk without a mouth, for a long time afterward carried it hung around his neck by a string, and to his wondering countrymen told what he saw it do.

The art of writing, however strange and mysterious it seemed to the savage tribes of men, was developed from steps of invention. Uncivilized men took the first step in writing by making pictures of such natural or artificial objects known to them.

In one picture-writing, used by hunting tribes of American Indians, there is recorded an expedition across waters, led by a chief on horse-back, having a Magical drumstick in his hand.

In that graphic, there were fifty-one men in four canoes, the first being led by an ally of the chief whose name was Kishkemunazee (Kingfisher), as shown by the bird. The land tortoise, the emblem of land, shows that they reached the other side of the water, the picture of the three suns under the sky indicating three days in crossing. When the tortoise is painted to represent land it is not a mere imitation, but has become an emblem or symbol. The bird does not represent a real kingfisher, but a man of that name; this becomes the first step toward phonetic writing or by sound, i.e., to make a picture stand for the sound of the word to be spoken. Tylor says (p. 169): "How men may have made the next move toward writing may be learnt from the common child's games of rebus, i.e., writing words 'by things.' Like many other games, this one keeps up in child's sport what in earlier ages was man's earnest. Thus if one writes the word 'waterman' by a picture of a water-jug and a man, this is drawing the meaning of the word in a way hardly beyond the American Indian's picture of the kingfisher. But it is very different when in a child's book of puzzles one finds the drawing of a water-can, a man being shot, and a date fruit, this representing in rebus the word `Can-di-date.'

"For now what the pictures have come to stand for is no longer their meaning, but their mere sound. This is true phonetic writing, though of a rude kind, and shows how the practical art of writing really came to be invented. This invention seems to have been made more than once, and in somewhat different ways. The, old Mexicans, before the arrival of the Spaniards, had got so far as to spell the names of persons and places by pictures, rebus fashion.

Even when they began to be Christianized, they contrived to use their picture-writing for the Latin words of their new religion.

Thus they painted a flag (pan), a stone (te), a prickly pear (noch)-which were together pronounced pa-te-noch-te and served to spell pater noster, in a way that was totally exact for Mexicans who had no r in their language. In the same way they ended the prayer with the picture of water (a) and aloe (me) to express amen."

"This leads on to a more important system of writing. Looking at the ordinary Chinese characters on tea-chests or vases, one would hardly think they had to do with pictures of things. But there are fortunately preserved certain early Chinese characters, known as the `ancient pictures,' which show how what were at first distinctly formed sketches of objects came to be dashed off in a few strokes of the rabbit's hair pencil, till they passed into the meaningless looking cursive forms now in use.

"The Chinese did not stop short at making such mere pictures of objects, which goes but little way toward writing. The inventors of the present mode of Chinese writing wanted to represent the spoken sounds, but here they were put in a difficulty by their language consisting of monosyllables, so that one word has many different meanings. To meet this they devised an ingenious plan of making compound characters, or `pictures and sounds,' in which one part gives the sound, while the other gives the sense. To give an idea of this, suppose it were agreed that a picture of a box should stand for the sound box. As, however, this sound has several meanings, some sign must be added to show which is intended. Thus a key might be drawn beside it, to show it is a box to put things in; or a leaf if it is to mean the plant called box; or a hand, if it is intended for box on the ear; or a whip would show it was to signify the box of a coach.

"This would be for us a clumsy proceeding, but it would be a great advance beyond mere picture-writing, as it would make sure at once of the sound and the meaning. Thus in Chinese, the sound chow has various meanings, as ship, fluff, flickering, basin, loquacity. Therefore, the character which represents a ship, chow, which is placed first in the figure as represented afterward with additional characters, to show which particular meaning of chow is intended.

"These examples, though far from explaining the whole mystery of Chinese writing, give some idea of the principles of its sound, characters, and keys of determinative signs, and show why a Chinese has to master such an immensely complicated set of characters in order to write his own language.

"Next as to the cuneiform writing, such as is to be seen at the British Museum on the huge man-headed bulls of Nineveh, or on the flat baked bricks which were pages of books in the library of Sennacherib. The marks, like wedges or arrow-heads, arranged in groups or rows, do not look much like pictures of objects. Yet there is evidence that they came at first from picture-writing; for instance, the sun was represented by a rude figure of it by four strokes arranged round. Of the groups of characters in an inscription, some serve directly to represent objects, as man, woman, river, house, while other groups are read phonetically as standing for syllables.

"The inventors of this ancient; system appear to have belonged to the Akkadian group of Nations, the founders of early Babylonian civilization. In later ages the Assyrians and Persians learned to write their language by Cuneiform characters, in inscriptions which remain to this day as their oldest records. But the Cuneiform writing was cumbrous in the extreme, and had to give way when it came into competition with the alphabet. To understand the origin of that invention, it is necessary to go back to a plan of writing which dates from antiquity, probably even higher than the Cuneiform of Babylonia, namely, the hieroglyphics of Egypt.

"The earliest known hieroglyphic inscriptions of Egypt belong to a period approaching 3000 B.C. Even at this ancient time the plan of writing was so far developed that the scribes had the means of spelling any word phonetically, when they chose. But, though the Egyptians had thus come to writing by sound, they only trusted to it in part, combining it with signs which are evidently remains of earlier picture-writing. Thus the mere pictures of an ox, a star, a pair of sandals, may stand for ox, star, sandals. Even where they spelled words by their sounds they had a remarkable way of adding what are called determinatives, which are pictures to confirm or explain the meaning of the spelled word.

".... part of the pictures of animals and things are letters to be read into Egyptian words. But others are still real pictures, intended to stand for what they represent. The sun is shown with a one mark below, and followed by the battle-axe, which is the symbol of divinity, while further on comes a picture of the horizon with the sun on it. Besides these, some of the figures are determinative pictures to explain the words, the verb to walk being followed by an explanatory pair of legs, and the word enemy having a picture of an enemy after it, and then three strokes, the sign of plurality. It seems that the Egyptians began with mere picture-writing, like that of the barbarous tribes of America, and though, in after ages, they came to use some figures as phonetic characters or letters, they never had the strength of mind to rely on them entirely, but went on using the old pictures as well. How they were led to make a picture to stand for a sound is not hard to see. In the figure a character may be noticed which is read R. This is an outline of an open mouth, and indeed is often used to represent a mouth, but the Egyptian word for mouth being R, O the sign came to be used as a character letter to spell the sound R O or R wherever it was wanted.

So much of the history of the art of writing may thus be read in a single hieroglyphic sentence."

The Last Sortie.
Firmly believing that the guiding hand of an all-wise and overruling Providence has conducted mankind from his earliest appearance on earth, commencing, as we have endeavored to show, with his primitive notions of things and his efforts to illustrate his first crude and imperfect ideas and clearly to demonstrate his gradual advancement in expressing those ideas, until he had accomplished the same by framing alphabetical writing-as shown in the earliest written languages - we will endeavor to demonstrate that it must have been by Divine Revelation that this was finally accomplished in the gradual development of man's inventive genius implanted by Divine Providence in the "Three Revelations."

It would seem evidently proper in the examination of symbolisms in connection with the ancient religions that we should also examine that religion which, commencing with Moses and the children of Israel, has gradually advanced and spread over the whole world.

CHAPTER II

THREE REVELATIONS

The "fall of man," or the loss of innocence, was well acknowledged in all the ancient theologies and philosophies, and that a "restoration" was to take place was also acknowledged; the effort in every mythology was to complete that restoration by means of a "divine savior."

In our Masonic system of the first era there is no question whatever in the minds of all impartial examiners that the authors of the system designed to teach the dogmas peculiar to Christianity. The revolution of 1717 divested Masonry of most of its Sectarian dogmas, and opened the way for the admission of all who would merely confess a belief and trust in a Deity. Nevertheless, in subsequent years, measurably between 1760 and 1800 A.D., the several lectures introduced, gradually, a more complete acknowledgment of the Christian elements than existed from the revolution in 1717 to the former date, 1760.

The lectures, now used in every State of the Union, clearly teach those dogmas.

The use of the Sacred writings, holding as they do a position representing, par excellence, the "Great Light," evidently demonstrates the belief in their direct inspiration from God himself, or the whole matter is an imposition and should be removed from our ritual. To declare solemnly that the Bible "is the inestimable gift from God to man" is a "solemn Mockery " if it be not the acknowledged " Holy Writing."

It is, therefore, the conceded guide for all of our conduct, and if not inspired by that confession, then we are defrauding every candidate who receives the Entered Apprentice's degree.

Assuming that we are honest men in our declarations, we proceed with our argument.

First Subject. - Revelation in External Nature.

The Constitution of the World is but partially discerned by man, and the revelation of the Will of God is but dimly perceived therein. The light of conscience and direct revelation are necessary to assist him in understanding external Nature.

(a) External Nature may reveal to man somewhat of God's Will from its constitution, when in all its parts he may discover in the government of God therein that " there is a fixed connection between virtue and happiness and between vice and misery as the 108 result of cause and effect; and we may thus conclude that God has so constituted all Nature that he approves of Virtue and condemns Vice. "These Moral tendencies are universal, being everywhere observed in creation and providence, and in individual and social experience. They are inevitable: - vice, in the long run, producing misery; and virtue producing happiness, by a law as unchangeable as the law of gravitation. "Plato said, by the Sophist Hippias " Now, by Jove, I must here confess that I do perceive plain traces of a Divine Law; for that laws should bring along with them their own penalty when broken is a most rare device, to which no mere human legislator has even yet been able to attain."

There is, evidently, to every reflecting mind, in God's Universe "a Vast and Wondrous System of Moral compensations and Moral retributions embracing all the subjects of the Divine Government."

(b) Not easily interpreted. In this form it is very difficult to interpret the Will of God. That wonderful Man Paul said that the invisible things of God - his eternal power and Deity - may be made known by things that are seen, yet Man, limited as he is, bounded by the enslavement of the flesh, can see but dimly the record of the Moral attributes and Moral law by the results of causes in the Natural World. From these sources only those who have attained to the highest philosophy can even remotely see the rule of right from external Nature. Nevertheless, we may perceive, even if remotely, that God contemplated, in the Creation of the Universe, that all things should work together for a specific purpose, and in his infinite mind there could not be a separation of the Moral attribute from those essentially necessary in his character as the Supreme Governor and Creator of all things.

Second Subject. - Revelation in Man's Nature.

We presume that in the original creation of Man, the revelation of the Will of God, in Man's Moral Constitution, must have been clear and perfect. Is this the case now with Man?

And may we well ask, How and when did the change take place? Observation and our own personal experience clearly demonstrate the fact "That it is now defective and dim," and the teaching of revelation also confirms the truth.

The following is the immediate and practical rule: "A rule of right, in order to be in the highest sense practical, must be always at hand and in readable form. For a being essentially and always active, emergencies of Moral action must be constant and often sudden and unexpected, so that time is not always given for consulting some outward rule to be comprehended by the processes of reasoning. The Author of Man's being has, therefore, placed a revelation of the rule of right in the soul, to be read intuitively, and so to furnish a practical guide suited to his circumstances."

For Mankind in general, experience teaches us that this rule is the chief practical guide for Moral conduct. Professor Haven says: "Within certain limits, the Moral nature of Man decides, without hesitation, as to the Character of given actions, and approves and condemns accordingly. It is seldom at a loss as to the great dividing lines which separate the Kingdom of right and wrong. It is the voice of nature, essentially the same in all climes and ages of the World, approving the right, condemning the wrong. It is the voice of God speaking through the Moral Nature and constitution which has been bestowed upon his creatures. Thus it is that they which have the law within are a law unto themselves."

This inner sense of Moral rectitude can not be the Ultimate guide, for it is well known that education, location, customs, and habits control our ideas of right and wrong in the abstract ; and it is also true, that as we change from one Kingdom or Nation to others we do find the inner consciousness of Men differing - wherefore, we are forced to find the Ultimate principle, by which to decide between any two conflicting ideas of Moral rectitude; and we thus come to a direct revelation by "Scripture" which, when received as those of divine inspiration, we are of necessity to obey them, as the mind and will of God; and to which we must refer as standards for our government.

The Christian Theologians have, in all the past, written constantly in advocacy of the divine origin of the "Bible." It is not our province, in so short an Article as this must be, to enter at all into a discussion of the validity or the "Authenticity" of the Text of Scripture. Volumes have been written, and but few have been convinced, save those already "believers"; hence we content ourselves in this "dictum": As Masons, we receive it as the Ultimate Standard of our Morality, and by it, as our adopted " Constitution," we must inevitably be tried, and be acquitted or condemned. If it be but of human origin, it is nevertheless the foundation upon which every Moral principle in Masonry now stands; just as we are governed by the Constitutions, Rules, Regulations, and Edicts which are acknowledged as of human authority only, and do govern us in our common jurisprudence throughout the entire World of Masons, so do the Scriptures rule and govern our Ethics and Moral Conduct, whether they be human only, or of Divine origin. Those Moral principles, clearly enunciated in the Bible, appeal to the Moral consciousness of Mankind in general; and it is only in the Minds of those who have suffered their Moral principles to be atrophied, that there ever has been or ever will be anyone to deny this. Among all enlightened and good men it is "the most perfect expression of the law of human duty."

"In bringing to light new relations, as arising out of Man's sin, the ethical system of the Bible has vastly widened the sphere of duty." We must believe in the infinity of God; but the infinite God can not, by us, in the present limitation of our faculties, be comprehended, but only conceived. A Deity understood would be no Deity at all; and it is blasphemy to say that God only is as we are able to think Him to be. We know God according to the finitude of our faculties; but we believe much that we are incompetent properly to know.

The infinite God is what, to use the words of Pascal, is infinitely inconceivable. Faith, Belief, is the organ by which we apprehend what is beyond our knowledge. In this, all Divines and Philosophers, worthy of the name, are found to coincide; and the few who assent to Man a knowledge of the infinite, do this on the daring, the extravagant, the paradoxical supposition, either that Human Reason is identical with the Divine, or that Man and the absolute are one.

In Man's condition, growing out of his imperfect Nature and the uncertainties of a correct understanding of duties, a revelation became a necessity, so soon as his change from a sinless to a sinful state occurred. We here encounter at once the Skeptical view which denies the present sinful state of Man. Let us then assume Man as sinless and take tie following sketch of Cousin to illustrate the present condition of things - Good and Evil.

You will agree with me that Man is, 1st, sinful; or, 2d, Man is sinless. There is no middle term of this category.

"Good and Evil "-Distinction.

"If we do not admit the essential distinction between good and evil, between virtue and crime, crime founded on interest, virtue founded on disinterestedness, then human language and the sentiments that it expresses are inexplicable.

"Disturb this distinction, and you disturb human life and entire society. Permit me to take an extreme, tragic, and terrible example. Here is a man that has just been judged. He has been condemned to death, and is about to be executed-to be deprived of life. And why?

Place yourself in the system that does not admit the essential distinction between good and evil, and ponder on what is stupidly atrocious in this act of human justice. What has the condemned done? Evidently a thing indifferent in itself. For if there is no other outward distinction than that of pleasure and pain, I defy anyone to qualify any human action, whatever it may be, as criminal, without the most absurd inconsequence. But this thing, indifferent in itself, a certain number of men, called legislators, have declared to be a crime. This purely arbitrary declaration has found no echo in the heart of this Man.

He has not been able to feel the justice of it, since there is nothing in itself just. He has therefore done, without remorse, what this declaration arbitrarily interdicted. The Court proceeds to prove to him that he has not succeeded, but not that he has done contrary to justice, for there is no justice. I maintain that every condemnation, be it to death, or to any punishment whatever, imperatively supposes, in order to be anything else than a repression of violence by Violence, the four following Points 1st, That there is an essential distinction between good and evil, justice and injustice, and that to this distinction is attached, for every intelligent and free being, the obligation of conforming to good and justice. 2d, That man is an intelligent and free being, capable of comprehending this distinction, and the obligation that accompanies it, and of adhering to it naturally, independently of all convention, and every possible law, capable also of resisting the temptations that bear him towards evil and injustice, and of fulfilling the sacred law of natural justice: 3d, That every act contrary to justice deserves to be repressed by force, and even punished in reparation of the fault committed, and independently too of all law and all convention. 4th, That Man naturally recognizes the distinction between the just and the unjust and knows that every penalty applied to an unjust act is itself most strictly just."[335]

In the Scriptures we find all that is necessary for Man to do in his progress toward reinstatement to his original sinless condition. It is

---

[335] Cousin, "True, Beautiful, and Good," p. 223.

no argument against the Bible that Men differ in regard to the very language of it, and that such differences have created bigotry, fanaticism, hatred, persecution, and death; because all those results are the demonstrations, palpably true, of the sinfulness of Man, his selfishness, ambition, and lust for power, in utter opposition to those very teachings in the Bible by which they should be guided to a course of love, compassion, charity, and beneficence. In all ages Men have done precisely the same things to their fellow-Men before the Bible was written; and since then, when in utter ignorance of its existence, when there were no redeeming features in their savagery, inhumanity, and devilishness.

The influence of the Morality of the Bible has tended, continually, to change the fierceness of the Natural Man to those milder and heavenly virtues of Love, compassion, and Charity.

Third Subject. - The Written Revelation is the Perfect Form of the Supreme Rule; it is the clearest expression of the Divine Will.

Every intelligent Man will say that a Character modeled after the Morality of the Bible is a perfect Character: as was that of Jesus, the "Christos" of the Bible. Every departure from that perfect type detracts from a perfect Character. Let us refer to those Characters who were representdl centuries before his advent and see if in their Conduct they were up to his standard. Were "Chrishna " of India, Mithras of Persia, Osiris of Egypt, Dionysus, Bacchus, Orphaeus and Adonis, of Classic days, such as to be examples for us to follow?

Were they not all of them the mere creations of human imaginations? Who now believes that any one of them ever had a real existence?

They were all Characters of human origin in the Mythologic ages designed as the "Saviors" of Men, each one emphatically the representative "Christos," or Christ of his particular Nation; and the religious system designed to restore the lost and fallen race of Man. This idea was derived from the traditions of the fall of Man, by means of the Serpent, Kalinac. Chrishna, in the Ninth Avatar, is represented as the Good Black Shepherd stamping the head of the Serpent Kalinac with his heel, while he holds the serpent aloft by his tail. In the Tenth Avatar, which is yet to come, Chrishna, the "Anointed," is to restore the race of Man to its pristine innocence and happiness. Hence, we assert, that since God promised to Adam that the "seed of the Woman should bruise the head of the Serpent," Christianity, in some form, has existed ever since. The Old Testament writings throughout foreshadow the "Savior,

Christos," and the Jews are yet - looking for him to come, to restore them as the Children of Abraham to their National greatness once existing. Christians say he has come already. Now as Masons we decide not between these, but take all in as our Brethren, and the One God as our Heavenly Father, revealed to us as such in the Great Light of Masonry.

"Aristotle has said that Man was a political animal-he certainly is a religious animal, as the history of Mankind shows from the earliest ages."

In the twofold nature of Man no one has a right to exalt either side of this nature at the expense of the other; also in the double nature of his intellectual faculties we have no right to atrophy either the reason, on the one side, or the sentiments, in the opposite direction; but it is the result of true wisdom to keep them in due equipoise, for the proper development of the intellect, for the wisest and best of purposes. Moreover, it has been shown that Man in his relation to his fellow-Man must also be held in the twofold relation of egoism and altruism. Every animal instinct prompts him to a pure selfishness, continued until that instinct be satisfied.

In the sentimental Nature of Man we find the promptings to social life, and altruism becomes a balancing force which brings the animal instincts to the equipose, when controlled by reason. When the sentimental faculties preponderate, it is because the reasoning force has become weakened; where sentiment is suppressed, the reasoning powers have been unduly stimulated.

From time immemorial Man has manifested the sentimental part of his nature, in worshipping something, by him considered his superior. As has been shown already, his worship, in the form of sacrifices offered, has been to appease an offended Deity.

How did he know of a Deity? and how know that the Deity was offended?

Self-consciousness of wrong done was the inner monitor, which taught Man what was right and what wrong, in regard to a Superior power. That men, among themselves, soon made laws for their Moral government we can readily understand; but how did Man first comprehend that above him was a power to which he was responsible? That of himself he should arrive at any such definite conclusion as to require him to appease an offended being, is incomprehensible to us; it is out of all human categories and can only be referred to a direct revelation of God himself to Man.

Its universality renders it certain; no mere accident could have communicated such ideas from nation to nation, and keep up the superstitious notions so prevalent among the most .abject and deplorable savage tribes as are found in America and in Africa, where fetichism of the lowest, most grovelling kind, "keeps alive some memory of the old Truth in the human heart." To deny this is to deny everything concerning the Spirit history of Man, and closes our eyes to the broad daylight of facts, and challenges a logical proof of the shining of the Midday Sun itself; both, alike, self-evident propositions, requiring no proof, they are our axioms.

That God exists is as true as that the Sun Shines continuously, and spreads his light over the entire Solar System, interrupted only by partial clouds, as they screen the earth from his rays. As well might we deny the existence of the sun at Midnight, because we can not see him or any evidence of his light, as to deny God, because we can not see him directly or, in our estimation, any evidence of his overruling power; yet in all times and in every Nation Men have had faith in a Deity; they have put their trust in him; have worshiped him in some form or other; and have framed theories in regard to him, his nature and his attributes, and hence have arisen mythological systems, Philosophical hypotheses, and religious formularies by which Man can approach nigh unto that great August being, recognized as the great Force of the Universe; and however many diverse gods there may have been, and howsoever differently portrayed in the different Nations and separate Mythologies, yet they can all be traced to but one great Deity or Supreme God, of whom all the others were, originally, emanations, receiving names descriptive of their peculiar functions, which in time became humanized or personated and worshiped as distinct gods.

Again, in the Original Theocratic systems of India, Assyria, and Egypt.

Three persons are distinctly set forth in the Godhead, and their peculiar attributes, alike, each to each, as Creator, Preserver, and Destroyer, this last term evidently signifying the dissolution of animal form to reproduce a Spiritual regeneration and resurrection to immortality.

In the Indian system the Office of the second person of the Trimurti is that of the Preserver of Man, and in the Nine several Avatars or Incarnations he has indicated his office, and more particularly in the Ninth, where as the Good Black Shepherd, or Chrishna, "Anointed One," he treads upon and bruises the head of the Old Serpent Calinac, thus demonstrating the promise in Gen. iii., 15 verse.

Now what do all these well-known Myths refer to if not to the enmity between God and Man? the necessity of reconciliation and the provision made by the Deity for such reconciliation? As far back as we are able to extend our examinations into the history of Man, we find him striving to become in perfect accord with God. Hence all of his sacrifices to appease an offended Deity. We have the best of opportunities to study the Paganism of the earliest civilizations of the Old World, compared with that of all the intermediate centuries and the present day. We know from the Old Testament precisely the Ceremonial law and Observances of the Mosaic economy and the subsequent history of the Israelites to the present day.

We have the Koran from the day it was first promulgated by Mahomet to its spread of the principles and practices of the Many Millions now governed by it, and yet, when all these come into the light of the Gospel of Christ they vanish like the Morning Mist before the glorious sun as it rises above the horizon.

We are not ignorant of the objections urged by all skeptical writers as to the inaccuracies of the Old Testament as well as the New. Moses did not make so many mistakes as he is charged with by Volney, Voltaire, and Paine of the last century, and Colenso of this. They all forget that this is an age of inquiry and Theists are no longer afraid to read, study, and controvert infidel Authors. The discoveries made during the last twenty-five years or more, and which have been, in that time, before the reading World, in the very country over which Moses is said to have conducted his people, have demonstrated incontestably the truth of the entire narrative concerning the wanderings of the Children of Israel; and he who denies this, after reading those Official narratives in connection with the Mosaic account in Exodus and Numbers, must be set down to the account of "None so deaf as those who will not hear."

We are prepared to prove, analogically, geographically, topographically, and philologically, that the accounts in Exodus and Numbers must have been written on the spot, at the time, and by an active participant in the Scenes and places portrayed and described.

We are not now advocating any inspiration for the text, any more than we would for Gordon's "Annals of the Revolutionary War." He was a Cotemporary writer cognizant from day to day of the events of the times, and stated them as he saw or heard of them, liable to mistakes and receiving incorrect information. So with the books of the Pentateuch giving an account of the Exodus and Wanderings for the forty years between Egypt and the East banks of the Jordan. He who now should explore that country from Rameses through the Desert of Sinai, Et Tih, and old Moab, or should critically examine the Official reports of Scientific Men and Oriental Scholars combined, would be obstinately, willfully blind, if not convinced of the truthfulness of the Narrative, so far as the essential facts are at issue. It must be remembered, that all the books contained in the Old Testament have come down to us from the days of Ptolemy Philadelphus, almost pure and unaltered, save in some non-essential features, as the Septuagint, agreeing, not only with the Hebrew handed down to us from that people, but corroborated by Josephus, who wrote after our Christian era began. The differences between the Hebrew and the Septuagint are no greater than between any English translation and an original classic work. Beyond the time of Alexander the Great, back to the return from Babylonish captivity, we rely upon the Scribes, who professed to copy the sacred books precisely as given to them, from age to age, for the preservation of the text. Extreme care was observed and exactitude insisted upon, in every copy of the Law, the Prophets, Psalms, and Histories. To prove this conclusively, we have only to state the facts connected with the translation of the Hebrew Scriptures into Greek at Alexandria by order of Ptolemy Philadelphus, by the Seventy Jews (319 B.C.). A certified copy was furnished by the High-Priest at Jerusalem and it was forwarded to Alexandria, and the Seventy completed the translation into Greek. That version we have at the present day; it has been carefully compared with the Hebrew Scriptures handed down from Jerusalem and copies of which are in the hands of the Jewish people all over the world at this day.

It is found that no Material differences occur between the original and the Septuagint, than might be anticipated in a translation from an ancient to a more Modern tongue, and as between the periods of time, from 319 B.C. to A.D. 1610, when King James's translation in England was perfected and published, the most perfect translation of all times.

Every attempt, by Skeptical writers, to invalidate the historical argument has signally failed to overthrow the Authenticity of the Old Testament. It stands as the eternal Rock of Ages, against all the lashings of every element hurled against it for its overthrow, and it will continue to stand until time shall be no more, and all the enemies of the Truth shall have been overwhelmed with confusion, and either compelled to acknowledge the Truth, as thousands have already done, or to be cast aside with obloquy and shame.

No single work, which has had Man for its Author ever had the severe criticisms which have been urged against the Scriptures, both of the Old and New Testament; yet no other writings have been so triumphantly vindicated by the highest talent, learning, and genius as have been always displayed by the friends of Inspiration.

Yet, nevertheless, it must be admitted, that the claim made in behalf of the inspiration; by which the utterances were prompted, must challenge the freest investigation of all the evidences adduced, in support of that claim. Momentous consequences must follow the categorical decision. If the Bible be from God, dictated by his spirit, then its every mandate must be implicitly obeyed. A failure to comply with its commands and directions, according to its own utterances, must involve eternal banishment from the presence of God. To follow its dictates, as far as imperfections of humanity will permit, faith in all its utterances, and implicit trust in the Divine Author, according to the text of Scripture, will secure the highest blessings on Earth and the promise of an eternity of bliss. It is then highly essential, nay, it is of the utmost, absolute consequence that every one should settle the question definitely whether he will exercise that saving faith in the "Word of promise," and accept the offered blessings, or, casting away every offer, he will utterly deny the authority of Scripture and look upon the " Book " as of human invention, and if so, then, bearing upon its pages the evidence of deception and fraud, and altogether unworthy of the attention of reasonable Men and to be itself cast out.

In pursuing our discussion upon this all-important subject, it is of the utmost consequence that we should, each one for himself, definitely settle the question of the Authority of the Word.

If the Bible be true and given by the inspiration of the Spirit of God, then its dictates are to be strictly obeyed; its utterances on all subjects to be carefully considered; and every thought, word, and deed referred to, commands and dictates therein as the very center of authority whereby we are to be governed.

If the Bible be not true, then it is to be no more considered, than any other book, which treats upon the conduct and affairs of Mankind. The arguments, in favor of inspiration of Scripture have been fully examined by the highest order of minds that have ever graced our schools and colleges. They have impartially considered the whole subject and have given in their testimony and pronounced in favor of the claim to inspiration. Skeptics, like Lord Rochester, Lord Byron, Rousseau and many others, could not refrain from giving their testimony, as to the Value of the Bible as a Book of pure Morality. Bolingbroke declared that "the Gospel is, in all cases, one continued lesson of the strictest Morality, of justice, of benevolence, and of universal Charity."

Now consider the state of society in Palestine, and we may say all over the Roman Empire, when Christ came teaching the lessons in the Gospel, alluded to by Bolingbroke. Who was it that thus taught? Was it one from the eminent schools of that age, learned in Grecian and Roman philosophy, and prepared by a long course of studies to become a teacher? Nay, but an unlearned Carpenter's Son, a denizen from that most depraved of all the abandoned villages of Galilee - the proverbial Nazareth - he came, astonishing the World, with a system of Morals, so vastly above all that had ever preceded it, that it was incomprehensible to the then whole World of Man, and they utterly rejected Christ and his teachings.

A simple reference to the profane histories of that day will clearly demonstrate, that long prior to the coming of Christ, during his life, and for a century following his death, the whole world, or what portion of it was known to and conquered by Rome, was in the most debased condition as to its state of Morals. The question must then very naturally arise in the mind of the impartial investigator as from whence Christ derived his ideas of a Morality, so pure and infinitely above the whole conception of his age, as to command the respect and admiration of the highest civilization in all ages since he gave utterance to those precepts, as we find them in the Gospels? He certainly did not get them from his people, or by education in Nazareth or in any other town of Galilee; for when he commenced his Mission among the Cities of that country, he astonished all, even those who had known him from his birth, when he had finished the famous discourse recorded in Matthew, chapters v., vi., and vii. It is written:

"And it came to pass, when Jesus had ended these sayings the people were astonished at his doctrine: For he taught them as having authority, and not as the scribes." And well they might be; for it was so different in all its principles from the practices of his day, that it was incomprehensible to them. Yet in so far as it referred to the conduct of Men toward each other, in the ordinary transaction of life, the lowest and poorest classes could see clearly a broad road for their elevation; so different from the treatment they were in the habit of receiving from those above them. We make no allusion to the account given of Miraculous cures wrought by him upon the poor, deceased, and stricken people; or his production of food for the hungry; or his reported power over the elements; it is the -,quite as Miraculous and undeniable fact of his anomalous teachings, that we now have to deal with. The Miracles may be denied, but the principles taught by him are undeniable; and that, it must be confessed, was quite above the natural tendencies of his times; and the Morals and principles of the whole World of Man, from the lowest classes to the highest, most refined, and cultivated. It was the Augustan age in literature. In that age we find a Cicero, not only as Author, but as a leading Statesman ; Virgil, Ovid, Sallust as poets, and Annalist; also the historian Tacitus; Pliny the elder and younger, and other Latin Authors, familiar to all scholars at the present day.

The World was utterly ignorant of the fundamental principles upon which the Morality taught by Christ was predicated, viz., "To do unto others what you could justly wish should be done to your self." This was the dictate as to our conduct to our fellow-Man. In relation to our duty to God. If the World of Man ever came up to the Standard, even of Socrates, Plato, or Aristotle, it had long lost a knowledge of any true principles of that duty since the Roman Empire had succeeded the Grecian; and during the period between the decline of the Alexandrian successors and the rise of Roman domination and the growth of that luxury which overwhelmed the City of Rome, spread its baneful influences wherever the Legions and cohorts were established as a permanence; even over the Jewish provinces in Palestine, so that the severe discipline of the Scribes and pharisees, and the strictest sect of Sadducees, became utterly abandoned to the Roman influence, brought about by the Herods and their courts, between the first conquest of Palestine and the period when Christ commenced his peregrinations.

What we have said in reference to Christ is well authenticated history; just as reliable as the history of the conquest of Caesar, the history of Tacitus, and the accounts by Pliny, and the writings of Cicero, Works which no one denies.

We think it is clearly shown that the Morality taught by Christ was of divine origin. It is a well-known method of demonstration in Geometry to prove a proposition by demonstrating that the negative of it can not be true. Thus I have shown that Christ's Morality could not possibly have been of human origin, hence it must have been divine.

We have been led into the discussion of the "Three Revelations" through the examination of the antiquity of signs, symbols, and emblems. The very remains of Antiquity, from which we derive our knowledge of the sign language, show, conclusively, the earliest religious instincts of Mankind. It is to be here remarked that the original religions were designed to teach a pure Morality; all writers concur in this fact; and the gross idolatries, impure, and lascivious rites, came at a later day.

We copy the following testimony: A recent writer of no mean repute, a clergyman in the Church of England, says: "Christianity is, in fact, the reintegration of all scattered religious convictions, and this accounts for the adoption by the Church of so many usages belonging primarily to paganism, and for the doctrines of the creed resembling in so many points the traditions of heathenism."

"The use of the temple," says M. Gilliot, "of churches dedicated to saints, and adorned with branches of trees on certain occasions, incense, lamps, tapers, votive offerings made upon convalescence, holy water, asylum, festivals, and ember seasons, calendars, processions, the benediction of land, sacerdotal vestments, the tonsure, the marriage ring, turning to the East, devotion to images, even, maybe, the strains of the Church, the kyrie eleison, all of these customs and many others are of Oriental origin, sanctified by the adoption of the Church."[336]

Thus much as to what has come down from Paganism to the Church. Now, it is well known that when Freemasonry revived under the influence of the Church it was a Church affair, and its rites, ceremonies, and symbols were controlled by the Churchmen. The vows were to make its members true to Mother Church. Then the ceremonial of baptism was an essential feature, and in the English rite it is still preserved.   Now, let us examine that point, and we quote from the same author, viz.

"Baptismal ceremonial includes all purifications. The idea that man is held back from perfect union with God by his imperfection, uncleanness, sin, is widely diffused, and manifests its existence by water, blood, and fire baptisms, by mutilation of the body and maceration of the flesh."

"Among the Greeks the mysteries of Cotys commenced with a purification, a sort of baptism, and the priests of the Thracian goddess derived from this their title of Baptai."[337]

Apollo, deriving his name from Apolouo, to purify, was the god of expiation by baptism.

A festival of "cleansing" was celebrated in Thessaly. "Musaeus" was a complete ritual of purifications, and divided the ceremonies into two orders, "teletai" and "kalharmoi," the latter being 109 purifications and expiations accomplished by special sacrifices, the former resembled the purifications performed in the mysteries.

The usual mode was dipping, or by aspersion.   Immersion was called "loutron," the other "perirransis."[338] When Diogenes saw one baptized by aspersion, he said, "Poor wretch! do you not see that since

---

[336] Gilliot, " L'Orient, l'occident," etc.
[337] Suidas, sub. voc. Juvenal, Satin, ii., 92.
[338] Plat., "Craty," 47 ; Theophr., "Hist. Plaut.," ix., 12.

these sprinklings cannot repair your grammatical errors, they cannot repair, either, the faults of your life."[339]

Lustral water was placed at the door of temples for the priests to purify the profane. The hands and feet were washed before entering the temple. The brazen laver of the Mosaic tabernacle was for that purpose. Blood was sprinkled by the peristiarch, who had slain the victim when the proedrai had opened the assembly. The herald, taking the peristiarch's place, continued the lustration by burning incense. Fumigations constituted another form of purification. Sand was used, and salt, in default of water, which was regarded as possessed of the virtue of purification, and a symbol of incorruption; every impure act whatever demanded purification.

The Romans practiced baptism, as we learn from Juvenal, Satin, vi., 522, where he satirizes those who dipped their heads thrice, in the morning, into the waters of Tiber.

At the feast of Pales, Goddess of Flocks, shepherds purified themselves by washing their hands in new fallen dew.[340] A lustration was made by consecrated water shaken from a branch of laure,. or olive; and Propertius, like David, prays, "Spargile me lymphis," "purge me with hyssop."[341] The waters of Ganges have a purifying effect; children are bathed in it, the sick are sprinkled with its waters, the dead are plunged in it.

Drinking of the water washes away sin, and the Indians take it with them and use it in the ceremonies of their temples.

In Egypt it was held that the dead were washed from their sin by Osiris, and on the sarcophagi the departed is often represented kneeling before him, who pours over him water from a pitcher.

Purification with water and urine of cows and earth is the most prominent feature in the ceremonial of Zend. Among the Jews, was practiced the rite of baptism, to cleanse by immersion or aspersion with consecrated water. (Numb. viii. 7; xix. q, 13-20; xxxi. 23; Ezek. xxxvi. 25, 26; Psl. li. 2-7.)

Infant baptism was practiced in Scandinavia before the introduction of Christianity, and the child was then named.

The Druids practiced baptism by dipping or aspersion, also by fire, borrowed from the -Phoenicians. This was "passing through the fire to Moloch." "Beltein" is still observed in Ireland. Cattle are driven through fires built on high hills, on May 1st.

---

[339] Diog., "Laert.," Lib. VI.
[340] Ovid, " Fasti," iv., 778.
[341] Proper., vol. vi., 7.

Among the 'Mexicans, the new-born child was bathed, and these words spoken by the nurse: "Take this water, for the goddess Chalchiuhcueja is thy mother," etc.

The second baptism occurred later, and was by fire. A boy was passed four times through the flames.

This passing through the fire was customary with the Romans after their return from a funeral, to purify themselves. The same custom prevails in Syria. Throughout Europe, in the Middle Ages, was kept up the old custom of leaping through a fire, and driving cattle betwixt flames, and was condemned by the Councils of the Church. "Every purification," said Servius, "is made either with water, or fire, or air. In all sacred rites there are three purifications, for they are purified either with the torch and sulphur, or are washed with water, or are ventilated with air."[342]

In Portal's work on Egyptian Symbols, compared with those of the Hebrews, we find this under

Water.

"In Egyptian Cosmogony, as in the first book of Moses, the world was created from the body of waters. This doctrine, says Champollion, was professed in Egypt in the most distant times. Water was the mother of the world, the matrix of all created beings, and the word M SC H BR signifies matrix and waves.

"Man was considered as an image of the world, the initiate was to be born again to a new life, and the baptism thenceforward symbolized the primeval waters. It was on this account that the initiate was called MSCHE, Moses, a word signifying in Egyptian, according to Josephus (Antiq., II., q, § 6), saved from the water, or by the water; designated in Hebrew by MSCHBEE, unction, and MSCHE, to save."

Water was the symbol of purity (according to Horapollo) and designated the birth of the pure or initiates, as we shall show in the article Dow.

Under the article Frog, he says "Thus the profane is compared to primal matter, damp, and without form, over which the spirit has not yet moved, and which is born again from the waters of baptism."

Dew.

---

[342] In Aen., ii., 384; Ovid, " Metam.," viii., 261 ; Terque senem /lamma, ter aqua, ter dufure lustrat.

"The sign we give here is an abridgment of the scene representing Egyptian baptism, or shedding celestial dew on the head of the neophyte.

"Horus and Thoth-Lunus pour water on the head of the neophyte, which is transformed to divine life (ansated cross), and to purify (hoopoe-headed sceptre), and is thus translated: Horus, son of Isis, baptizes with water and fire (repeat four times).

"The baptism of water and fire, designated in the Zend by the characters that Leemans has explained, is identical in its exterior form with the baptism of water, the spirit, and of fire, in Luke iii. 16-17."

The name received by the baptized or anointed was given in the Bible to the chief of the Hebrews - Moses. This name exists on the Egyptian monuments; it is written by the sign of the dew or baptism, equal to Hebrew M, and the bent stalk, equal to Sheen, the group; in Hebrew SCH, M, or M-SCH-E is translated in Champollion's grammar by begotten; we give it the signification of regenerated or begotten again.

But why multiply examples from antiquity? Let it suffice that when Masonry adopted the symbolism of the ancients, how could the most important one be omitted?

Masonry is made up of symbolisms. The rite of consecration belongs to it, and by some form or other must take place; and we hold that every form whatever the " pious rite may bear," is "masonic," because that word expresses the original idea. The "genus," "York," "Scotch," "French," "modern," are the " species," or separate specific forms of ritualism; and we might go further, and class every "religion" that existed as specific forms of "masonry," for by that word we distinguish the true relation existing between the Creator and his creatures - that is, Masonry or Religion (re-ligo, to bind again).

www.ingramcontent.com/pod-product-compliance
Lightning Source LLC
Chambersburg PA
CBHW071143160426
43196CB00011B/1997